POSTMODERN PHILOSOPHY
AND THE
SCIENTIFIC TURN

POSTMODERN PHILOSOPHY

AND THE SCIENTIFIC TURN

DOROTHEA E. OLKOWSKI

Indiana University Press
Bloomington and Indianapolis

This book is a publication of

Indiana University Press
601 North Morton Street
Bloomington, Indiana 47404-3797 USA

iupress.indiana.edu

Telephone orders 800-842-6796
Fax orders 812-855-7931

Manufactured in the United States of America

Library of Congress Cataloging-in-Publication Data

Olkowski, Dorothea.
  Postmodern philosophy and the scientific turn / Dorothea
E. Olkowski.
      p. cm.
  Includes bibliographical references and index.
  ISBN 978-0-253-00112-2 (cl : alk. paper) — ISBN 978-0-
253-00119-1 (pb : alk. paper) — ISBN 978-0-253-00114-6
(eb) 1. Philosophy and science. 2. Postmodernism. 3.
Phenomenology. 4. Science—Philosophy. I. Title.
  B67.O425 2012
  190.9'04—dc23
                                    2011034963
  1 2 3 4 5   17 16 15 14 13 12

Dedicated to

CONSTANTIN BOUNDAS,
True Philosopher and True Friend

"Whatever is not explicitly forbidden is possible."

—SAYING HEARD AMONG PHYSICISTS

CONTENTS

PREFACE
POSTMODERN PHILOSOPHY

The object of this study is the condition of knowledge in the most highly developed societies. I have decided to use the word *postmodern* to describe that condition . . . it designates the state of our culture following the transformations which, since the end of the nineteenth century, have altered the game rules for science, literature, and the arts.

—Jean-Francois Lyotard, *The Postmodern Condition, A Report on Knowledge*

A book that sets out to engage with the topic of postmodern philosophy and the scientific turn might seem rather curious. Why refer to postmodern philosophy and not, for example, poststructuralist philosophy? What do we mean by the phrase *scientific turn?* Continental philosophers are familiar with the idea that a group of highly influential European philosophers rejected the claims of phenomenology and hermeneutics by making what is widely understood to be a *linguistic turn.* How then is it possible for continental philosophy to have taken a scientific turn? These and related questions are the subject of this inquiry.

Perhaps we may open up our inquiry by briefly examining these questions in relation to more general trends in philosophy, trends that arose out of the separation of philosophy from natural science and mathematics, both of which had once been thoroughly embedded in philosophical practices. Correlative to these trends, we might also remind ourselves of the various separations that took place within philosophy itself. Phenomenology, it appears, arose at least partly as a rejection of logical positivism and functionalism. Postmodern philosophy, in turn, sought to distinguish itself from phenomenological presuppositions and methods. What might be surprising is that at least some postmodern philosophies did so by turning back toward a version of formalism, which we have referred to as functionalism. Let us begin by examining precisely this surprising turn, which is, we will maintain, the scientific turn.

Philosophers of science credit Descartes with the notion of a feedback loop, which operates to justify theories and facts. Descartes believed that mathematics is a pure product of reason, reducible to purely logical relations, yet applicable to the world.[1] Descartes's difficulty was in finding a connection between the pure intelligible realm and the world. He argued that when we develop a theory based on observation we are perfectly justified in relying on further observations to support and sustain the theory.[2] The problem that this situation, this "Cartesian Circuit," presents is that of circularity between observation, theory, and observation again. It appears that there is no solid justification of the theory insofar as *something extra-logical must be the precondition of all such knowledge.*[3]

The situation today remains quite similar. Jean-François Lyotard has argued that to the extent science must legitimate the rules of its own game and produce a legitimation discourse, that discourse has always been philosophy. According to Lyotard, the term "modern" refers to any science that appeals to a grand narrative of philosophy as its metadiscourse, even though that metadiscourse itself must in turn be justified.[4]

By contrast, what Lyotard calls the postmodern condition of knowledge evinces incredulity toward all such metanarratives, especially those grounded in metaphysical philosophy, and in Lyotard's analysis, this has precipitated a turn toward what have been called "language games."[5] Briefly, this implies that postmoderns participate in communities whose cultural conventions are given to them. Words perform certain *functions* in this system and users are trained to observe these conventions. In this system, semantics is given in the cultural syntax.[6] But here too, the necessity of justification arises. Cultural conventions orient and justify individual language use, but what justifies cultural conventions? Lacking any grand metanarratives, postmoderns, it appears, have turned to a formalist justification. This is what has been called the *linguistic turn,* the process by which the philosophical model of consciousness was replaced with a model of the sign.[7] Both analytic and continental philosophy made this turn to the study of language itself, scouring it for alleged prejudices underlying reasoning processes, ensuring that language as a whole satisfies strictly linguistic criteria, while ignoring individual language use as irrelevant, since "unidentifiable subjective contributions" remain external to language and its conventions.[8]

This arose as part of an attack on representation. Specifically, as Manfred Frank has noted, the linguistic turn is linked to the idea that speech designates and *represents* simple ideas and immediate impressions, as well as connections between them established by reason. Against this, Ferdinand de Saussure and Ludwig Wittgenstein, among others, embraced a system in which the idea of a thought, perception, or representation independent of language arises from pure abstraction.[9] Different thoughts are thus an effect of expression, the manner in which significant units are combined and recombined, thereby unifying thought and speech. In this system there is no thought without speech and so the limits of knowing are one with the limits of speaking. Language systems are thereby intersubjective and transindividual. However, the meaning of intersubjectivity is altered, referring not to communication between subjects but merely to semantics; intersubjectivity is now no more than a matter of how one masters a language and how one has that mastery affirmed.[10]

The connection between Saussurian-Wittgensteinian poststructuralism and postmodernism lies roughly in the idea of a function. A word can have significance only insofar as it has a function. So, for example, the sentence "I know I feel fine" means precisely the same as "I feel fine." The word "know" serves no function here and is therefore meaningless.[11] As Frank points out, the difference in this regard between analytic philosophy and poststructuralism is that the former insist on formal semantics, the treatment of language as an algebra of symbols whose meaning derives solely from symbolic relations.[12] In its most extreme formulations, syntax is or produces all the semantics one needs. Poststructuralism similarly transforms philosophy into semiology, the theory of signs.[13] However, although addressing postmodernism and the scientific turn calls for us to take poststructuralism into account, insofar as we are examining the mathematical and scientific frameworks that influenced continental philosophy, we will utilize the term "postmodern" to discuss primarily the philosophies that are of interest in this regard, that is, those philosophies modeled on formal semantics or taking their cue from the limitations of formal semantics.

According to the mathematician Vladimir Tasić, it was the dream of modern science and the accompanying culture of modernism to eliminate the "Cartesian Circuit," that is, to eliminate metaphysical illusion as well as what are called "intuitions" and to replace them with positivist explanations, meaning logical constructs of immediate experience.[14] Formalists and functionalists hotly deny that intuitions can be a source of mathematical objects. Intuitionism in mathematics is the position that we can perceive mathematical objects, like sets, in a manner similar to our perception of objects in our world.[15] It is a position that we will examine in some detail in this work as it is closely linked with the philosophical position of phenomenology.

Philosophers are familiar with Immanuel Kant's concept of an a priori intuition of space and time as the condition of the possibility of the experience of objects. As mathematicians have noted, these intuitions are the form of our experience, a conceptual framework that describes them, but also a necessity in that we cannot have an experience of a physical object without intuition.[16] Left to its own devices, reason can generate opposing and contradictory statements, known as antinomies, therefore mathematical knowledge requires that our concepts correspond to possible experiences.[17] Nevertheless, the question arises, how is it that we know that intuitions shape our experience, since like any object, we know only ourselves in space and time? Kant and other philosophers have argued that we have an awareness of ourselves (the object = x) that arises with each of our acts of consciousness.

Similarly, Edmund Husserl famously argued that passive synthesis, or what he often referred to as passive intuition, is the necessary basis of the genesis of existent physical things.[18] It is a genesis that begins "in 'early infancy,' . . . [when] the field of perception that gives beforehand does not as yet contain anything that, in a mere look, might be explicated as a physical thing."[19] We adult meditating egos are capable of penetrating into formations antecedent to the intentional constituents of experiential phenomena. There, we discover that the ego has an environment of objects arising from an original becoming acquainted, a primal instituting whereby everything now affecting that developed ego has arisen from infancy in a genesis, a universal principle of passive genesis Husserl calls, somewhat boldly, association.[20] As with the temporal synthesis, this is not, of course, the empiricist concept of association, subject to "naturalistic distortions."[21]

The form of internal time, the subjective process, is not connected part by part externally but is immanently associated. This will be the case for passive genesis as well. If time is the stage, the passive genesis is the action on that stage. Here association receives new fundamental forms that allow us to make sense of continuity. These forms are sensuous, a sensuous configuration in coexistence and a sensuous configuration in succession designating an innate and a priori realm without which no ego is understandable.[22] It is the realm of temporality; for Husserl, it is the realm of everything new. For the already developed ego, there are certainly constituted objectivities, an objective universe, a fixed ontological structure. But for immanent temporality and sensuous, receptive life, the new arises and takes shape.[23] This is implicit in the formulation that while consciousness constitutes partly explicit objects, various moments and parts of those objects that have not yet come into relief may yet be taken into account as affecting the ego.

We can see how commensurate Husserl's position is with that of the mathematical intuitionists, and this reminds us that Husserl's PhD was in mathematics. In mathematics, "Intuitionists accept the 'obviousness' of mathematical entities and place them on par with objects such as chairs and tables."[24] From this it follows that for intuitionists, we perceive mathematical objects like sets in the same way that we perceive ordinary objects in the world. "Gödel suggests that 'we do have something like a perception of the objects of set theory, as is seen from the fact that the axioms force themselves upon us as being true.'"[25] So it is not the perceiver who determines the truth of her perceptions, rather it is the perceptions themselves, through their perceptibility, that bring their own truth into perception. For intuitionists, mathematics, like art, is created and not discovered, and "the role of a creator is best exhibited when the mathematician has to exhibit proof for all existential mathematical assertions."[26]

Nevertheless, the dream to end the Cartesian Circuit and to eliminate intuitions was the shared provenance of logical empiricism and logical positivism, which chose to treat mathematics as purely symbolic manipulation, meaningless in relation to reality, and meaningful only in its structural relationship. This formalism or functionalism, we have noted, was named *the linguistic turn*. It is not identical to the Saussurian-inspired linguistic turn in continental philosophy. For in analytic philosophy the so-called linguistic turn was, in reality, a turn toward the language of logic only and, eventually, a turn toward discrete and formal computation.[27] Nevertheless, a number of postmodern philosophers and theorists have embraced even this more radical postmodern form of the turn even while embracing cultural norms.

Recognizing the modern dilemma embodied in the Cartesian Circuit, science studies theorist Bruno Latour claims that the term "modern" refers

to two sets of practices. One creates hybrids or mixtures of nature and culture and the other tries to purify them by creating two distinct ontological
zones: that of human beings and that of nonhumans. The hybrids utilize
culture, the practices of a community, to justify their natural science, or they
use the idea of pure rationality to justify their politics. The purification processes try to separate nature from culture. The dilemma, for Latour, is that
the rational rule of mathematical demonstration in science, which excludes
the need for experiment, can be very much mistaken about the nature of reality in the face of the scientific community of trained experimentalists who
test out theories in the artificial space of the laboratory. Latour's conclusion
is that politics is impotent without science and science is impotent without
communities.[28]

Thus, Latour celebrates hybrids. Nature, he argues, is present through
the communities of scientists (the society) who speak in its name, and societies are present through the objects (nature) that ground them. The circuit exists in the form of the "object-discourse-nature-society," a return, he
thinks, to a premodern condition.[29] Yet if half of politics is constructed in
science and half of nature is constructed in society, then it seems that another sort of formalism has emerged, the formalism of hybrids. In other
words, nothing is authored by a person, everything is constructed by a hy-
brid thinking machine, a series of unknown and unknowable forces subject
to discontinuous, thus random, fluctuations in the overall system.[30]

Yet what, more precisely, do we mean by formalism? The mathematician David Hilbert is widely considered to be among the most important
sources of the formalist tendency in contemporary, including postmodern, thought.[31] The claim has been made that due to the vast expansion of
mathematical knowledge, mathematicians themselves took on the role once
inhabited by philosophers like Immanuel Kant. This occurred as concept-
formations rose to higher levels of generality and as conceptual abstractions
and systematic fundamental ideas undid the notion of meaning.[32] Moreover,
to the detriment of the Kantian approach, any notion of an a priori spatial
intuition became much less relevant to geometry.[33]

Beginning with his *Foundations of Geometry* (1899), Hilbert set out a
new system of geometric axioms using the criteria of simplicity and logical completeness.[34] What was revolutionary in Hilbert's methodology was
that the demand that each axiom express an a priori truth was dropped.
One simply chose empirical statements or hypotheses as axioms, particu-

larly in the application to physics, as the idea that geometry is an empirical science found more and more support.[35] However, with the construction of comprehensive systems that incorporated Euclidean geometry but were nevertheless raised above spatial intuitions, the necessity of separating the mathematical/logical realm from the spatial/intuitive became clear.[36] Hilbert was able to eliminate spatial intuitions and representations not only from his proofs but also from axioms and concepts. Terms like "point" and "line" were not associated in any way with intuitive spatial objects but were taken to designate *initially indeterminate relations* that were implicitly characterized through the axioms in which they occur.[37] Thus axioms were no longer taken to be initially either true or false but *had a sense only in the context of the whole axiom system,* which itself was not taken to be a statement of truth. In this way, the logical structure of axiomatic geometry could be understood as a purely hypothetical structure.[38] It is a system of connections that must be mathematically investigated according to its internal properties, its logical relations.[39]

Of great interest, for our purposes, is that Hilbert "envisaged the point of view of the uniformity of the axiomatic method in its application to the most diverse domains."[40] In describing the method as setting up a theory, what is given is an arrangement of facts by means of a framework of concepts, where a few propositions suffice for the logical construction of the theory, then going from there to considering the framework of concepts as a possible form of a connection of relations in its internal structure.[41] This means, of course, that certain conditions must be satisfied. There must be consistency; all the relations expressed in the axioms must be logically compatible. This condition takes the place of the old demand that each axiom be a statement of truth. Then there is the question of logical dependency, whether or not any of the axioms are superfluous because they can be proven from others, and the question of whether the axioms can be reduced to more fundamental propositions.[42] Once set out, this method was thought to be applicable to any theoretical domain.

One further consideration lay in the necessity of proving consistency. It must be the case that the modes of inference do not ever result in contradiction when the object of investigation is the proofs themselves and not the objects to which they refer.[43] This is the level of the metanarrative analogous to the philosophical critique of reason, which mathematicians refer to as mathematical logic. It involves the mastery of the forms of logical inference through the symbolic denotation of the simplest logical relations: "and," "or," "not," and "all," essentially, what are called grammatical dummies analogous to the "it" of "it is raining."[44] Hilbert stripped the intellectual content of the inferences from the proofs he investigated, replacing proofs of analysis with purely formal manipulation of signs according to definite rules.[45]

By this means, we enter into the domain of pure formalism, and mathematics becomes the general theory of formalisms. Perhaps we can now see more clearly why Tasić takes Hilbert to be one of the key sources of postmodern philosophy. For postmodern philosophy, as for Hilbert, only the formal, structural relations among signifiers are of interest, and what they signify can be anything, as the signifier-signified relationship is arbitrary.[46] Signs are immediately graspable finitary objects, that is, a finite number of symbols and propositions that are foundational, along with rules of inference regardless of semantics.[47]

The formalist system has certain guarantees. It is a consistent, compatible, noncontradictory extension of reasoning; it is equally accessible to all members of the community; questions about meaning are irrelevant.[48] And so the thought or intuition of finitary objects of mathematics became the source of social consensus, the minimum that a mathematician cannot deny. Yet the logician Kurt Gödel proceeded to raise serious objections. Hilbert replaced the vague notion of "truth" with formal demonstrability. Gödel agrees that demonstrability is definable in formalist mathematics and that a proof is a finite sequence of symbols of a certain kind.[49] Yet if we insist that all provable statements are true, the converse, that all true statements are provable, is certainly not the case, thus there are true mathematical statements that are not provable. The conclusion is that "either mathematics is false, or there are true mathematical statements that are not provable (in a chosen formalization). This is usually referred to as 'incompleteness.'"[50]

Otherwise stated, the conceptualization of mathematical truth goes beyond a particular formal language, and the important realization for our purposes is that it is the same with postmodern philosophy. Truth exceeds any particular formal language. In mathematics, the manipulation of finite strings of symbols and the formalization of this process is roughly what is known as computation. Mathematician Alan Turing based his notion of a calculating machine on an analysis of how humans perform computations. And although a Turing machine can do all the computations a human mind can do and more, the human mind can do many things that the machine cannot do. The machine can do only what it has been programmed to do. But if, as seems to have happened, the computer has become the model for the mind, computation is "a universal spirit of which we are but physical realizations."[51] It has also been pointed out in many different ways that "all sufficiently strong systems of formal reasoning, including that of a Turing machine, have some randomness inscribed into them."[52] Before celebrating this, let us see what it implies.

We saw that Hilbert wished to separate the notion of truth from that of provability. Mathematical symbolic objects such as "the square root of -1" appeared initially as a result of a process for finding the formula for the solution of certain kinds of equations.[53] This so-called imaginary unit eventually became an object of study. Because it appeared in the process of finding a formula for a solution to a problem, the credit for imaginary numbers is often attributed to science itself, to the mathematical language extending itself and not to the individuals involved in the task.[54] The question this raises is, does the same thing happen with a concept like truth? The logician Alfred Tarski proposed the theorem that no adequate formal language can formulate its own notion of truth, but that higher-level concepts are needed, concepts that only emerge over time. This implies that it would take an endless amount of time for truth to emerge in an endless conceptual becoming. If we are to grasp any notion of truth, it must then exist outside of formalist methodologies.[55]

Postmodern philosophy, for the most part, has abandoned any concept of truth in favor of the proposition that meaning is in the method, and the method continues throughout history, if not beyond. Postmodern philosophers have thereby endorsed ignorance rather than knowledge, and formal rather than temporal flux or flow, as well as signifying chains rather than truth. Some mathematicians, notably Gödel and the Dutch mathematician L. E. J. Brouwer, and some philosophers, notably Edmund Husserl, expressed the hope that mathematics is based on some type of truth that is invariant even though the manner in which it is formalized may alter, thus that there is something beyond formal methodology.[56] One question we must explore then is, if so, what might this be?

We have attempted in this preface to set out, in as simplified form as possible, the formal mathematical framework of postmodern philosophy, the scientific turn. Tasić speculates that postmodern philosophy is courting the extreme aspects of science, whose goal is to construct a thinking machine. The postmodern subject, he claims, is another "grammatical dummy," an effect of events in a formal structure.[57] For philosophers who take this beyond language, projecting mathematical structures onto physical reality, we might find ourselves in something more tangible than the "prison-house of language."[58] We might find that these philosophies place us in a prison-house of sensation, perception, thought, and experience from which there is no escape insofar as the "house" is a field of immanence, a wholly determined vector field where random events occur, but lacking any reference to truth and ultimately leading to no consequences for human behavior and action.

What such a structure implies is that when syntax alone produces semantics or meaning, material expression and participant's intentions are irrelevant. They are game pieces on a game board that plays itself.[59] Thus no word or deed can be true or false, and no one is responsible for the consequences of any word or deed because there are no authors. No "one" is playing, everyone is played. In the face of these structures, we will look at the possibility of alternatives: An alternative logic, an alternative theory of mathematics and physics, and alternative philosophies. Philosophies according to which human beings and human actions have consequences insofar as "truth" remains, in some sense, operative. Thus not merely a formal structure of relations, but a world, a universe, in which ethical behavior is possible.

Chapter 1 opens with an account of the controversial, fake essay written by the physicist Alan Sokal and published in 1996 by the cultural studies journal *Social Text*. The essay begins with the statement that "there are many natural scientists, and especially physicists, who continue to reject the notion that the disciplines concerned with social and cultural criticism can have anything to contribute, except perhaps peripherally, to their research." Of course, it is precisely what scientists have called "radical claims in popular books," implying that "fundamental flaws have been found in the scientific worldview and that one has to rethink the notion of law of nature" that so aroused the fury of natural scientists. Whether or not the development of a worldview based on a dominant scientific paradigm is an error, such worldviews have been and continue to be posited, so it is important that we ask what the consequences of each worldview might be, beginning, for purposes of this analysis, with the classical model of nature, which arose along with Newton's classical physics.

Chapter 2 leads off with Michel Serres's account of the battle of science against philosophy, described as one in which two human combatants are sinking into quicksand, yet failing to heed the very earth on which their contradictions take place. This description calls for some scrutiny, from the point of view of ontology and ethics as well as from the point of view of the natural sciences.

In philosophy, in the realm of moral and political discourse, the issues raised by Serres take us to Hannah Arendt, who argues that the modern cardinal virtues—success, industry, and truthfulness—did not come from political communities or theories, but from the learned societies and royal academies of scientists, which proscribed rules of behavior and standards of judgment. Arendt's argument is that modern science began with the Archimedean point of view, the view of Earth from far out into the universe, where only very general, statistical patterns can be observed. This is how mathematics emerged as the science of the structure of the human mind, treating geometry, the extension of nature and the world, as expressible in algebraic formulae. When analytical geometry proved that numerical truths are fully representable in terms of space, it was no longer necessary to begin scientific investigation with an immediate, sensible intuition; a distanced, Archimedean, and mathematical one would do.

Chapter 3 introduces the conceptual break of science with strict determinism when it was recognized that the motions of individual particles of gas could not be predicted and that only their behavior in structures turned out to be somewhat predictable using methods of statistical sampling. This view correlates well with David Hume's philosophy. If the stability of human ideas and reason is directly dependent on nature's regularity and predictability, but nature turns out to be merely probable and not certain, then reason is doubly probabilistic. It is a train of ideas grounded in habit, which itself is grounded in an uncertain nature, statistically probable but no longer classically, deterministically predictable, not even in an ideal sense. The classical model was further undone when the first and second laws of thermodynamics were formulated, implying that the universe is not symmetrical with regard to time, at least whenever there are complex processes. The conclusion that has been drawn is that if nature is probabilistic rather than determined, and reason is an effect of natural principles, then reason too tends toward the probable and not the certain.

Chapter 4 takes up the postmodern view, especially in the philosophy of Gilles Deleuze. Non-equilibrium thermodynamics' view of nature seems to bring it closer to phenomenology, the study of lived experience. Yet postmodern philosophers are not interested in modeling nature on lived experience. Gilles Deleuze is exemplary in this regard as he remains firmly committed to the Archimedean point of view and limits the role of human experience. Deleuze formulates his philosophy from the notion of a plane of immanence that arises from some consequences of the second law of thermodynamics, which states that in a *closed* system, where no new matter or energy enters, disorder must increase. Deleuze proposes that this system can be formalized mathematically by means of differential calculus and vector fields. In mathematics (specifically linear algebra), the rules of *association, commutation,* and *distribution* define vector space without reference to magnitude or directions, thus they may be utilized in a variety of fields whose terms are not material or physical. Deleuze argues that these rules *apply to nature.* This means that the rules have ontological status and that nature is associative, commutative, and distributive.

Chapter 5 examines the consequences of maintaining the classical scientific worldview and correlates this with current theories in both analytic and continental philosophies of language. Although Arendt has suggested that the statistical view is the most banal view of all, she maintains that potentially, under certain conditions, it gives rise to unethical behavior as extreme as the most evil of crimes, genocide. In a related line of thought, Simone de Beauvoir addresses the mathematical view of classical science in its most contingent form, the clinamen, where this term represents what mathematicians now call deterministic chaos. She asks if such a structure, which gives rise to "being and nothingness," is appropriate for human life and ethics, and why it does nothing to put an end to gulags and death camps. The problem that arises is that in view of the natural equality of atomistic individuals and universal natural law, the only moral law *thinkable* is one that maintains universality. However, nature seems to be sublimely indifferent to human beings and to language. This permits the replacement of what is sensuously given by a system of mathematical equations where all real relationships are dissolved into logical relations between man-made symbols.

Arendt's objection is that the deterministic certainty or probability of natural processes can still be challenged by the finitude of individuals, by the temporality of their lives. Arendt and Beauvoir are shown to agree that the act that brings and keeps people together is not the force of deterministic laws of nature, but the choice to recognize past, present, and future, to engage in noble words that narrate the stories of others and noble deeds that are the context and meaning of life. An extended analysis of the logician Lewis Carroll's *Alice in Wonderland* critiques the formalism of both analytic and postmodern philosophies insofar as neither seem to yield an account of truth or causality, both of which are necessary for ethical action.

Chapter 6 proceeds with caution, recognizing the widespread application of differential equations to human behavior, while recognizing the limits of such an approach, limits such as the "three-body problem," where the introduction of more than two bodies in a system produces chaotic behavior. But can we not also take into account the ethical phenomenologies of Arendt and Beauvoir, which seem to utilize intuitionistic and not formalist concepts? We will grapple with these questions so as to find a way to mesh the interests of natural science with those of philosophy and ethics. It may be the case that this ethical view can be correlated with recent work in quantum physics. A recent theory in physics argues that geometric time, the spacetime of the classical model, emerges out of the microscopic fundamental time of quantum gravity, since at the high energy levels of the early universe there is no geometric locality. Matter and with it geometry only make an appearance when the universe starts to cool down. Reversing the commonly accepted formulation, geometry could be conceptualized as a property of matter. The conclusion of this reversal is that physically and philosophically, we may have trapped ourselves inside a physical structure or a system of knowledge, which we think organizes our behavior, but in truth it is the effect of the collective action of matter in nature as well as the collective action of those who feel, act, and think in culture. Thus it will be our responsibility to do more than simply study the structure of society. We must, as Arendt and Beauvoir propose, understand and guide the actions of people in that society.

ACKNOWLEDGMENTS

The theme of this book is that no creature or event in the evolving universe is merely the result of random, atomistic collisions. The existence of this book is perhaps the strongest evidence I have for that position. No doubt, my very gradual awakening to the correlation of mathematics and natural science with postmodern philosophy and phenomenology arrived due to the influence of a multitude of sources and situations. Nevertheless, some of these left a particularly deep and powerful mark on me. Constantin Boundas, as always, my friend for many years and a visionary philosopher, pointed the way to the role of mathematics and science in the work of Gilles Deleuze. I would like to dedicate this book to him, for it was really Costas who influenced me so long ago and whose idea was the strong current that carried me in this most recent, albeit difficult, direction.

Helen Fielding encouraged and supported me more than I can ever say, applying these ideas broadly, finding numerous instances of their applications, especially in Merleau-Ponty, Foucault, and Irigaray. Her constancy and friendship are the true meaning of those words. Veronica Vasterling woke me up to the depth and breadth of the philosopher Hannah Arendt.

My amazing and loyal students, Claire Eavenson, Robb Vawter, and Kumeko Norris, not only took class after class where these ideas were developed, but each in their own way took them to the next level. I have learned so much from them. Marek Grabowski responded to my many requests for definitions and clarifications of numerous concepts in physics and mathematics. Angela Scordo-Polidori and I shared many philosophical ideas, and my steadfast friend Kate Petley, an artist of great gifts and the very model of perseverance, picked me up and dusted me off time after time.

Dee Mortensen, of Indiana University Press, supported and promoted this project. Her encouragement came at a truly important moment in the development of this book. Claire Colebrook and Andrew Cutrofellow generously read and commented on the manuscript. The many points and questions raised by Andrew gave me the incentive to dig much deeper and the insight to clear up serious inconsistencies and ambiguities in the text. It is a much, much better book for this.

The University of Colorado, Colorado Springs and the Department of Philosophy supported both a fellowship in the fall of 2010 and sabbatical in 2011, allowing me to revise and rework the manuscript. The University of Western Ontario, Rotman Institute of Philosophy Fellowship in the fall of 2010 gave me time and a wonderful opportunity to work on philosophy of mathematics. I was inspired by the graduate students in the institute who were so outstanding, as well as by the graduate students in Helen Fielding's feminist theory and philosophy and art classes at the University of Western Ontario.

I am grateful to all of these persons and institutions. Because much of this book relies on accounts of mathematics and natural science, I have used the books and papers of practicing mathematicians and scientists throughout in an attempt to be as accurate as possible. Mathematics and natural science are overwhelming in their complexity and highly context-dependent. It is my hope that I have not misrepresented mathematical and natural scientific ideas, nor overstated either the presuppositions or the possible consequences of various structures in mathematics and natural science. If I have, I look forward to correcting this in any future work.

Thank you to Edinburgh University Press for permission to reprint sections of chapters 4 and 5, which were originally published as "The Interesting, The Remarkable, The Unusual: Deleuze's Grand Style," *Deleuze Studies* 5, no. 1 (2011): pp. 118–39; and "After Alice: Alice and the Dry Tail," *Deleuze Studies, Deleuze and Gender* 2, no. 3 (2008): pp. 107–22.

Thank you also to Rodopi for permission to reprint sections of my essay "Science and Human Nature: How to Go From Nature to Ethics," which originally appeared in *Metacide*, ed. James R. Watson (Amsterdam and New York: Rodopi Press, 2010), pp. 107–22.

POSTMODERN PHILOSOPHY
AND THE
SCIENTIFIC TURN

NATURE CALLS

SCIENTIFIC WORLDVIEWS AND THE SOKAL HOAX

Cooler Than Thou?

The controversial, sham essay, written by the physicist Alan Sokal and published in 1996, possibly to its great mortification, by the cultural studies journal *Social Text*, begins with a statement that is no hoax but that rings true for many, if not most, researchers in the natural sciences.[1] The statement is that "there are many natural scientists, and especially physicists, who continue to reject the notion that the disciplines concerned with social and cultural criticism can have anything to contribute, except perhaps peripherally, to their research."[2] This view is affirmed by Steven Weinberg, a Nobel Prize winner in physics, in comments appearing in *The New York Review of Books*. Admitting that he found the news of Sokal's hoax amusing (a view shared by other physicists who have spoken or written about these events), Weinberg goes on to confirm Sokal's position. "Those who seek extrascientific messages in *what they think they understand about modern physics* are digging dry wells. I think that, with two large exceptions, the results of research in physics (as opposed, say, to psychology) have no legitimate implications whatever for culture or politics or philosophy."[3] Weinberg adds that until "we" learn the origins of the universe or the final laws of nature, philosophers and cultural theorists might avoid making statements about what they think "they" understand. Apparently, "we" is a set that does not include either of the latter two groups.

In a sentence that can only be read by any practicing physicist as dripping in irony, Sokal goes on to write that natural scientists "cling to the dogma" of the existence of an external world whose properties are independent of "humanity as a whole" since they are encoded in eternal physical laws.[4] *Humanity* can obtain partial and imperfect knowledge of these laws through the objective procedures and structures supplied by the scientific method. From the perspective of the natural sciences, especially physics, it is quite possible that no truer words were ever written. From the perspective of contemporary philosophy and cultural theory, as well as associated fields such as science studies, there is little question that each of these statements is, at least, problematic. Even philosophers who do not espouse postmodern views would have been most likely taken aback, and some seriously offended, by the notion that culture or politics and even philosophy remain totally peripheral to the work of the natural sciences. The claim that research in physics holds no legitimate implications whatever for culture or politics or philosophy may also be deeply shocking because in spite of the often-heard claim that even the educated public knows little about science, these same theorists have often been deeply invested in the natural sciences. Philosophers, historians, and social scientists have linked changes in natural scientific methods and theories to changes in *worldview,* where the latter is defined as "a system of beliefs that are intertwined, interrelated, interconnected."[5] These worldviews or systems of belief may be variously designated. Recent literature in the history and philosophy of science describes two overarching scientific worldviews, the Aristotelian and the Newtonian. The former incorporates numerous "mini" worldviews or systems: the Ptolemaic, the Copernican, the Tychonic, that of Kepler, and finally that of Galileo, which is strongly continuous with what came be the Newtonian worldview.[6] The advent of the special and general theories of relativity and the development of quantum theory might be said to be part of an ongoing transition to yet another, still undefined worldview. Scientists and historians have also studied the pervasive influence of scientific theories such as evolution and thermodynamics, each of which seems to have impacted academic disciplines from philosophy to economics.[7] So it can be shocking to philosophy and the social sciences when a theoretical physicist claims that philosophy, history, and sociology bear little relation to changes in the sciences and should avoid making claims based on their interpretation of those changes. Not surprisingly, it is precisely what have been called "radical claims in popular books," implying that "fundamental flaws have been found in the scientific worldview, and that one has to rethink the *notion* of law of nature," that have apparently aroused the fury of natural scientists.[8]

It seems that the first question that looms over us is, specifically, the matter of this gap between the view of at least some physicists and that of philosophers and others. We noted above the position asserted by Sokal regarding natural scientists who maintain their belief in the existence of an external world whose properties are *independent of humanity* as a whole because they are encoded in eternal physical laws. This is an established position, already set out in the writings of Galileo, who contrasts natural science with law and humanities insofar as the former is not dependent on human judgment but acts in accordance with immutable laws, caring nothing for the limits of human understanding.[9] Cultural theorists, against whom these arguments have been directed, have replied that it is intellectually incompetent to set up an opposition between truth and objectivity on the one hand, and nihilistic, relativistic constructionism (postmodernism) on the other.[10] Nevertheless, as Barbara Epstein points out, there are strong and weak versions of postmodernism, and for the strong version, it is indeed the case that there is no "truth," because all perception of reality is mediated by discourse, which has no external standard by which to measure it.[11] The effect of this position is that all claims to truth have equal status, leading to the conclusion that postmodernism is "relativistic."[12] Ultimately, she argues, postmodern literature adopts an attitude of radical skepticism with respect to truth claims and objective reality. As we articulated this in the preface, postmodern formalism, modeled on mathematical formalism, equates truth with demonstrability, but formal languages cannot formulate their own notion of truth. Higher concepts of truth do not lie in a single proof but in the process of finding formulas for different problems in a conceptual becoming that has no end.[13] With respect to the strong versions of formalist postmodern theory, it is not simply a matter of continually revising truth claims as knowledge changes and grows, but of maintaining an extreme social constructivism with respect not only to social and political positions, relations, and identities, but also with respect to epistemology itself.[14]

Ironically, at least some of the impetus for the postmodern relativistic view may have come from the noted physicist Werner Heisenberg. To the dismay of more "measured" physicists, Heisenberg wrote that for quantum mechanics, it is no longer possible for physicists to speak about the behavior of particles independently of observing them, thus their objective existence in space and time is also called into question, and science therefore is not an objective observation of nature, but alters and refashions its objects of investigation.[15] Even if a physicist were able to accept this loose account of quantum uncertainty (the theory that light acts as both a particle and a wave), it would be inappropriate as a characterization of certain methods universally utilized in physics. We cannot, for example, ignore the predictive power of differential equations.

> In the 300 years since Newton, physicists have come to realize that the laws of physics are expressed in the language of differential equations. This is true for the equations governing the flow of heat, air and water; for the laws of electricity and magnetism; even for the unfamiliar and often counterintuitive atomic realm where quantum mechanics reigns. In all cases, the business of theoretical physics boils down to finding the right differential equations and solving them. When Newton discovered this key to the secrets of the universe, he felt it was so precious that he published it only as an anagram in Latin. Loosely translated, it reads: "It is useful to solve differential equations."[16]

It is perhaps because such mathematical tools do exist and are universally acknowledged and utilized that Epstein claims that some theorists were uneasy about postmodernism from the start. The postmodern embrace of instability called for the dismantling of classical values even while allowing a new set of values to establish themselves, unacknowledged and without any critical scrutiny, a celebration of fragmentation without an accompanying search for coherence.[17]

Although, as several critics have pointed out, postmodernism came to the United States via diverse routes, many of these different discourses found inspiration in the work of Michel Foucault. In *Power/Knowledge* in particular, Foucault makes a number of arguments advocating the ascendancy of subjugated knowledges, which, he claims, had introduced instability through discontinuous, particular, and local criticism but had been disqualified by the "inhibiting effect of global, totalitarian theories."[18] Although most of the subjugated knowledges described by Foucault arise in relation to historical knowledge, local or regional knowledge, or experiential knowledge, this is quickly obscured by claims that such knowledges were policed in the name of "Truth" and "science," "*an idea that is as arbitrary as any other*," and that genealogies (knowledge of subjugated knowledge) are "anti-science."[19] Although Foucault states that he does not advocate ignorance or deny the possibility of knowledge but merely wishes to oppose the more egregious effects of scientific discourse, nevertheless, since the claim that some knowledge is a science is for him a claim to power, and since he believes that the scientific hierarchy responds to genealogies with immediate co-option, recodification, and recolonization by what he calls "unitary discourses" such as science, then the task of genealogy is to expose what is at stake in the struggle against power that is nothing but the demand for a unitary discourse and power that invests *scientific discourse*.[20] But in addition to scientific discourse, Foucault goes on to link power to the deployment of force in struggle, conflict, and war, thereby taking the struggle against the unitary power effects of scientific discourse out of the purely discursive realm and bringing it into the concrete, material world.[21] Warfare is everywhere. There is no institution that is not at war and the war against science was declared.

Foucault's position appears to have been highly influential among social scientists. In tracing the responses to the Sokal essay from various postmodern intellectuals, Epstein cites in particular the argument of Bruce Robbins, one of the editors of the journal *Social Text*. Robbins argues that scientific "truth" had been utilized to oppress women, African Americans, gays, and lesbians, in other words that "the concept of truth is questionable on political grounds."[22] As Epstein sees it, he is using the "truth" of postmodernism to combat the "truth" of science, a tangled web indeed. She agrees that some claims about these groups are not true, but she asks, does this mean that the *concept of truth* should be rejected or that we should merely reject *false assertions*? When Robbins goes on to make ad hominem attacks against theorists who supported Sokal (such as Katha Pollit, a feminist journalist, and Epstein herself, a professor of the history of consciousness, among others), we are left, she argues, with self-righteous posturing, striking poses that convey moral superiority, and "the sneer built into postmodernist discourse, a *cooler-than-thou* stance."[23]

Robbins's position might be contrasted with that of Meera Nanda, a PhD in science and technology studies, a self-described "one-time biologist, science writer and partisan of science-for-the people movements," as well as author of *Prophets Facing Backward: Postmodern Critiques of Science and the Hindu Nationalism in India*.[24] Like Epstein, Nanda argues that "strong programme" sociologists and epistemological relativists advocate a fundamental asymmetry at the core of their ideas. This is that statements of facts about nature are suspect as value-laden, even as social and cultural values are beyond rational criticism and reasoned change.[25] Moreover, she wonders what the results of so-called interactionism in science might be, since it invites disregard for external consistency with the existing body of scientific knowledge, thereby weakening the goal of any shared, publicly recognized standards that would in fact keep subjective biases in check.[26] Finally, she emphasizes that modern liberties, including feminism, came about only with the release of the natural from the dominance of the moral order.[27]

Expressing concern over the assertion of the Bharatiya Janata Party (BJP) in India that Hindu material science must have ultimate authority over what aspects of Western science and technology are allowed in schools, Nanda ventures into the defense of scientific realism. Her position is that "although not free from cultural biases, scientific reasoning does incrementally lead to knowledge that corresponds to the actual state of affairs in the world."[28] This is of particular importance for those who have long been oppressed by so-called situated knowledges. In India, women, lower castes, and working people need transcultural truths that are capable of exposing and challenging the local knowledges under which they have suffered.[29] She reminds us that in India, the popularization of science and the view of science as a tool of criticism against traditional authority had once played a prominent role in progressive politics. But students who are currently being taught nothing but the local mathematical knowledge–Vedic mathematics, for example–have limited tools, useful only for computation, rather than the more advanced conceptual tools of algebraic geometry that allow them to enter into the "real-world" mathematical problems they will encounter as scientists and engineers.[30] This is perhaps equivalent to denying history students knowledge of current theories and worldwide historical events and sequestering them in family history and interpretations, while deriding any wider historical views. The problem with elevating subjugated knowledges, for Nanda, is that an account of knowledge that makes the standards of validity internal to culturally conditioned consensus cannot escape epistemo-logical and judgmental relativism. Modern science, she argues, is not some-thing to be deconstructed and overcome. Instead it must be utilized to play an active role in progressive political movements the alternative to which, she believes, is nothing less than religious fundamentalism.[31]

Robbins's position might also be contrasted with that of Paul Boghos-sian, a philosopher of science from the analytic school of philosophy. Bog-hossian opposes what he calls "equal validity," that is, that there are many radically different yet equally valid ways of knowing the world, and that sci-ence is no more than one among them.[32] Regarding the hoax, Boghossian makes at least one salient point, which is that Sokal "peppers his piece with as many smaller bits of transparent nonsense as could be made to fit on any given page," including claims that the mathematical constant "pi" is actually variable, that complex number theory is recent and speculative rather than well-established and dating back to the nineteenth century, and that quan-tum field theory *confirms* Lacan's theory of the neurotic subject.[33] In the end, it is the unintelligibility of much of Sokal's text that leads Boghossian to the conclusion that the editors of *Social Text* simply do not understand the mathematical and physical ideas invoked. He cites Linda Nicholson, who in the introduction to her anthology *Feminism and Postmodernism* writes that the historicist claim that any inquiry is influenced by the values of the inquirer is indeed a very weak counter to the norm of objectivity.[34] Thus it seems to Boghossian, to paraphrase Robbins above, that the concept of objectivity is being made questionable on political grounds and that if one wishes to question the norm of objectivity, it is better to let a presumed objectivist such as a physicist do it without questioning the values that he brings to the project. In their own defense, the editors of *Social Text* claimed that theirs is just a magazine that publishes unreviewed essays, but one won-ders if they would have allowed publication of a text on, say, Foucault that blatantly misrepresented or distorted his views.

Boghossian writes at length about the nature of objectivity, confronting in particular philosophers such as Richard Rorty, a pragmatist, and Nelson Goodman, an analytical philosopher. Like Hannah Arendt and Edmund Husserl, whose positions we will discuss later in this volume, these philoso-phers identify Galileo's invention of the telescope as a defining event in the development of modern science. Summoned to the Vatican by Cardinal Bel-larmine, Galileo offered the cardinal the opportunity to look with his own

eyes, but the cardinal refused. It would have been so simple! It did not require any particular effort on the cardinal's part, no sea voyages, no dangers
of any kind, just the effort of looking, and yet he refused, citing the Bible as
his only source of evidence on the nature of the heavens.[35] The question that
arises from the cardinal's refusal is, what constitutes evidence? Certainly the
mathematically based Ptolemaic, Earth-centered view of the universe conformed to the view put forth in scripture, so that one cannot really accuse
the cardinal of being unscientific for following scripture.[36]

If we are to question this response, it must be on some other grounds,
and Rorty's claim that we reject the cardinal's response for being unscientific
does not stand, for it is certainly scientific in the Ptolemaic system.[37] The
cardinal is content with scripture because it has been widely substantiated
by the mathematically verified Ptolemaic *worldview*. Thus the cardinal uses
deduction to predict that what has been proven mathematically and scrip-
turally to be the case will hold true. Although the cardinal operates with a
different worldview, his rationality is the same as Galileo's.[38] However, since
using the telescope requires empirical, visual observation, and the cardinal
has been using his eyes as well as centuries of observations made by others to
verify the Ptolemaic system, he already has a crucial component for verifying Galileo's claims at his disposal. What might be said to be irrational is the
cardinal's decision not to look with his own eyes, since he knows already that
observation is certainly a necessary part of verification.

The View From the Cosmos

Clearly, Galileo hoped to convince the cardinal to use observation to
question the worldview under which he had been operating. Meera Nanda
alerts us to potential problems arising from a system that has no external
standards by which to assess its truth. That this is as much a concern for
humanities disciplines as for science is a point we must also raise. But for
the moment what is initially most strange about the contemporary situation is the demand made by Sokal that cultural theorists and philosophers
ignore science, that it has nothing to say to them. Under what constraints,
we might ask, have physicists arrived at the conclusion that there exists a
near absolute separation between what Sokal calls the external world with

its eternal physical laws and *mere humanity*? Must there be an unbreachable abyss between the world described by physical laws and the concerns of humanity? If so, why? And if not, why not? Is this abyss the only way scientists believe that they can keep cultural relativists out of their discipline? And even if reconciliation between physics and, at least, philosophy is possible, do philosophers and social scientists really want a single theory (set out either by philosophy or by physics) that governs them all? A single theory of everything? Perhaps the conception of an absolute break between the point of view of physics and that of philosophy is not the only viable alternative to a single theory? And if not, might it be possible to conceive of this break between the laws of physics and humanity in less catastrophic terms?

Although Isabelle Stengers has also been targeted by critics from the natural sciences, she has nonetheless addressed the conflict between the natural and social sciences directly, appealing to researchers in social science studies to understand the point of view of the natural sciences.[39] Scientists, she confirms, are indignant that their activities are becoming an object of study for philosophy, history, and sociology. They wish to differentiate clearly between those who have the right to intervene in scientific debates and those who do not.[40] They point out that the strong programme in sociology asserts that the proofs and refutations of science are simply effects of belief. Who, they ask, is this person, the philosopher, social scientist, or cultural theorist who claims to speak for *us*, for science and scientists? Scientists must protect their autonomy. The preservation of the scientific community is therefore of the greatest importance, serving as the norm and condition of the possibility for carrying out scientific activities. Within the confines of a specific research program, scientists do not need to justify, in advance, their priorities nor explain the appearance of unexpected or disconcerting results. The scientific community is indifferent, Stengers argues, toward difficulties, incomprehensible results, or anomalies unless and until they prove to be of use in countering the interpretations of other scientists, ideally leading to a new paradigm. The competent scientist is one who can evaluate the research in his domain, "his" own and that of other scientists.[41] However, the abyss between science and those who study it from outside or seek to project its discoveries onto a worldview appears to be rooted in something more profound than the distinction between the scientific and nonscientific communities. The correlation between formalist methodologies in mathematics and postmodern philosophy has deep roots as well as critics.

To this end, philosophers have acknowledged not merely the importance of Galileo, but the shift in the conception of truth that resulted from
his discoveries. Edmund Husserl refers to Galileo's mathematization of nature. Contrasting this with the approximate and fluctuating nature of the
intuitively given world, Husserl emphasizes that geometry is concerned with
carrying the perfection of ideal shapes as far as possible and enabling mental
manipulation in a world of pure *ideal geometrical* objects.[42] This is of particular importance because "geometry is to be understood as the foundation
for the meaning [*Sinnesfundament*] of exact physics."[43] However, although
mathematical demonstration makes possible the mental manipulation of
the world of ideal geometrical objects, Galileo had a good laugh at the "glo-
rious folly" of some unnamed philosopher in Padua who refused to look
through the telescope, preferring logic to the evidence of the experimental
apparatus.[44] In other words, as we have seen in the case of Cardinal Bellarmine, experimental verifiability is crucial. Logic cannot tell us which pure
concepts are merely logical possibilities and which are possible to verify.[45]

Stengers goes on to argue that what sets Galileo's account of the law of
motion apart from the interpretation of philosophers lies in the distinction
he draws between the causes of acceleration (the question why), about which
philosophers express different opinions, and the properties of accelerated
motion applicable to registers animated by a naturally accelerated falling
motion. In other words, there is a profound distinction between opinion
and demonstration.[46] But let us not forget that Galileo first conceives of and
constructs the experimental setup, a wood molding with a single smooth
straight groove along which a "very round" bronze ball is rolled when the
wood is placed in a sloping position, one end raised above the other, along
with an ingenious device for measuring time.[47] But then, as Stengers points
out, he withdraws, letting the phenomenon *speak for itself,* and in so doing
it silences his rivals. Nonetheless, what the apparatus says is governed by
the conception of speed as formulated by Galileo: speed gained when the
moving body changes altitude, the speed of the moving body at a given moment, and the speed of its horizontal, uniform motion. The three notions
are related insofar as "the instantaneous speed characterizing the moving
body at the end of its fall is equal to that which it had gained in the past and
to that which in the future will characterize its uniform motion."[48] Stengers
characterizes the law of motion as an abstract (meaning purified of extraneous elements), created fact, an artifact of the experimental construct, but

it is something more than this. It produces truth with regard to a reality it discovers, or rather invents. To illuminate this aspect of modern science, let us turn to the analyses of Hannah Arendt.

The Demise of Great Words and Deeds and the Rise of Necessity

Hannah Arendt is overwhelmingly identified as a political philosopher who objected to the discipline's privileging of contemplation over the political. But as Margaret Bentz Hull points out, this is due primarily to Arendt's objection to the hierarchical ordering of contemplation over politics.[49] Hull's thesis is that Arendt's philosophical dimensions lie in her commitment to human interaction and plurality, which resulted in the creation of a "philosophy of mankind" that respects both the philosophical and political plurality of human beings.[50] Plurality, in this instance, refers to "the concrete living and interaction of 'men,' . . . [who are not] 'endlessly reproducible repetitions of the same model, whose essence and nature were the same for all and as predictable as the nature or essence of any other thing,'" a characterization Arendt refers to as multiplicity.[51] Nevertheless, the distinctness of each person is formed only through interaction with others in a public realm.[52] Arendt's idea of human interaction, Hull points out, arises from her appreciation of the philosophy of Immanuel Kant, in particular Kant's notion of judgment as interactive and interdependent, reliant on others with needs and wants in order to form any human expression.[53] In other words, "a plurality of competing wills and intentions combine into events not singularly willed" in accordance any one person's intentions.[54]

Unlike most readers of Arendt, Hull reminds us of her philosophical training in phenomenology, which ensures that the existential existence of the plurality of human beings is the core of her philosophical thinking. Arendt's correspondence with Karl Jaspers clearly lays out the position that philosophy only theorizes human beings as abstract, therefore identical individuals, thereby ignoring the ontological nature of their plurality.[55] Although every person inhabits a perspective on the world, Arendt proposes that insofar as the same world opens to everyone, there is a common world and a shared humanness.[56] As Hull points out, even thought, for Arendt, is an interaction with oneself and therefore not a solitary activity.[57]

Of equal importance is Arendt's phenomenological analysis of appearance. Although our bodily organs and brain structures are more or less the same "inside," this inside does not appear to us. Rather, the world appears in the mode of what Arendt calls "it-seems-to-me," which depends on perspectives determined by a being's location in the world as well as its organs of perception, including the relentless succession of inner sensations that never assume an identifiable presence.[58] This leads to other important questions. The first among them might be, what is it that grounds appearance?

Were we to assume the necessity of a transcendent ground of appearance, a Kantian thing-in-itself, this ground would be nothing more than our inner organs, their sensations and perceptions. A strange sort of divinity, Arendt points out.[59] No isolated senses or sense object can produce reality. Thus generating a concept usually attributed to Gilles Deleuze, she states that this is why art, which transforms sense objects into thought-things, tears them first of all out of their context to de-realize them and prepare them for a new function.[60] Moreover, without thought, we would lose the ability to produce thought-things like works of art as well as the capacity to ask questions whose answers once seemed unattainable.[61] Conversely, she adds, no consciousness of an acting self that had suspended faith in the reality of intentional objects would have been able to convince us of our own reality had we been born without a body and senses and without fellow creatures to confirm that they perceive the same thing.[62] Ultimately, Arendt maintains, our faith in the independent existence of objects depends on those objects appearing to others, and out of this we experience a sensation of reality, a feeling of realness that we must take care to differentiate from thought.

We examined in the preface the manner in which formalists sought to replace truth with proof and demonstrability. However, for Arendt, thinking is completely incapable of proving or disproving the sensation of reality, *le bon sens*, literally the good sense, because thinking withdraws from appearance and from sensation.[63] Nevertheless, we have seen that it is mathematics, which is the farthest removed from *le bon sens*, that has played the largest role in modern science. This has led to the conviction in modern and postmodern philosophy that mathematical reason should be the paradigm for all thinking, even though it remains the case that only factual statements are scientifically verifiable, because, as Arendt reminds us, "a triangle laughs" remains a meaningless statement.[64] Thinking is powerful insofar as it allows us to extend reason beyond the limitations of sensation and the sensory world. Yet Arendt agrees with Kant that pure reason produces no knowledge and does not move in the realm of appearances, and so cannot be the source of deception and illusion, which belong to *le bon sens*, but only nonsense and meaninglessness. The problem is that ideas of pure reason demonstrate nothing, but they pursue only their own interests: God, freedom, immortality, meaning the disjunctive, the hypothetical, and the categorical logical functions of the understanding.[65] With this account of Arendt in hand, let us proceed to Arendt's analysis of modern science and philosophy, using it to address our thesis concerning postmodern philosophy's scientific turn.

We have noted in the preface that, with extraordinary insight into the workings of science, Arendt argues that the modern cardinal virtues–success, industry and truthfulness–did not come from political communities or theories but from the learned societies and Royal Academies of scientists, which proscribed rules of behavior and standards of judgment. From the seventeenth century, scientists were organized so that the "collective effort of the best minds of mankind" could take on the overwhelming task of investigating nature.[66] It is, she maintains, one of the great ironies that persons considered to be the least practical and the least political were the only ones capable of acting, which is to say, acting as a community with moral standards and a code of honor.[67] But what sort of a community are we talking about? To answer this question Arendt contrasts the organization of contemporary scientific communities, and their political offshoots, with the ancient Greek view.[68]

When Aristotle designated freely chosen ways of life, she maintains, labor was not among them. Labor was the way of life of the slave forced by necessity, as well as of the craftsman and the merchant, each of whom was thought to have lost the freedom of movement and activities.[69] By contrast, for Aristotle, the free life involved the enjoyment of beautiful things, the carrying out of beautiful deeds in the *polis*, a particular kind of activity that Arendt specifies as the *vita activa*, the human life of active engagement. The only free alternative was the contemplation of beautiful because eternal things.[70] Neither labor nor work were considered to be forms of the active, free life; quite the contrary, they were taken to circumscribe the life of necessity. Although the term was already waning in the thought of Plato, by the time of Augustine the term *vita activa* lost its philosophical and political meaning of free action, action untainted by securing the necessities of life in the realm of human affairs. Already it was transformed into an aspect of necessity, leaving contemplation (*bios theōrētikos*) as the last and only remaining free and quiet way of life.[71] As Arendt argues, the term *vita activa*, once it took on the negative connotation of an unquiet activity, came to be connected with the Greek distinction between things that are *physei* (what they are by themselves) and things that are *nōmō* (things that owe their existence to man), with the implication that nothing made by men could equal the beauty and truth of the physical realm, the *kosmos*, which only contemplation can discern.[72]

A second distinction comes into play to influence this development. The ancient Greeks, Arendt maintains, sought immortality in a world in which they alone seemed to be mortal. They sought this through their ability to make things, through great deeds, great words, and great works.[73] Preferring immortal fame to mortal things, not content to live and die like animals, the Greeks characterized the life of the citizen as the *bios politikos,* the life of political speech and action, which constituted the *vita activa.* By contrast, philosophers from Plato forward privileged the eternal over the immortal. The eternal was posited as a kind of death, because it no longer required living among men, but instead called for removing oneself from the company of other humans, because striving for immortality was judged to be vanity.[74] Thus the contrast with the former view of the *vita activa* could not be stronger, for the latter is specifically rooted in the human world, implying that the political creature is political and free only in the human world and only in the presence of others.[75] This reduction of the supreme importance of the political life and the presence of others, which alone was thought to offer the chance for immortality, that is, for great words and deeds, leads eventually to its identification with something quite different, something that excludes the possibility of immortality, that is, it gives rise to the social. But the social, Arendt cautions, is only *that sphere that human life has in common with animal life.*[76]

The Greeks considered the social to be a limitation imposed by biology and therefore part of nature and not an aspect of the *bios politikos,* which included only action (*praxis*) and speech (*lexis*), activities in service to immortality, each of which exclude anything useful or necessary.[77] If, as Arendt maintains, finding the right words at the rights moment is action, then surely the ancient Greeks already understood the power of the linguistic performative, that one can do something by saying something, but with the proviso that violence is mute and will never be seen as greatness. In other words, "to live in a *polis* meant that everything was decided through works and persuasion and not through force and violence."[78] In this way, the political animal of the Greek *polis* was a human capable of persuasive speech rather than a simple, rational animal, and certainly not a mere social animal. In addition, the function of the *polis* was entirely distinct from that of what today is called society. This is because of the manner in which society emerged from what the Greeks took to be the purely private sphere whose driving force was life itself and the sphere of necessity that life invokes.[79] Life was understood to be preoccupied with the maintenance and survival of the body, the sphere of necessity where slaves labored ceaselessly in accordance with the rhythms of nature's cycles. Only the *polis* was understood to be a sphere of freedom, the sphere of immortal speech and action where one's daily acts were not restricted by necessity, the necessity of protecting the faithful, protecting property, protecting acquisition, or protecting jobs.[80] In short, for the ancient Greeks, the political realm is to be clearly distinguished from nature's necessity, nature's chaos, and natural hierarchical and cyclical processes in general. This, as we will see, is what the modern scientific revolution put an end to once and for all.

What changed involves at least two things: one, the modeling of all human relations on the household, and two, the overcoming of even the social by the organic, by nature understood as a process, giving rise to philosophies of life. If, according to Arendt, the ancient Greeks considered the *polis* to be the sphere of freedom, then the privacy of the home and household were entirely devoted to necessity, to life itself; maintaining the body and the species, nourishment, reproduction, and all economic activity were taken to be a thoroughly private affair.[81] In the household, only the head of the household could be considered free, because he could leave necessities behind to enter the *polis*, the realm of speech and action open only to peers.[82] Jean-Pierre Vernant claims that by the end of the seventh century BCE, the Greeks began questioning their entire system of values, leading to legal and ethical reforms, but that the starting point of the crisis was economic.[83] The aim of these reforms was to re-establish justice (*dike*), a principle both common to and superior to all, subject to discussion and modification, but expressing a sacred order.[84] The Greeks had strayed from their former rejection of aristocratic excess (*hybris*), which by accentuating social inequalities increased the distance and dissimilarities between individuals, giving rise to envy and discord.[85] The purpose of justice was to guarantee equitable, although not equal, distribution of duties, honors, and power.[86]

But in this movement of reform, we see already the first articulation of what Arendt takes to be the origin of philosophies of life, that is, the elimination of the boundary between activities that serve "only the purpose of making a living, of sustaining only the life process" and the political realm, the blurring of the borderline between raw life and the *polis*.[87] Vernant points to "a brief but suggestive remark of Aristotle's" in the *Politics* in which Aristotle wishes to show that the *polis* is like an extended family, formed by the merging of villages that themselves merged out of individual households. In this way the domestic family (*oikos*) becomes a natural community (*koinonia*) and the model for society in general.[88] By referring to members of the family as those who share bread and eat at the same table, Aristotle further evokes the Spartan institution of giving citizens the feeling that they are brothers by sharing food prepared at the same hearth and eaten at the same table.[89] Perhaps this is also the point of Plato's edict in *Republic,* that guardians will not have private families but will maintain a life in common, a public form of the formerly private life.[90]

Greek society condoned slavery in order to be free, that is, slavery was the attempt to exclude labor and necessity from life, but modern philosophers do not distinguish the labor of the body from the work of making, nor even from the life of, speech and action.[91] Moreover, the modern philosophers brought labor out of the private sphere and into the public realm. According to Marx, laborers do not sell their labor, "what they actually sell to the capitalist for money is their labour-power. This labour-power the capitalist buys for a day, a week, a month, etc. And after he has bought it, he uses it up by letting the worker labour during the stipulated time."[92] Labor-power produces what it needs to reproduce itself and yields a surplus beyond what it needs, thus *what it produces is life and nothing but life,* and because of its surplus productivity, the labor of some suffices for the life of all.[93] Moreover, "political economy knows the worker only as a working animal–as a beast reduced to the strictest bodily needs."[94] But it is not only the unskilled who are reduced to the labor of necessity. According to Marx, "the bourgeoisie has stripped of its halo every occupation hitherto honoured and looked up to with reverent awe. It has converted the physician, the lawyer, the priest, the poet, the man of science, into its paid wage labourers."[95]

As Arendt points out, when there is no distinction between menial tasks and the making of durable things, between skilled and unskilled, manual and intellectual tasks, then society has arrived at a one-dimensional, social point of view in which all things belong to the life process as objects of consumption.[96] Every individual sells labor-power and nothing but labor-power. The physician, lawyer, priest, poet, and scientist are simply menial servants and nothing more.[97] Their labor, like that of the slave, is now considered to be utterly consumable. When all making, speech, and activity are reformulated in terms of labor and the necessities of life, when the philosophical realm is reformulated in terms of the cyclicity of nature's eternal recurrence as the highest principle, then human life is no different from the biological life of any other animal species, that is, it is species life, deathless and everlasting, cyclical and repetitive, like all of nature.

The Community (of Scientists)

Does this characterization of all human activity as reduced to a single dimension, that of labor in service to necessity, also characterize the community of scientists? And if so, then on what basis do they differentiate themselves from philosophers, sociologists, and cultural theorists? According to Arendt, the difference between modern science and philosophy is clear. Observation is the oldest scientific methodology known to Western science. What made Cardinal Bellarmine so secure that his idea of evidence was modern is the addition of mathematics. But the mathematics of Bellarmine was still Euclidean, still tied to the three-dimensional human perceptual realm, the close range of the senses. Had he observed the heavens through the telescope, he would have experienced the Archimedean point of view, which, when combined with modern mathematics, made modern science possible.[98] The modern transformation of science by algebraic geometry, a transformation contrasted with and problematized by our human, earth-bound terrestrial nature, also contributed significantly to the separation of modern science and philosophy. The viewpoint of modern natural science, a view that commences approximately with Galileo and continues into the present, arose from the wholly "un-Platonic subjection of geometry to algebraic treatment, which discloses the modern ideal of reducing terrestrial sense data and movements to mathematical symbols."[99] It is un-Platonic insofar as throughout Plato's oeuvre, the philosopher is represented as someone who comes to know the ideal of the forms beginning from sensation. This is clear, for example, in both the encounter with beautiful individuals of the *Symposium* and in the confusion and squalor of the sensible life in the cave, described in *Republic*. In the former, the ideal of beauty is filtered out of the sensible encounter that begins with a single beautiful body; in the latter, the sensible is revealed to be what is initially encountered as reality, but is then revealed to be nothing but the dark shadow existence or degenerate form of the good.[100]

In contrast, while acknowledging the importance of experiments to convince others, Galileo seems to have felt no need to make them for himself or to make the least possible number of experiments. He may have been guided by more than the mere insight that the universe is structured mathematically, that valid conclusions can be drawn from even a single experimentally discovered causal fact, conclusions that may then be extended well beyond the initial experiment.[101] What makes the difference between the cardinal's mathematics and Galileo's is the remoteness of the latter, the Archimedean point of view.

> Under this condition of remoteness, every assemblage of things is transformed into a mere multitude, and every multitude, no matter how disordered, incoherent, and confused, will fall into certain patterns and configurations, possessing the same validity with no more significance than the mathematical curve.[102]

Echoing this understanding, Edmund Husserl (himself a mathematician) argued that modern science provided a method for constructing, a priori, the infinitude of causalities that constitute the world. And although Husserl emphasized that this began not just with experiment, but with direct experience, such experience is admittedly fuzzy. The new mathematical methods made it possible to idealize an infinitude of bodies and to show, through measurement, that one can descend from idealities to empirical realities, obtaining thereby objectively true knowledge.[103] Mathematization of the world made possible general numerical formulae that express general causal interrelations, otherwise known as "laws of nature."[104]

Unlike any other language that we know about in the history of humankind, the language of modern science is mathematical, but in a specific way. It is *nonspatial and symbolic,* but it makes it possible to grasp geometrical dimensions and concepts, symbolically, geometrical dimensions and concepts such as the infinitely small or large. These are concepts that exceed the limitations of the human mind, in other words, concepts that cannot be actualized in lived space and time. This capability arose out of the algebraic treatment of geometry, which led to a completely novel approach to understanding nature, an approach utilizing symbolic representation rather than empirical observation as its starting point. For this reason, mathematics was elevated to the rank of the noblest science, "purified of human sensuality and mortality as of material perishability."[105] The goal of this method, as established by Galileo and his successors, has been described as that of "*obtaining quantitative descriptions* of scientific phenomena *independently of any physical explanations.*"[106] By the seventeenth century, mathematicians were aware of both the limitations and the capabilities of geometry and algebra. Geometry provided information about bodies in the world; algebra made it possible to reason about abstract and unknown quantities and to mechanize and minimize the reasoning process.[107]

Ingeniously, René Descartes combined geometry and algebra. By this means, he was able to represent a curved line by an equation that uniquely describes the points of that curve, and, conversely, to represent each equation as a curve. This association constituted a radically new way of thinking.[108] It constituted the power of nonspatial, purely symbolic representation such that mathematics ceased to be concerned with appearances at all. Arendt's powerful and compelling argument is that mathematics became *the science of the structure of the human mind,* treating geometry, the extension of nature and the world, as expressible in algebraic formulae. Conversely, as Arendt explains, when the new mathematics, called analytical geometry, proved that numerical truths are fully representable in terms of space, nothing beyond mathematics was needed for physical science. In other words, to the extent that the formulas of analytical geometry were able to be projected into concrete, extensive examples, their validity was secured. It was no longer necessary to begin scientific investigation with an immediate, sensible intuition. A distanced, mathematical one would do.

What does this really mean for human beings? What does it mean if observation-based reflection on lived experience, which had been the basis of philosophical thinking and political speech and action, is no longer operative or even valid in the natural sciences? Minimally, it seems to imply that thinking and theorizing about reality were removed from the web of human interactions into a private sphere, the private, symbolic corner of the rational mind. "*In this science man could move, risk himself into space and be certain that he would not encounter anything but himself, nothing that could not be reduced to patterns present in him.*"[109] In short, human beings would encounter only the mathematical order and mathematical operations inherent in their own patterns of thinking, but these patterns reflect exclusively the new universal standpoint. The arithmetization of geometry made it possible to formalize all spatiotemporal shapes using algebra. Spatiotemporal idealities, arising out of the human, terrestrial view, were transformed by purely numerical configurations so that in calculating them, there is always a tendency to forget that the numbers signify magnitudes.[110]

So perhaps it is not surprising that some scientists take these formulae to be nature itself since they are what make it possible for us to "produce processes which do not occur on the earth and play no role in stable matter but are decisive for the coming into being of matter."[111] This ability is what makes modern science universal rather than terrestrial insofar as Earth is just a special case of these universal laws. These numerical configurations are not, Arendt stresses, ideal forms–ideal forms would be ideal measures of sensually given data. Rather, they are the translation of such data by human mental structures, a translation accomplished by distancing the mind to a remote and uninvolved position as far from phenomena as possible. From this remote vantage point, "every assemblage of things is transformed into a mere multitude," and each multitude, regardless of how disordered, incoherent, and confused it appears to be, will be assimilated into some pattern or configuration, subject to mathematical treatment but lacking any other significance, including philosophical, historical, or cultural significance.[112] Thus we see that Sokal's position on the irrelevance of science for culture is nothing new, but was long established by scientists who were equally mathematicians and philosophers, and who began to think solely from a distanced and remote vantage point.

This may be why Husserl claims that the arithmetization of geometry led inevitably to the emptying out of its meaning and to a formalist point of view. When we forget that numbers signify magnitudes, when "pure analysis" is applied to geometry and results in universal formalization, the formal and logical idea of a world-in-general, and when it is no longer obvious that formal, symbolic concepts represent an abstraction and approximation, then the life-world is abandoned as the meaning-giving source of natural scientific techniques.[113] It is, Husserl claims, still the pregiven world that is the horizon of everyday, meaningful induction, which grew into induction according to the scientific method.[114] But this world, the world of sensibility and common sense, failed to be absolute, objective, immutable, and mathematical, and so was judged to be merely relative, subjective, fluctuating, and sensible. Not the realm of divine and human knowledge but that of opinion and illusion.[115]

Thus, as proposed by Galileo but embraced as well by philosophers such as Thomas Hobbes and John Locke, it was necessary in all instances to distinguish primary qualities, such as number, figure, magnitude, position, and motion, from their sensible secondary effects, taste, smell, sound, touch.[116] The sensible world is merely subjective; it is not real. As Husserl points out, this makes all truths of prescientific experience appearance and it makes extra-scientific life merely subjective. Thereby, it is devoid of value, nothing but a vague indication of the reality that transcends it.[117] If, as we noted above, the formulas of the universal science of analytical geometry could be projected into concrete, extended, and spatial reality, and if it appears that the truth of nature is mathematical, then our world is determined by a science and technology whose "objective truth and practical know-how are derived from cosmic and universal, as distinguished from terrestrial and natural laws."[118]

So perhaps we should not be too surprised that that there looms an abyss between those practitioners of the natural sciences and those of philosophy, history, social sciences, and cultural studies. Little might we wonder at the frustration of nonscience theorists who wish to understand their world, including the scientific view of it formed at a distance from and outside of that world. Little wonder too that social scientists and philosophers have sought to develop methodologies grounded in formalist natural scientific methodologies and worldviews, since it is these latter that claim to describe the truth of nature. But given this situation, there are several important questions to ponder. To what extent can this seeming abyss between natural science and philosophy be bridged, or is it unbridgeable? What are the limits of formalist natural science and what are the limits of formalist philosophy along with the other social sciences and humanities utilizing postmodern methodologies? To answer these questions for ourselves here and now, we might want to begin by examining some contemporary attempts to work this out, attempts that may be only partially successful but that nonetheless point to some of the difficulties we face.

2

THE NATURAL CONTRACT AND THE ARCHIMEDEAN WORLDVIEW

The Natural Contract

In *The Natural Contract,* Michel Serres makes a case for the juridical nature of knowledge in the natural sciences. "The sciences proceed by contracts. Scientific certainty and truth depend, in fact, as much on such judgments as such judgments do on them."[1] How does this occur? The claim is that science engages in a dialectics or dialogue that results in a contract between scientists and the world of things, a synthesis of human verdicts and the realm of objects.[2] This arises, according to Serres, from a fundamental situation in which two subjects find themselves in *violent contradiction* with one another yet bound by a legal contract that affirms that their war is a legal state in the theater of war that defines nature. The social contract guarantees that the combatants share a common language, that of the contract, and oppose a common enemy, which is anything, any *noise,* that would jam or shut down their voices.[3] Through the centuries, the violence of the combatants escalates, as the means for destroying one another becomes technologically more sophisticated and more devastating. But each time the combatants contradict one another, their confrontation results in a new synthesis, an objective state of violence.

The final state of the dialectic comes into view when their violence is finally "unleashed against the world," and not merely against other combatants. The effect of technological advancements in warfare, according to Serres, is to unleash violence that goes beyond two combatants (individuals or nations). So powerful are their weapons that rather than destroying one or the other, they destroy Earth, which has served as the theater of their warfare. The destruction of Earth, the destruction of the very the theater of war, thereby puts an end to history, such that history is stopping, stopping in the face of nature.[4] In this new and possibly final theater of dialectics, war has been declared on things, and Earth is the victim. Thus, for Serres, this *objective violence* against Earth is the violence that must now be the focus of our ethical concerns. What were once merely subjective conflicts between individuals or states have become objective war against Earth, evidence that the dialectic of violence returns eternally, and conflict or war is in fact not merely the motor of history, but has ontological status, that it is a newly discovered structure of nature and amounts to a new naturalism. Seemingly without limit or rule, war now appears to be an effect or force of nature, on par with that Hobbesian war of all against all before the social contract was put into place.[5]

Serres imagines the battle against nature as one in which two human combatants are sinking into quicksand, yet fail to heed the very Earth on which their contradictions take place. This dialectical account, dramatic and appealing, nonetheless calls for some scrutiny, from the point of view of ontology and ethics as well as from the point of view of the natural sciences. There is no doubt that Earth is our immediate environment, both for humans and for nonhuman living creatures, however broadly one is able to define that. Likewise, it is possible that, as Serres proclaims, "I am also an agent with a remote chance of having effects on a global scale measurable by the physical sciences" and that "collectively, we have powerful and weighty effects on the entire world of all the natural sciences."[6]

Nevertheless, we might ask if any of this matters from the point of view of nature, Earth, the solar system, or the universe? Or might it not be the case that environmental destruction is an issue of supreme importance only for humankind and that nature and the cosmos beyond have their own resources and orientations that are not those of humans? Quite possibly the claim that, collectively, humans have become as powerful as nature can be understood as a reflection of Arendt's focus on the Archimedean viewpoint of modern and contemporary mathematical natural science. Arendt's position is that the recent desire of humankind to be free of anthropomorphism and to ground thinking in purely formal structures may have unpredictable, possibly bizarre consequences such as the possibility that even the most remote and fanciful constructions of pure mathematics will one day be validated by currently unanticipated applications.[7] It seems that it is precisely these applications, such as the ability to convert mass into energy and energy into mass, that have led to our current destructive power. The indifference of the universe with respect to human concerns fuels the continued investigations of modern science and leaves the rest of humanity to clean up the trail of destruction left by the interactions of the application of these symbolic formulations.

Nevertheless, Serres is convinced that "monopolized by science and all the technologies associated with property rights, human reason conquered external nature in a combat . . . that sped up relentlessly with the industrial revolution."[8] To compensate for this, he argues, we must change our ways of thinking and being. But can we agree with Serres that we must become like men at sea, men who would perish if they were not bound by the necessity of a social contract of nonaggression and courtesy, since it is only for them that nature's elements come through, but only when they hear the voices of the Sirens, those "strange women who sing in the enchanted straits"?[9] Can we also agree with Serres that the all-important primal ontological scene embodies God the power, man the knower, and woman the pleasurer, and that we must return to this scene in order to re-establish an ethical relation with nature?[10] Clearly, these and other remarks call for more thorough investigation and thought.

Many scientists and mathematicians of the sixteenth and seventeenth centuries, including Copernicus, Kepler, Galileo, Descartes, Fermat, Huygens, Leibniz, and Newton, devoted themselves to the discovery of the mathematical relations that hold for the physical universe. The new mathematics of calculus made it possible to determine the instantaneous speed, that is, the rate of change of distance compared to the time, for objects moving at varying speeds.[11] By providing a theoretical description of universal gravitation and the laws of motion thought to govern all objects, Isaac Newton made possible the science of the motion of bodies that came to be called classical mechanics. Among science theorists especially, Newton's world of matter was "a world possessing mathematical characteristics, fundamentally," a world composed of indestructible particles corresponding to the philosophical category of "primary qualities."[12] Hobbes, for example, agrees with Newton's position, declaring that what we take to be sensible qualities are actually the motions of matter and nothing more–they are "extended bodies in motion, external to us, which cause by their motions the phantasms within."[13]

The goal of classical mechanics is to tell us how the universe evolves over time; for large objects, classical mechanics gives what have been called excellent results.[14] But classical mechanics is not *mechanical*. Rather, Newtonian mechanics describes something much more abstract and difficult to comprehend. It describes *forces* acting on a system where "forces are at each instant of time determined by the state of the system at this instant."[15] Gravity is the exemplary force. Newton theorized that the force of gravity between two celestial bodies is inversely proportional to the square of the distance between them. He sought to explain how variation in the state of a system over time is related to forces, such as gravity, that are acting on the system. Using Newton's equations and beginning with the initial state of the system, one may determine how this state varies over time and determine the state of the system at any other moment, future or past.[16] As the physicist David Ruelle points out, these ideas were quite shocking. Descartes, in particular, rejected the very notion of forces as absurd and irrational because he could not accept the idea that there is no contact between bodies.

Newton's mathematical science calls for a specific set of necessary presuppositions. Newton asserted that to understand space, time, and motion we should consider things themselves and not rely on our senses and our sensible measures of them.[17] Newtonian or classical mechanics has been described as giving us a specific representation of the world. First of all, it is *deterministic*. "Given the initial position, mass, and velocity of every entity in the system, a completely specified set of forces operating on it, and stable closure conditions, every subsequent position of each particle or entity in the system is in principle specifiable and predictable."[18] In other words, knowledge about the state of the universe at some particular time makes it possible to determine its state at any other time, where state refers to the positions and velocities of bodies in that system.[19] Formulated by Pierre Simon, Marquis de Laplace, the principle of determinism has presuppositions of its own. It calls for an intelligence who would know all the forces animating nature, as well as the situation of all the elements composing it, both the largest bodies and the smallest atomic bodies. Submitting this information to analysis would reveal, with certainty, the past as well as the future.[20] However, in order to sustain determinism, classical mechanical systems must also be *isolated or closed.* "If they were open to outside influences, none of the laws governing force-induced changes within the system could be expected to hold."[21] As we can see, an obvious implication of determinism is that classical mechanical systems are also *time reversible.* "(In the absence of friction and its analogues). . . . The laws specifying motion can be calculated in both temporal directions."[22] And finally, "Newtonian systems are strongly *decomposable* or *atomistic.* All changes in nature are due to the motions of atoms which are permanent in nature.[23] Newton committed himself to a 'corpuscular' or atomic theory of matter, and even to the corpuscular theory of light, long before any direct evidence for such a theory was forthcoming because he needed an ontology of point masses and additive quantities of matter and force."[24]

Newton's discoveries eventually led to the idea that the motions of all bodies, those on Earth and those of heavenly bodies, are governed by the same set of natural laws. It has been argued compellingly that the clockwork conception of the universe is truer of Laplace's theory than of Newton's and that the latter was greatly aware of nonperiodic perturbations sufficient to threaten the stability of the solar system. But Newton worked on developing successively more and more accurate approximations so that the deterministic model of the universe can be said to serve as an ideal limit.[25] Newton makes this explicit in his *Rules of Reasoning in Philosophy* where he also clearly establishes the importance of what he calls experiments. "We are certainly not to relinquish the evidence of experiments for the sake of dreams and vain fictions of our own devising; nor are we to recede from the analogy of Nature, which is wont to be simple, and always consonant with itself."[26] In other words, we make many inferences based on our experience, but as experience is subject to more and more precise measurements, these "experiments" are always subject to being made more accurate or even reversed as our ability to measure phenomena improves. "All these inferences from phenomena count as deductions from phenomena in the wide sense in which such empirically warranted propositions are contrasted with mere hypotheses which are not sufficiently backed up by measurements from phenomena to count as serious rivals."[27]

Given the reactionary and repressive, if not bloody, atmosphere of the seventeenth century, it is not that difficult to understand why mathematics and science, along with mathematical rationality, were eagerly embraced and why their capacity to explain a wide variety of phenomena, both natural and social, was welcomed with relief.[28] We recall, for example, René Descartes's joy at being released from the authority of a tradition, in whose faith in common sense and the senses Descartes finds only confusion and ambiguity, if not disaster, since its adherents threatened even his own well-being and peace of mind.[29] What was embraced as both beautiful and magical in Newton's formulations was that "a correct theory (e.g. Newton's theory of gravity and his second law of motion) combined with correct mathematical logic (the calculus) is a more trustworthy purveyor of truth than the purely empirical approach."[30] This approach was put to the test by Newton's mathematical derivation of Kepler's third law of planetary motion, which showed that Kepler's data, based entirely on empirical observations, was slightly incorrect.[31]

Among mathematicians, scientists, and philosophers, human reason was exalted, and mathematical reasoning applied to nature came to be regarded as the "purest, deepest, and most efficacious form of all thought," such that not only science but "philosophy, religion, politics, economics, ethics, and aesthetics were to be recast, each in accordance with the natural laws of its field."[32] Thus, the reach of Newtonian insights did not stop with predictions concerning the motions of earthly and heavenly bodies. Newtonian principles were, it seems, elevated, raised to the status of a generalized worldview, "an intertwined, interrelated, interconnected system of beliefs."[33]

Nature was postulated as a place of perfect freedom to order one's actions and possessions, but only within the bounds of the newly discovered natural laws. *Freedom came to mean independence of another man's will*, insofar as the free man would be guided solely by nature's laws. In this way, according to the philosopher John Locke, nature's laws and not other men determine the limits of human action, and nature came to be defined as a state where no man has authority over another; in other words, it is a state of *equality*.[34] If creatures of the same "species and rank" are born to the same advantages of nature as well as to "the use of the same faculties," each is and should be the equal of every other in every possible way.[35] Duties and rights as well as charity and justice are given their foundation in this equality of natural advantages and faculties. And reason, derived from the system of nature, is now called the *law of nature;* it determines that in a state where all are equal and independent, no one ought to harm another's life, health, liberty, or possessions.

The first rule of reason, derived from the laws of nature, is preserve oneself (God's servants cannot destroy themselves, for they may not disturb natural equilibrium); the second, do not take away or harm the life, liberty, health, limb, or goods of another (for the same reasons).[36] Men, therefore, can be restrained from invading other's rights or hurting others.[37] Equilibrium can be maintained among men just as nature's laws maintain it among the planets and stars. If it is the case that the tendency of a planet to fly off on a tangent is restrained and balanced by the gravitational pull of other bodies in its neighborhood, then this law can also be applied to the realm of men. Transgressors of other's rights are equally transgressors of the laws of nature and therefore can be restrained and balanced by other men. In other words, they can be punished. In nature, each man guards equilibrium. Simultaneously and significantly, each man is an individual. But this means only that each has the same faculties and advantages, thus each has the same rights and duties. Each individual is a little planet, a mass of matter, following the laws of nature.

Labor and the Revaluation of Values

Analogously, Hannah Arendt reasons that lacking any more solid basis for the establishment of private property, for taking it out of the commons, Locke founded it on the body, the property of one's own person, so that the labor of the body was, for the first time, identified with the work of the hands.[38] As such, property could also be understood to be the result of a natural process, that of the body and its labor, which cannot be shared but is given to each person for her or his private use. This implies that to put a check on private labor and its products amounts to an inappropriate intervention in a purely natural process, an intervention that would place the processes of individual bodies as well as the life of the society in which they flourish out of equilibrium.[39] The rise of modern science and its influence over all areas of experience may have produced or at least corresponded to a radical shift, not only in science and philosophy, but in society, in the role of labor and the understanding of life. We have seen Arendt's argument that for the ancient Greeks, labor was the way of life of the slave forced by necessity, as well as that of the craftsman and the merchant, who were seen as having lost the freedom of movement granted by free activities.[40] We noted her claim that neither labor nor work were considered to be forms of the active, free life; they clearly belonged to life's necessities. And when the term *vita activa* lost its philosophical and political meaning, that of free action untainted by securing the necessities of life in the realm of human affairs, the free life of speech and action came to be associated with necessity, leaving contemplation (*bios theōrētikos*) as the last and only remaining free and quiet way of life.[41]

We also have seen that in Arendt's version of history, what took the place of the *vita activa,* the life of noble words and deeds, was society.[42] The rise of society was made possible by the absorption of the private family unit into corresponding public social groups whose equality was constituted as equivalent to that of household members in the face of the despotic power of the household head.[43] The most significant change arising out of these transformations is far from trivial. The tendency of mass society to absorb social groups into one vast society resulted in the equalization of individuals, in effect replacing the *vita activa* with conformist behavior; "the rule of nobody . . . may indeed, under certain circumstances, even turn out to be one of its cruelest and most tyrannical versions."[44]

If Arendt is correct that the modern disintegration of the family coincides with the rise of society and the absorption of the family unit into corresponding social groups, then indeed equality is simply the equality of all under a despotic rule.[45] Mass society absorbs social groups into a unified, homogeneous society that views all persons from afar as statistically equal and more or less similar to one another, thereby making conformity the standard model for the good citizen.[46] The modern science of conformist behavior, Arendt asserts, is economics, because it relies on statistics whose laws are "valid only where large numbers or long periods are involved" and where individual acts are no more than deviations and fluctuations whose meaning and significance as historical or political deeds are simply erased, obliterated by the increasing validity of statistics, which, as populations grow and nonconforming behavior is less and less tolerated, become more and more accurate.[47]

Conformist behavior, as opposed to immortal speech and action, requires the introduction of a single guiding interest such as Adam Smith's "invisible hand," the "rule of nobody" that harmonizes conflicting interests and which itself is an interest proposed and substantiated as one with the life process.[48] This is because modern communities became "centered around the one activity necessary to sustain life," that is, all members of society, regardless of their education or activity, were transformed into laborers and jobholders.[49] Labor, that activity most intimately connected with the biological life processes, with repetitive and cyclical processes inherent in organic life, emerged from the private into the public realm and put an end to both the private sphere as the sphere of necessity and the political sphere as the higher realm of speech and action.[50] In the end, the Archimedean point of view has been projected onto the entire realm of human interactions through the mechanism of social contract theory.

As we will see, social contract theory does not directly protect the private realm; rather, it protects wealth, but without constant accumulation, wealth can be consumed and used up. For this reason, it was necessary, as Locke and Smith both make clear, to transform as much wealth as possible into something more durable that does not spoil. Thus the importance of capital. But capital also circulates, passes from hand to hand, just like a natural process, and so it never provides a truly stable structure for public or private life.[51] Those workers who have mastered the use of money have the ability to raise themselves above mere necessity. The so-called "masters" have no need to work but because all human activity has been defined in terms of labor, the masters are said to be condemned to a static life of leisure and consumption, or at best to a natural cycle of repetition, engaging in combat to enlarge their domain or defeat another master who threatens.[52] The master treats the laborer as a thing, a tool for the satisfaction of the master's wants. The laborer works on, to satisfy her or his own life-sustaining needs and to provide for the necessities of the master.

However, it has also been claimed that the worker learns to suppress all animal desires and to work for the sake of duty and self-discipline.[53] In this way, the laborer begins to transform nature, to transform nature's materials in a reverse Platonic manner, that is, by beginning with a concept or an idea that is then materialized, a mathematical concept that can be projected into physical and material reality. So we see that "modern and natural science is not the invention of idle masters, who have everything they want, but of slaves who are forced to work and who do not like their present condition."[54] In other words, even the Archimedean realm of abstract thought, the realm of mathematical abstraction, is labor, and the work of our most creative scientists is taken to be nothing but the labor of slaves. If labor represents freedom because it represents the ability to transform nature, to do so as a laborer is not to escape necessity, it is simply to redefine nature.

In other words, with the rise of labor, not only does the *vita activa*, the realm of free speech and action, cease to be held as the highest value, but the natural world itself alters. So we find, in place of the ancient Greek world-view according to which the Earth was situated at the center of the universe, where objects had essential natures and natural tendencies, and where sublunar phenomena inhabited a place of imperfection in comparison to the perfected superlunar world, that something new emerged.[55] The laborer masters nature; *he does this by utilizing his idea,* the idea of a calculable and predictable world on the model of classical mechanics. What emerged from this idea was an empirical world of testable hypotheses, a mathematically deterministic world organized on the basis of atomistic sense data and the external association of ideas derived from that sense data, giving rise to a social contract whose rules would guarantee a social and economic reality that would itself be closed, deterministic, atomistic and, if need be, potentially reversible (able to be dissolved into its original atomistic elements should that be necessary).

If the social realm participates in nature and is subject to the same laws as nature, we must not forget that these laws are established on the basis of "the certainty of mathematical demonstrations."[56] In order to make society deterministically certain, so that once rational rules were put in place society would operate in an orderly and predictable manner in accordance with those rules, the social realm must be organized by the same principles as nature. It would be closed so that as few as possible external influences could intervene in the social order, atomistic so that the rules would govern the movements of atomistic individuals in their purely external relations with other atomistic individuals, and temporally reversible so that the individuals making up the society could, if need be, dissolve the social contract and return to the state of nature. Thus we might not be surprised that the rise of modern natural science and the alacrity of those who engaged with its ideas rapidly produced a qualitative change in the relation between scientific knowledge and the political and economic process, beginning perhaps with the idea of mastering nature, that is, justifying the cultivation of what once had been common land in the name of transforming worthless "wasteland" into bountiful, private property.[57]

Out of the Quicksand

We have seen the claim from Serres, a claim affirmed by other combatants who contradict Serres's view of nature even while standing on the same quicksand, that once invented by the Europeans, the idea of mastering nature became the universal possession of all rational human beings.[58] The cultivation of land and the appropriation of whatever has been removed from the state of nature (private property) may be seen as simply a means to this end. For these dialecticians, the determinism promised by a closed political and economic system opened the eyes of Europeans to the idea of a progressive and continuous unfolding, a mechanism guided by natural rules, discoverable by reason. Once these rules were put into place, they would result in a stable, predictable political and economic system as long as it remained closed, deterministic, atomistic, and (in principle) reversible.

It appears to be Serres's aim to enact this reversibility right back to its primal scene, to end what he calls our *parasitism* with respect to nature and its objects, and to reinstitute reversibility. The arrow of time, he claims, often characterized by what the natural sciences call thermodynamics, takes everything from nature and gives nothing back. What is needed, he believes, is what he calls judgment; what is needed is to give something back, to reestablish equilibrium between men and nature, something only the judicial can accomplish as it brings flows into balance through exchange and contracts.[59]

However, does not such a return require a revival of the classical model of nature, that same system in equilibrium proposed by Newton that gave rise to the social contract? Is this nostalgia for equilibrium supportable? Or is it precisely the injection of classical natural law into the *vita activa* that has contributed significantly to bringing humankind to our current situation of mastery and possession with respect to nature? Is the thermodynamic arrow of time truly parasitic, as Serres claims?

For Serres, as for his combatants, those whose views contradict his own, the newly proclaimed natural right of self-preservation (new to the seventeenth century), extendable through labor to private property, leads to the rationally deduced claim that every individual or state has the natural and rational right to destroy whatever threatens *them* with destruction.[60] And, as was noted above, following the formation of a society governed by a rational and mathematical social contract, this right passes to the body politic. The implications and impact of implementing this structure and this right are generally taken to be so banal as to raise little interest or concern. Modern states must be large enough to protect themselves from external intervention, so there must be national unity. They must be able to mobilize resources on a national level, which requires a strong centralized state with the power to tax and regulate. Moreover, since technologically advanced societies have a decisive advantage in war and conflict, states have to break down regional religious and kinship ties so as to produce an elite capable of producing and using technology. And they must open the door to the enfranchisement of the poor so they can rely on these classes in case of war. Conflict, it is said, rather than cooperation, induces "men" to live in societies and to develop the potential of those societies.[61] By which is meant, war forces nations to accept the social and economic structures that support the modern liberal state.

Perhaps then, this how and why the model of modern natural science applied to the social contract has been elaborated in terms of the progressive conquest of nature for the satisfaction of individual human self-interest, which is to say, for the economic development of atomistic individuals that will, in principle, contribute to the development of all. Given the command to preserve ourselves through the cultivation of the formerly common "wasteland," an act of self-preservation that, as we have noted, transforms the land into private property, self-interest becomes a necessity. Not to act out of self-interest is irrational behavior. "The rational economic agents portrayed by Adam Smith 'maximize' their self-interest, a property supposedly rooted in their very nature as rational, economic atoms, by getting the most profit for the least expenditure of inputs like rent, labor, and raw materials."[62] But self-interest alone is not adequate to establish a science. The potential for unpredictable initiative remains, thus the need to introduce a scientific concept such as the invisible hand that guides economic activity apart from individual intentions.[63]

So in the end, it is not just individual behavior that counts but the stability of the market as a whole. Just as stable planetary orbits are constructed out of a moment-by-moment balance between inertia and gravity, a free market, into which producers and consumers can enter and exit at will, will produce stable patterns of production, exchange, and consumption. In this way the economic sphere will be run by laws analogous to those of a Newtonian system.[64]

Thereby, as Arendt has maintained, the social order seems to have been extended to include the economic order, that realm the ancient Greeks had deemed to be the sphere of necessity and which they kept separate from the free and active life of great words and deeds. Together, the socioeconomic sphere was posited as constituting a relatively autonomous system: closed, deterministic, atomistic, and reversible. Such a system could function properly only if left undisturbed, only if guided by the rule of no one, the *invisible hand*. In other words, since God need not interfere with the stars and planets once put in place, neither should governments interfere in the socioeconomic life of society.[65] Quite possibly, this led to the conclusion that if there was to be intervention, it should come only from the mathematicians, those laborers who are able to apply their mathematical ideas to the social sphere to create and apply the science of economics. In this way, insofar as each distinct society is closed (and the threat of conflict ensures that it remains closed), only the mathematical and rational laws of economics should inform the socioeconomic structure of the social contract.

For these reasons, Adam Smith may have felt able as well as obligated to give an account of the success of the new science of economy. "The causes of [the]. . . . improvement in the productive powers of labour, and the order according to which its produce is naturally distributed among the different ranks and conditions of men in the society, make the subject of the first book of this Inquiry."[66]

As atomistic, labor in a liberal democracy must be divided into the smallest possible portions for maximum results. "The division of labour, however, so far as it can be introduced, occasions, in every art, a proportionable increase of the productive powers of labour."[67] As the system is deterministic, that is, governed by pre-established rules, self-interest would guarantee that what is in the individual self-interest is in the interest of all.

"It is not from the benevolence of the butcher the brewer, or the baker that we expect our dinner, but from their regard to their own interest."[68] In accordance with atomism and reversibility, money was introduced.

> In all countries, however, men seem at last to have been determined by irresistible reasons to give the preference, for this employment, to metals above every other commodity. Metals can not only be kept with as little loss as any other commodity, scarce any thing being less perishable than they are, but they can likewise, without any loss, be divided into any number of parts, as by fusion those parts can easily be re-united again; a quality which no other equally durable commodities possess.[69]

Concerning the first of these principles, the division of labor, Arendt adds that when activities, including the activities of scientists, are divided into so many parts that each laborer needs little or no skill, then what is bought and sold is really nothing other than *labor-power,* which each laborer possesses in approximately the same amount. The implication of the concept of labor-power is that laboring activity possesses a productivity of its own, which is the human power to not merely produce enough to reproduce oneself but to leave a surplus. It is due to the surplus of human labor-power that "the labor of some suffices for the life of all," and it it this, Arendt maintains, even more than the division of labor, that is primarily responsible for the productivity of labor.[70] And, we might add, it is this that makes it possible for there to be so-called masters who live the life of leisure and consumption.

What is interesting for our purposes is that already in Smith we find that any and all activity is deliberately characterized as a species of labor, and that all productions are characterized as objects available for consumption. As Arendt points out, if this is the case, the worldly, objective quality of material things disappears, and material objects are understood only as products of labor available for consumption. Thus the so-called attack on things Serres decries began long ago when, under the influence of the classical view, all human activity was determined to be a species of labor, and life was defined in terms of production and consumption.[71]

In Western Europe, putting these economic principles into action is reported to have resulted in per capita income growing tenfold from the mid-1700s to the present.[72] Technological improvements contributed to market expansion, then to economies of scale through increased rationalization of the organization of labor. Specialized tasks are most profitable when sold to an entire nation or an international market, so increased productivity requires enlarging the internal and external markets while simultaneously creating an even greater division of labor. These developments, in turn, called for consistent, large-scale changes in social structures. The permanent relocation of populations from the country to cities was necessary to assure that there would be a steady supply of available labor for production. Increased urbanization guaranteed that cities would have the infrastructure to support specialized enterprises. And, along with urbanization, labor had to become increasingly mobile; workers cannot remain tied to a single job, locale, or set of social relations. They must be able to sell their labor to the highest bidder and to learn new tasks quickly in order to keep up with technological changes.[73]

The effect of this, we would argue, is deterritorialization, the undoing of traditional social groups: tribes, clans, families, religions, all of which lost out to labor organized by rational principles of economic efficiency. But individuals, freely acting and speaking human beings, were not simply set free. As Arendt's account implies, what deterritorialization set free was labor-power, the power of productivity. Initially, deterritorialization or expropriation deprived the laboring poor of the protection of family and property, exposing them to misery. Eventually, membership in a social class, in a socioeconomic group, replaced the family, and the nation-state replaced privately owned property.[74]

Of course, for all the efficiency and determinability of this system, certain questions remained. What if social and economic calculation are not all? What if they do not wholly and completely account for so-called human nature? What if some other human sensibilities persist? Moreover, what if nature, now so knowable, so predictable and stable, what if nature itself improbably altered, which is to say, did not act as required according to the Newtonian hypothetical-deductive method, even when understood as experimental philosophy? That is, what if, using mathematics to explain and predict the motions of physical objects and then testing these predictions, something else emerged, something that did not confirm the predictions?[75] Is it enough to say, as Newton did, that successively more accurate approximations will resolve contradictions and discrepancies? Perhaps, as human thinking has evolved, we are ready to answer these questions and perhaps these questions will be our guide in proceeding from nature to ethics.

3

SEMI-FREE

THERMODYNAMICS, PROBABILITY, AND THE NEW WORLDVIEW

From Determinism to Probability

What might be surprising about modern science, what might go against our expectations, at least if we follow Arendt's account, is that it already revealed the human capacity to "think in terms of the universe while remaining on the earth . . . to use cosmic laws as guiding principles for terrestrial action."[1] The view that the sun is the center of our solar system, for example, requires the idea that the universe is not a small, cozy place, that the stars are too far away to manifest any parallax (the apparent shift in the position of objects due to the observer's motion), and even the possibility that the universe is infinite, that it has no center and no periphery, so there is no motion either toward or away from the center of the universe. It requires the ability to imagine that humans are not the center of creation but just specks of dust in a universe of empty space.[2]

So, perhaps, although alienation from enduring, worldly things in favor of what can be produced and immediately consumed may describe the socioeconomic development of modern society, *earthly alienation,* the view of nature from a point in the universe beyond the earth, might in the end be the more persuasive and pervasive structure. At the same time, if the same sort of mathematical structures allow human beings to understand both heavenly and terrestrial bodies, if the ideas of philosophers only gained acceptance when validated by the factual consequences of repeatable experiments carried out in the newly developing natural sciences, then what is meant by "naturalism" might well be a function of the "demonstrable and ever-quickening increase in human knowledge and power, which in turn arose as earth alienation and the instruments developed to measure it which ushered in the modern age so as to create the very idea of science."[3]

For example, Kepler's three laws of planetary motion were based on his and Tycho Brahe's observation of planets. Derived originally from empirical observation, the application of these laws was limited to calculating elliptical motion, equal areas of motion, and the periods of revolution around the sun of the actually observed planets.[4] By contrast, Newton's laws of motion and gravity involved observable, meaning measurable, phenomena and mathematics. For this reason, they were able to be applied to an amazingly vast variety of phenomena, to light and sound, to electricity and heat, to liquids and gases and other chemicals, and even to biology.[5] As Arendt and others have observed, from the eighteenth century on, natural science became more and more mathematical in content, language, and method.[6] "Galileo and Descartes had proposed a program and philosophy, namely, that nature consisted of matter in motion and, that science had but to discover the mathematical laws of these motions."[7] Debate among mathematicians about whether or not axioms must be proven to be true rages on, but the axiomatic nature of Newton's laws of motion and universal gravitation are accepted by physicists who make use of them, and physics has become, more and more, the creation of mathematicians. Physicists adopted axioms, propositions requiring no formal demonstration, because they are accepted as self-evidently true or have been established as true, and because other, useful abstract structures may be deduced from them with what has come to be called certainty.[8] From the eighteenth century up to the present, "mathematical laws begin to make such sweeping affirmations about the universe that they jeopardized the titles of the traditional philosophic and religious rulers of the realm of truth. . . . revealing a new order and plan of the universe more majestic than any ever offered before."[9]

Philosophers, it seems, were not immune to the influence of the "mathematical spirit."[10] This was clearly affirmed by Descartes, who states that to guard against the weakness of memory and error, it is preferable to represent matters that do not require our immediate attention by means of highly abbreviated symbols such as those used by arithmeticians, for they are preferable even to geometrical figures.[11] Descartes elaborates, reasoning that we ought to begin our reflections with simple intuitions of simple propositions, which he calls *axioms,* in order to compare these with what we know, and to reach compound truths through deduction and deduction alone. Errors arise when we begin our deductions from particular or contingent facts instead of universal and necessary propositions. The pathway to certainty is lined only with self-evident intuitions and necessary deductions from those intuitions.[12]

It seems that the advancement of mathematics as the pre-eminent tool for thinking arose from a re-evaluation of its source and that this produced a re-evaluation of the very meaning of reason, as well as a re-evaluation of the content of our rational propositions. The philosopher Thomas Hobbes agrees with Galileo that bodies in motion follow the laws of physics; they stay in motion unless externally hindered. Sensible qualities are indeed caused by these motions of matter pressing on our organs, producing motion in us and leaving behind images.[13] The transition from one image to another, where these images are derived from our sensible qualities, form a train of thoughts to which names have been attached for the sake of remembering.[14] However, rather than relying merely on the order of images in memory, human beings make use of reason, that is, reckoning, adding, and subtracting. "Adding together two *names* to make an *affirmation,* and two *affirmations* to make a *syllogism;* and *many syllogisms* to make a *demonstration,* and from the *sum* of *conclusion* of a *syllogism,* they subtract one *proposition* to find the other."[15] In other words, the capacity to reason is a mathematical skill. It requires that one is able to go beyond what is merely given in the order it is given through the use of addition and subtraction, and this is what defines reason. As such, we can see that reason is not merely the result of the orderly flow of sensations. It is something much more and different.[16]

Hobbes asserts that philosophers should begin their thinking with definitions, but specifically definitions such as those used in geometry. Then they are to proceed from one certain consequence to the next until they can reduce those consequences to general rules called theorems or aphorisms, reasoning not only numerically, but utilizing whatever can be added or subtracted. Knowledge of consequences, the relation of one fact to another, when it is discovered through syllogisms, can be called science, whereas sense and memory are merely knowledge of fact.[17] In this light, we must pay attention to Hobbes's argument that reason proceeds in accordance with those theorems or aphorisms which are general rules, so that it is no less absurd to speak of a *round quadrangle* than of *free subjects, free will,* or any sense of freedom other than that of being hindered by opposition.[18] Nevertheless, Hobbes's conclusions regarding the symbolic and mathematical nature of reason remain vague, and a more precise account of what it means to reason mathematically was advanced by those philosophers who followed him, especially Locke and Hume.

Locke's philosophy has been called "an almost perfect reflection of the contents of Newtonian science."[19] Speculating, perhaps wildly, that the mind is a white paper, void of characters and ideas, Locke proposed that the materials of both reason and knowledge arise from our experience of external sensible objects or our experience of the internal operations of our own minds.[20] Perceptions provide the mind with the experience of sensible qualities, but more important, for the argument being advanced here, is the perception of the operations of our own mind, having nothing to do with external objects. The perception of the operations of our own mind is an internal sense, an experience of the ideas of perception such as thinking, doubting, believing, reasoning, knowing, and willing.[21] Mathematics does indeed figure large among the operations of our own minds. Perhaps there is no more forceful statement of the priority and privilege of mathematics for certainty and its source in the human mind than this one from Locke. "I doubt not but it will be easily granted, that the knowledge we have of mathematical truths is not only certain, but real knowledge; and not the bare empty vision of vain, insignificant chimeras of the brain: and yet, if we will consider, we shall find that it is only of our own ideas."[22] We cannot, perhaps, overestimate the significance of Locke's view that the knowledge a mathematician holds of, say, a geometrical figure like a circle is true, even of real things insofar as real things agree with what Locke calls "*those archetypes in his mind.*"[23] Whatever mathematical ideas have an ideal existence in the mind of the mathematician will be found, *for this reason,* to have a real existence in matter.

While acknowledging the existence and significance of this position is of supreme importance in and of itself, for our purposes what follows from this is equally profound. What follows is the statement that "moral knowledge is as capable of real certainty as mathematics."[24] Locke's justification for this position is that certainty lies in the perception of the agreement or disagreement of our ideas, and that the perception of the agreement of our moral and mathematical ideas is all we need for the demonstration of their certainty. But recall, this is not sensible perception; it is the perception of the operations of our own mind. This is so because our moral as well as mathematical ideas are themselves archetypes. They are always adequate and complete ideas and all the agreement or disagreement we find in them produces real knowledge, knowledge for both the moral and the mathematical realms.[25] Locke's meaning here is clarified in a later section of the *Essay Concerning Human Understanding*. Knowledge and certainty are the result of determined ideas. Determined ideas are ideas that answer to their archetypes and not to actually existing things. "All the discourses of the mathematicians about the squaring of a circle, conic sections, or any other part of mathematics, concern not the existence of any of those figures; but their demonstrations, which depend on their ideas, are the same, whether there be any square or circle existing in the world or no."[26] And if this is the case for mathematics, it is equally the case for the truth and certainty of moral discourses which abstract from the lives of men and the existence of virtues, and which exist nowhere but in the ideas of those thinkers who have given us these rules. What is true in idea is true in reality, and it is the former and not the latter that give it its certainty.[27]

Hume extends Locke's position to its furthest consequences. In principle, Hume's work uses reason to unseat the mathematical certainty that reason had attained. However, the circularity of this gesture is not without consequences and perhaps, paradoxically, Hume's efforts to refute all claims to certainty seem, in the end, to reaffirm, on the grounds of probability, all he would deny on different grounds. For Hume, all we know arises naturally from the association of ideas. When an impression strikes the senses it gives rise to a sensory perception, a copy of which remains and is taken by the mind to form an idea.[28] Such ideas are initially organized by the imagination in accordance with their resemblance to one another and their contiguity in space and time. Additionally, from the regular arrangement of such simple elements arises something completely natural but nevertheless profound. Of all the arrangements of impressions of sensation and ideas, only causation produces a connection that also allows the mind to go beyond what is immediately present to discover a relation of objects or to discover the real existence of an object.[29] Yet causation arises not from any immediate sensation, but only secondarily from the *relation* among impressions and ideas. For example, we find that causes and effects are, at first, merely contiguous in space and time, and it is the constant conjunction of one thing and another, as well as the priority in time of one over the other, that leads us to call one cause and the other effect.

Of course, Hume insists that the actions of matter are necessary, that as Newton's laws define matter, "every object is determined by an absolute fate to a certain degree and direction of its motion and can no more depart from that line than it can convert itself into an angel, a spirit or any superior substance."[30] However, as Hume emphasizes again and again, the relations between matter and mind are perfectly "natural" relations, and this means that the origin of the impressions and the ideas that give way to the relations between them is entirely unknown to us. In other words, we can never know the ultimate cause of impressions that arise from the senses, but the claim that matter follows necessary laws and the relations between matter and mind are natural remains effective and powerful. Impressions are like an afterimage when we close our eyes. But perhaps shockingly, in the quest for certainty, nature fails us here. This is because it fails to give us a causality that would validate the system of natural science that requires nature to be not only deterministic but absolutely certain.

Hume states that the actions of matter are necessary actions, that they follow the dictates of Newton's laws of motion. As we have noted previously, according to Newtonian mechanics, for a given system, knowing its state at a given time makes it possible to determine how it varies over time and therefore to know the state of the system at any other moment.[31] However, under the specific conditions asserted by Hume, the constant union of bodies and the inference that they are necessarily connected, it will always be impossible to decide with certainty whether impressions arise immediately from objects or as a product of the creative powers of the mind, or if they come from God.[32] Equally problematic, there is no original impression of causality (nor of space or time for that matter) and no impressions of deduction. "Habitually or customarily, merely because nature gives us the instincts to do so, we happen to believe that objects exist outside the mind, that things really are connected causally and that inductive inferences are probably true."[33] If nature fails us, Hume concludes, reason fails us as well, for "we can never prove that the future will yield the same as the past."[34]

Reason, it turns out, is only a sort of "instinct" that carries us along certain trains of ideas, ideas grounded in nothing more than the externally connected association of ideas, where external refers only to that proximity of one idea to another, based on resemblance, and producing habit. Habit is, however, a principle of nature and derives all its force from nature. In other words, if nature is stable, so will be our ideas and our reason.[35] But if nature were to turn out not to be highly predictable and closed, as the classical view promised, then human reason is likewise limited. As it turned out, such instabilities were not long in being revealed. Perhaps few scientists were aware of Hume's conclusions, but Hume's philosophy seems to have accurately reflected the scientific revolution in progress.

Dynamics and Thermodynamics

In a conceptual move not far removed from that of Hume, already by the seventeenth century Robert Boyle (1627–1691) had begun experimenting with gases. "After his experimental refutation of Hobbes's theory of the nature of the air, no important thinker dared again to promulgate a physics composed of deductions from general principles without careful and exact experimental verification. . . . [However, reason or] understanding remains the judge."[36] Boyle showed that air is compressible, meaning that air is composed of particles with space between, and that gas volume is inversely proportional to pressure and temperature (Boyle's law).[37] More important for scientists and philosophers, however, was the eventual conceptual break of science with strict determinism when it was recognized that the motions of individual particles of gas could not be predicted. Only their behavior in structures turned out to be somewhat predictable using methods of statistical sampling when gases were studied as aggregates of particles rather than as individual particles.[38] The significance for philosophy, and the resonance of Hume's view, is hard to ignore. If the stability of human ideas and reason is directly dependent on nature's regularity and predictability, but nature turns out to be merely probable and not certain, then where does this leave reason? Doubly probabilistic, it is a train of ideas grounded in habit, which itself is grounded in an uncertain nature, statistically probable but no longer classically, deterministically predictable, not even in the ideal sense Newton proposed.

Importantly however, Boyle remained committed to mathematics. Geometry—the science of magnitude, figure, and motion—was required to understand the operations of matter and the relations between its magnitude, figure, and motion, so that the entire world seemed to have a fundamentally mathematical structure.[39] The fact that any successful explanation of nature required mathematical principles convinced Boyle that mathematical principles and the axioms of logic are ultimate truths, superior even to God, transcendent truths, the universal foundations of all knowledge.[40] Boyle contributed significantly to clarifying the mathematical structure by insisting upon the need for precise definitions. He defined nature as a system of mechanical laws, a world of matter and motion, and in so doing provided a definition that could be qualitatively measured because it could be mathematically structured.[41]

Soon after Boyle's experiments with gases, Nicolas Leonard Sadi Carnot (1796–1832) formulated the first and second laws of thermodynamics. By quantifying the relation between heat and work, he discovered that energy is conserved yet not all heat can be turned into work. The first law of thermodynamics is concerned with quantity; it states that in an isolated system the total quantity of energy, whatever its transformations, will remain unchanged. The second law is concerned with quality and states that in an isolated system, high-quality energy is lost to friction in the form of heat as the effect of the fast-moving atoms. This erosion of the quality of energy implies that the universe is not symmetrical with regard to time. In other words, in addition to deterministic prediction, another key feature of classical systems, reversibility, is apparently lost wherever there are complex processes. Complex processes, it seems, have tendencies, they have directions, whereas with respect to particles or simple processes, reversibility can generally be maintained.[42] Like all classical systems, classical thermodynamic systems have specific requirements. They are not merely closed (allowing energy but not matter to be exchanged across boundaries) but isolated, thus without contact with any external events. Additionally, their final state is one of equilibrium where no further changes take place. Finally, their temperature must be held constant during the transfer of heat. If the system is externally heated, heating must be accomplished slowly with as little turbulence as possible.[43]

Thermodynamics studies energy, work, and heat, where energy is defined as the capacity to do work either by virtue of its position (potential energy) or its motion (kinetic energy) and matter is a potential reservoir of energy. Heat and work are means for transferring energy; the former transfers it into coherent action and the latter does it via temperature gradients. What is important about heat and work is that they describe *processes,* not things or beings. Work transfers energy via coherent motion but heat warms, making the thermal motions of a body more chaotic, more incoherent.[44] Although the rehearsal of these concepts may seem tedious to philosophers and other humanist thinkers, they are of great importance in contemporary philosophy–at least insofar as, as Arendt has noted, philosophers have taken up the study of processes over that of things in an attempt to solve philosophical questions brought to the fore by modern science–in particular, the question of determinism and freedom.

In thermodynamics, chaos refers to "random, uncorrelated, disordered, fundamentally unpredictable events."[45] More recently, some scientists have adopted the ancient Greek interpretation put forth by Anaxagoras, that chaos was the formless, equilibrated entity from which an ordered universe and an earthly "perfect mixture" arose. Mathematicians, using computer models of dynamic systems, have calculated that they can unmix perfectly mixed systems, retrieving the "original algorithmic state of the universe," recreating the so-called "generative mind of God."[46] It is important for our purposes to recognize that such reversibility is mathematical only, thus the result of an idealized process and, in this instance, a computer model. The possibilities for such a process occurring in nature are slim.

Mathematical dynamic systems, such as that proposed by Gilles Deleuze, are oriented by a related but distinct concept of chaos, that of deterministic chaos. "D chaos," as it is commonly called, belongs to systems whose initial conditions and whose mathematical rules of operation are known but which nevertheless do not have deterministically predictable trajectories due to uncertainties arising from initial conditions and boundary conditions. For our current purposes it is important to point out that these are theoretical and computer-based systems, which means a branch of "experimental mathematics," and that at present "*chaos is extremely difficult to identify in real-world data.*"[47] The models for such systems are limited to two or three variables and require large sets of accurate data, thousands or even millions of observations, which limits their usefulness in complex systems such as biological or ecosystems.[48]

In thinking about complex systems from a process point of view, some physicists have even posited that nature's laws may evolve. However, to the extent that this is conceivable, it is, as we will see, due to process irreversibility, as stipulated by the second law of thermodynamics, which has been called "the rule of rules."[49] Contrary to expectation, the second law is needed precisely to explain complex processes. The patriotic Carnot discovered that temperature differentials, called gradients, produce more energy for steam engines, allowing the English (who used them to produce coal, steel, and guns) to defeat Napoleon. But heat must flow . . . it must flow *into the cool,* meaning, atoms with higher average velocities, thus warmer temperatures, will mix with atoms of lower average velocities and correspondingly cooler temperatures in a situation where larger gradients produce more power.[50] If the world of idealized steam engines seems to be less than riveting philosophically, we must nonetheless persist in our study of gradients in order to understand nature's small-scale operations and to realize the role of thermodynamics with respect to living organisms, for gradients also operate for living organisms.

Gradients "are the source for the cyclical buildup of energy in natural machines that then seek out more energy to keep themselves going," extracting energy not from temperature gradients as do mechanical engines, but from chemical gradients, ultimately from that "great solar gradient the sun."[51] Let us note in this the central idea that energy can change forms but is not lost (the first law), yet that something is always lost in the transformation of energy from one form to another (the second law). Scientists like Robert Boyle, fascinated by machines, measured and predicted the behavior of huge collections of particles when a piston compresses gas in a cylinder.[52] It fell to Rudolf Clausius to divide heat, a measure of the quantity of energy, by temperature, a measure of the intensity of energy, and to show that over time this ratio increases. In other words, it has a definite direction. This ever-increasing quantity was given the name *entropy,* the principle of energy changing forms, able to be used until it could no longer change or make other things change.[53]

Phenomenological and Fundamental Laws

Here it may be also useful for our purposes to pause and make note of another important distinction prevalent in the natural sciences. In a recent work, science philosopher Isabelle Stengers reminds us of the important distinction between phenomenological and fundamental laws. This distinction is of consequence insofar as phenomenological laws are correlated with irreversible evolutions and so-called fundamental laws are correlated with the reversible processes of classical physics. Laws of physics are said to be fundamental insofar as they go beyond appearances to unify the diversity of physical phenomena. From this perspective, at least for classical physics, the distinction between before and after, past and future, is only phenomenological. It is a matter of appearance, such that uncertainty regarding the future is interpreted by at least some if not most physicists as ignorance.[54] In other words, under ideal conditions, meaning given more and more precise information and given the unlikely advent of a theory that can handle so much precise information, the expectation (or possibly hope) is that certainty would once again be possible.

For Stengers, what the distinction between phenomenological and fundamental laws indicates, and what some physicists may not take into account, is the existence of two types of deterministic laws. One is a science of movement or dynamics, for which the velocity at a given instant is equal to the cause producing it. If the velocities of all the points of a system are reversed the system would retrace all the states it went through during the previous change of state.[55] In the case, for example, of a pendulum, the velocity must be sufficient to allow the body to regain the altitude it lost, thereby joining past and future through the sign of identity. In this case, identity is understood as a syntactic rule, a rule defining velocity, force, and acceleration.[56] The second type of deterministic law is based on the study of unstable dynamic systems and allows a rapprochement of sorts between fundamental laws and phenomenology. Therefore, in a highly unstable system, starting from quasi-identical states, originally indistinguishable systems will behave dissimilarly and only a God capable of defining the instantaneous state of a system with infinite precision could calculate their trajectories.[57] This distinction exposes the limits of the physicist's ideal without abandoning fundamental laws.

Closely related to the distinction between stable and unstable systems is the question of change, that is, are changes in a system imposed from the outside or are they immanent to the elements of that system? Modern science and modern empiricist philosophy set themselves up in opposition to the latter, establishing the dominance of the idea of change as nothing but movement, yet with two possibilities. Either change is due to chance collisions of atoms or there is a force exterior to masses responsible for and governing movement.[58] Indeed, such a force was put into place in the form of the mathematical universal laws of dynamics, which imply that an object of dynamics can be completely understood and that the totality of its past and future can be deduced. And yet Jean-Baptiste Fourier's (1768–1830) formulation of the law of heat diffusion, insofar as it characterized the intrinsically irreversible process of heat flow, the first to be given a mathematical expression, led to the realization that dynamics, the description of nature as obedient and controllable, is a particular case of nature's behavior and not necessarily ubiquitous. Dynamics does not account for unities such as photons and electrons, whose processes imply irreversible interaction with the world.[59] One of the goals of our work will be to introduce alternative concepts that take into account not only the second kind of determinism, characteristic of nonlinear thermodynamics, but even more radical evolutionary possibilities mentioned above as well.

Eternal Return?

For the moment, what is philosophically striking in our study is that thermodynamics seems to put into question Nietzsche's principle of eternal return, the idea that everything that can happen will happen repeatedly an infinite number of times, as randomized conditions prevail in processes on their way to equilibrium. Contrary to this, the claim of statistical thermodynamics is that life processes grow more complex. For advocates of irreversibility, the rationale for eternal return, "the repetition of all particle combinations in a closed space over infinite time, and the intrinsic inability of dynamics based models to distinguish past from present," might be taken as philosophically driven rather than strictly physical.[60] But for most physicists, eternal return, the so-called ergodic hypothesis holds, and Ilya Prigogine's position (which we will examine in more detail below) is taken to be a philosophical prejudice.[61] That means that time or process reversibility would be a consequence of repetition or eternal return, but only in a closed or, more likely, a truly isolated space over infinite time. For a classical, complicated system such as that of molecules in a liter of water, if the system is isolated, over an infinite time "all configurations of positions and velocities of the particles that have the right total energy would be realized."[62] In other words, eternal return. Nevertheless, this is a highly idealized situation requiring total isolation and infinite time, something that has never been realized among the natural processes of our earthly lives. Of course, it is always possible that the oxygen atoms in a room will, for example, gather in a corner, leaving the inhabitants gasping for air, but statistically it is highly improbable, so you don't need to hold your breath.[63]

The main problem with the notion of eternal return is time–it requires infinite time–but one solution to the question of time is scale. Newton's deterministic laws of motion tend to operate for systems with a lot of mass, like planets. For bodies with small masses and sizes, thermodynamic statistics, probability, functions appropriately. For objects with tiny masses and sizes, such as atoms and molecules, the statistical distribution of energy microstates in a system, but not that of individual particles, can be predicted, although only probabilistically. What this implies is that in nature, the question of scale is of great importance. Some theoretical suppositions seem to be appropriate only at certain scales and no others. Additionally, the concept of eternal recurrence requires an isolated system with an inexhaustible energy supply, whereas if it is the case that our cosmos is an open system that is expanding infinitely, it may evolve eternally with no repetition at all.[64] As we can see, with every scientific advance there is a corresponding loss of predictive certainty. We have moved from the laws of motion understood as transcendental ideas that we can put to use to obtain certain knowledge, to the laws of thermodynamics, transcendental ideas that are merely regulatory principles, time-oriented and probabilistic, not reversible, and deterministic.[65]

At first this seems like a remarkable turnabout, probability rather than determinism. Are we not deliriously free, free of mechanical determinism? That is, if nature is probabilistic rather than determined, and reason is an effect of natural principles, then reason too tends toward the probable and not the certain. Otherwise stated, reason too would be no more than regulative and would give us no certain knowledge, justifying Hume's empiricist skepticism. In any case, following this model, it seems that human beings must be at least semifree, regulated with respect to how they think and act but not *determined* with respect to what they think and do.

But what really do we mean when we claim that the laws used to calculate the motions of particles are probable rather than deterministically certain? And what do we mean when we say that the ideas of reason are regulative? We have stated that according to the second Law of thermodynamics, in an isolated system where no new matter or energy enters, disorder must increase. So, for example, in the classical mapping of gas particles distributed in two chambers, there are far more disordered states (mixtures of particles in various states) than ordered states (mixtures of particles in a limited number of states). When we say that there are many more ways for particles to be distributed evenly (in various states) than lopsidedly (clustered, for example, in one corner of a room), what is meant is that probability is on the side of disorder, mixing, and dissipation. In other words, the probable state of particles is one in which their energy–once unconcentrated–is *of little use*. So, for example, heat on a sidewalk is of little use relative to the sunlight that generates it.[66]

Once again, we have arrived at the so-called arrow of time and left reversibility behind along with certainty, but such disorder might well be met with disappointment if not dismay. In the world of time asymmetry, classical thermodynamics studies structures whose complexity decreases, machines that lose the capacity to do work–isolated or closed systems sealed to incoming matter.[67] At equilibrium, when molecules diffuse from higher to lower concentration, in other words when molecules are most disordered (unstructured), then everything is homogeneous and *nothing interesting, remarkable, or unusual* can happen. And what is often called "complexity," meaning the tendency toward order, is matched equally by the tendency toward disorder–heat and entropy.

Dissipative Structures

Reflecting upon the modern classical view of nature and society in terms of scientific rationality, Isabelle Stengers and Ilya Prigogine contrast it with scientific ideas about nature that grew out of the discovery of the laws of thermodynamics. They note that if "in the classical view, the basic processes of nature were considered to be deterministic and reversible. . . . Today we see everywhere, the role of irreversible processes, of fluctuations."[68] Following from this, Stengers and Prigogine articulate a concept of of nature as open, complex, probabilistic, and *temporally irreversible*, the sphere of organisms dwelling in the world of energy and material flux, the sphere of open rather than isolated or closed systems.[69] This concept, proposed by Erwin Schrödinger in 1943, states simply that organisms feed on negative or, more accurately, free entropy; they defy the second law of thermodynamics by *importing* high-quality energy–light quanta from the sun–using it to increase their organization, to resist thermodynamic equilibrium.[70]

But Schrödinger analyzed life as a material process in two senses, as energy and as information.[71] The term "entropy" has been used to describe both information systems and thermodynamic living systems, both data and energy. "In information theory, *entropy* describes the uncertainties associated with the utilization of characters in sending and receiving messages," while in thermodynamic systems, entropy values are based on the "uniqueness of a system's matter-energy distribution at a molecular or atomic level"; thus the system has only one particular microstate out of all that are possible.[72] Dynamic systems theory is the mathematics of informational entropy the subfields of which are focused on unpredictability, incompressibility, asymmetry, or delayed recurrence. It is expressed in terms of the abstract properties of mathematical figures, whereas entropy in thermodynamics measures irreversible processes, the decrease in the quality of energy–tiny particles measured by temperature–when matter reaches more probable distributions.[73]

That there is no unproblematic link between the entropy of dynamical systems and that of energy is of some importance to our project here insofar as some philosophers–Gilles Deleuze, Michel Serres, and possibly others–appear to operate with the assumption that the link is clear and well established. Nevertheless, there has been some agreement among mathematicians and physicists that "the principles and mathematics of information theory can substantially contribute to the formulation of thermodynamics and the expression of its content."[74] It may be useful to keep in mind, following Schrödinger, that living beings possess both information- and energy-handling abilities, the former in the form of the genetic, language-like order, chemical data processing derived from parents, and the latter in the potential for functioning as an energy transformer.[75] "Life" seems to be such an energy transformer, a dissipative, metastable process in continuous flux, whose energy comes from the sun.[76] It is this aspect of thermodynamics that is the focus of Stengers's and Prigogine's work.

Stengers and Prigogine have contributed significantly to informing philosophers about the relation of thermodynamics to philosophy in their account of the conceptual transformation from classical science to the present, particularly as it applies to the macroscopic scale, the scale of atoms, molecules, and biomolecules. They pay special attention to the problem of time, a problem that arose out of the realization that new dynamic states of matter may emerge from thermal chaos when a system interacts with its surroundings. These new structures were given the name *dissipative structures* to indicate that dissipation can in fact play a constructive role in the formation of new states insofar as they grow more complex by exporting entropy into their surroundings.[77] Stengers and Prigogine take us from the static view of motion, that of classical dynamics, a view based on time reversibility and applicable to particular scales, those of molar and molecular phenomenon, to an evolutionary view arising with nonequilibrium thermodynamics, which is based on time irreversibility, especially on the microscopic scale. What is of additional value in their work, for our context, is that they also concern themselves with the "strong interaction of the issues proper to culture as a whole and the internal conceptual problems of science in particular."[78] Thus the reorientation from the classical to the contemporary view is, for them, reflected in tensions between the natural sciences and the social sciences and humanities. Nothing, it seems, could be further from Sokal's view than theirs.

If, for the average person or even the apparently well-informed academic, the development of science has been understood to shift away from concrete experience toward abstraction, they believe that this at least in part a consequence of the limitations of classical science. In order to free itself from traditional modes of comprehending nature, science isolated and purified its practices so as to achieve greater and greater autonomy, leading it to conceptualize its knowledge as universal and to isolate itself from any social context.[79] Over the decades, important results may have been repressed or set aside if they failed to conform to the classical model, further limiting its ability to give a coherent account of the relationship between humans and nature. Michel Serres refers to this new abstract, scientific view of nature as transcendence, something that can only be verified apart from human law, something that was necessitated when Galileo was brought to court to defend his ideas. Thus, in his own defense, Galileo invoked the world of things, appealing not the laws of men but to nature, the ultimate reference point beyond which no further appeal can be made.[80]

In spite of the tendency of modern science to abstract and isolate itself, Stengers and Prigogine are alarmed by contemporary criticisms of science, such as that of the philosopher Martin Heidegger, who in their view levies an unrestricted condemnation of the natural sciences, whose aim he identifies with the subjection of nature.[81] We will take this up again later, but for the moment, suffice it to say that there is some concern that these views threaten to take philosophy in the direction of mysticism, something that greatly concerns Stengers and Prigogine. Like Serres, who at times equates the transcendence of science with that of religion, mysticism does not appear to Stengers and Prigogine either as a viable alternative to or explanation of the naturalism of classical science.[82] Their concerns and the structure within which they articulate them are quite similar to those of Hannah Arendt.

The enthusiasm for modern science that took shape in the sixteenth century, and in many respects continues unabated today, arose, they posit, as an extension of the ages-old effort of humankind to organize and exploit the world and to understand humankind's place in nature. However, while the ancients remained preoccupied with the question of *why* certain natural processes occur, the moderns ask only *how;* they ask what is the process. Answering this question involves activity, the manipulation of physical reality rather than its passive observation. Thus, unlike its scientific predecessors, modern science learned to prepare and isolate physical reality to make it conform to an ideal conceptual scheme.[83] As we saw already in our discussion of Newton's experimental science, experiment is an art with no guarantees of success. It requires choosing an interesting question that embodies a theory's implications, abstracting a natural phenomenon from its environment, and staging it to test the theory in a manner that is both reproducible and communicable. Additionally, modern science can engage in a thought experiment, governed entirely by theory.[84] What is crucial here is *that the scientist cannot force nature* to respond the way the scientist wishes; there is, in effect, a dialogue between humans and nature, not a dictatorship. This conversation, however, is not so easily accomplished.

First of all, as we have noted throughout this chapter, science writes in mathematical language, and from the mathematical point of view the world appears to be homogeneous. In other words, what is simple can always be used to explain what is complex. Moreover, it is possible, as Serres also argues, that the scientific view may have arisen in part due to the mutual amplification of theological discourse and science—a resonance located in the medieval insistence on the rationality of God who could be counted on to provide a basis for the world's intelligibility. Nonetheless, when humans

sought to view the world from same divine viewpoint, they did so by invent-
ing scientific experiments rather than by proclaiming miracles and revela-
tion. To the extent that this is the case, Serres's near conflation of religion
and science fails to express the reality of science. Such views may contribute to Stengers's caution that "philosophers were requiring of the sciences
(which they do not practice) that they justify the practice of the philosophers of science; that sciences illustrate a definition of scientific rationality
which the philosophers could then *disengage,* so as to know better than the
scientists, what defines scientists as such."[85]

This caution does not prevent Stengers from expressing concern about
the general autonomy of the natural sciences in relation to the world they
study, including the "condemnation of nature to exploitation, the subject
and object to separation," and "the splintered figure of the other of the identity of science."[86] And for this reason, she takes up the claim held out by
Sokal and Weinberg that contemporary science and contemporary humanities, philosophy in particular, have nothing to say to one another. Stengers
begins by engaging with the dominant philosophies of science to clarify the
epistemological and social relations between philosophers and scientists.
What she finds is that autonomy, the preservation of the community as the
norm and as condition of the possibility for a fruitful exercise of science, is
all-important in freeing scientists from the necessity of continuously justifying their research priorities and methods.[87] Yet insofar as scientists do,
in actuality, draw on all the resources of society, resources ranging from
social and political support to technological innovations, she believes that
it is essential for both sides not to construct differences using language that
leaves irreducible oppositions and provokes hateful misunderstandings that
rigidly draw the lines between science and nonscience.[88]

So we might wish to be just as cautious as Stengers about pitting the
interests of the mind against the interests of everyday life.[89] Rather, let us
consider the possibility that scientific theories require the invention of a
world that they then render intelligible and to which they give signification.
In place of the ideal of a pure mathematical and experimental science juxta-
posed against an impure external milieu that constantly threatens to invade
it, Stengers suggests an alternative. She suggests that the scientific paradigm
is a manner of intervening in the world, an intervention that creates what
it explains in a competent, discussable, and astute manner that constitutes
the paradigm as an event.[90] Thus even if the aim of modern science was

to discover the unique truth about the world, and this means a truth that excludes the observer, this was possible only to the extent that the questions they asked of nature and the responses they received from their experiments conformed to the model of intervention.[91]

Specifically, for modern science (science of the sixteenth and seventeenth centuries), we have noted that the central theoretical and practical problem was to find a way to define a continuously varying speed, instantaneous changes in position, velocity, and acceleration, and the state of a body at a given instant. Any pair of material bodies, planets, or atoms are linked by the same force of attraction, called gravity, which operates in the universe as a whole, any local variations being too small to have an impact. Given an initial state, the general law deduces the series of states the system will pass through, and a single state is sufficient to define both the future and the past of any system. This is what *reversibility* implies. We can see Stengers's point that classical dynamics required bold, possibly godlike assumptions, a world in which all trajectories are reversible, in which whatever occurred could be undone. And yet the active experiments carried out by scientists remained extraneous to the idealized, reversible world they describe.[92] In other words, the real world of living human beings, of scientists and citizens, did not appear to be able to be reversed, even though the idealized and isolated world they describe was reversible. This sort of tension between science and society remains thematically central. Stengers and Prigogine are quite explicit that they seek a convergence between nature and the mind that knows, perceives, and creates science. The divine ideal of a being who could calculate the future and past of the world starting from the observation of an instantaneous state is not the ideal they endorse.[93]

And yet, as powerful as modern science appeared to be, it was immediately confronted by a rival that defined the conditions of the possibility of experimental and mathematical knowledge of nature. Immanuel Kant's transcendental philosophy decidedly identified phenomenal reality, which can be known with science, and science with Newtonian science. According to Kant, phenomena, as the objects of experience, are the product of the mind's synthetic activity. So the scientist is, in effect, the source of the universal laws discovered in nature, the source of what Arendt calls the Archimedean point of view. However, for Kant, philosophy assumed a dominant position with respect to science, since Kant's critique reveals the limits of scientific knowledge.[94] Scientists know only appearances; they will never know the objects of the transcendental Ideas, the Ideas of God, World and Self, because this would require knowledge of infinity. Thus transcendental Ideas give us the limits of human knowledge. Beyond those limits, philosophy engages with transcendental Ideas for what they can do, for how they regulate our activities in the realms of ethics and aesthetics, the noumenal realm that belongs to philosophy alone.[95]

Unlike Kant, who at least proposed a sort of harmony between philosophy and science, G. W. F. Hegel's philosophy systematically denied the principles of Newtonian science, insisting that simple mechanical behavior is qualitatively distinct from that of complex living beings who can become self-conscious, and denying that nature is itself homogeneous and simple. Stengers and Prigogine concede that "Hegel's system provides a consistent philosophic response to the crucial problems of time and complexity," but ultimately fails insofar as no science can support it.[96] But if Kant examined the limits of what individual humans can know, we might suggest that Hegel takes up the point of view of knowledge itself, which reaches the stage of self-knowledge, enabling Hegel to claim that what is rational is real and what is real is rational.[97] Unique to Hegel, as Stengers and Prigogine imply, is that although antinomies appear at every step, rationality evolves. These distinct approaches suggest solutions to the ongoing question: what *is* the relation of philosophy to science and to scientific rationality? The Kantian problem implies that science is the realm of knowledge and philosophy the realm of action. This might seem to correspond to Arendt's claim that what we have lost are noble words and deeds, but does this mean that philosophy contributes no knowledge? In other words, is the division into what can be known by science and what can be done in philosophy and other humanities absolute? Or is it possible that philosophy and science once again may if not develop together, at least in some manner mutually influence one another? It is precisely these questions that must be addressed and that we will take up in the chapters to come.

4

BURNING MAN

THE INFLUENCE OF NONEQUILIBRIUM
THERMODYNAMICS AND THE SCIENCE OF FLOW

Broken Symmetry: The Science of Flows

We saw in the previous chapter that for Stengers and Prigogine, questions about the relationship of philosophy to science are closely associated with their understanding of processes that, they claim, no longer appear to be explicable in terms of time or process reversibility. Concepts associated with irreversible processes can, they hope, bridge the divide between spiritual and physical aspects of nature, including human nature. Moving from the study of heat to the conservation of energy, the first and second laws of thermodynamics, linear and nonlinear thermodynamics, self-organization, chaos, dissipative structures, evolution, complexity, open systems, relativity, uncertainty, and finally to temporal evolution in quantum systems leads them to the conclusion that the reversibility of classical dynamics is a characteristic of closed or isolated dynamic systems only, and that science must at least remain open to a pluralistic world in which reversible and irreversible processes coexist.[1] For classical dynamics, time was a geometric parameter, and as such this conception was part of a general drive to eliminate temporal evolution, to reduce the different and the changing to the identical and permanent. The proposal that Stengers and Prigogine put forth is that in place of general, all-embracing schemes that could be expressed by eternal laws, there is time. In place of symmetry, there are symmetry-breaking processes on all levels. Moreover, they claim, time irreversibility can be the unifying source of order on all levels. Among philosophers who engaged with the sciences, can we not find philosophical precedents for these ideas?

Although in 1922 Henri Bergson attempted to introduce and defend (against Einstein) the possibility of a multiplicity of coexisting "lived" times, for Einstein intelligibility remained tied to immutability.[2] Bergson's cone of memory appears to be a truncated Minkowski space-time light cone with the past flipped over to the top so that the future appears as contracted into the present point and the past of sensible memory is brought into the present by the immediacy of the call of perception.[3] In *Matter and Memory*, Bergson describes the cone of memory in terms of time dilation and space contraction evolving to a single point of view, terms that are also characteristic of descriptions of special relativity as Einstein described it in 1905.[4] The motion of memories is relative to a point of view, the point of view of a present perception. Time dilates when memories are called up and put into motion, but distances between memories contract as those memories are brought into the present perception. Thus consciousness consists of a double movement; it contracts and expands. Memory responds to the call of present perception contracting to meet that perception, and also, rotating upon itself, memory dilates as if our recollections were repeated an infinite number of times. Memory therefore appears to be relative to the perceptual experience that calls it up. Moreover, memory is relative to each person's point of view, as well as to every other person's point of view and to that of other isolated systems.[5]

However, not all properties are relative. The speed of light is an invariant, as is the so-called space-time interval, the distance between events measured in terms of both space and time.[6] Bergson seems to want to maintain that it is possible for a consciousness to exist absolutely within the same frame of reference as another phenomena, thus for there to be an experience of simultaneity. His famous example, that of sugar dissolving in a glass of water, seems to exemplify this. The consciousness of the observer dissolves along with the sugar. Her frame of reference is, for Bergson, exactly the same as that of the dissolving sugar in the glass. Rather than existing relative to one another, their lived time is simultaneous. "It is no longer a relation, it is an absolute."[7] Perhaps this brings Bergson perilously close to an idealism such as that of Berkeley, especially since Bergson argues that we live the duration immanent to the whole universe.[8] In fact, Bergson does argue that Berkeley perceives matter to be a thin, transparent film between man and God through which God expresses himself, possibly thereby bringing Berkeley's position closer to his own, a position according to which absolute and relative spacetime appear to coexist as do matter and memory.[9]

Bergson's conflict with Einstein arose precisely because Bergson insisted on the simultaneity of time in contrast or really, in addition to Einstein's conception of relative time. Bergson's conceptualization of the existence of absolute time would make it possible for what seem to be two distinct points of view to experience time as simultaneous rather than as relative to one another.[10] In Aristotle's and Galileo's concepts of spacetime, absolute "horizontal planes of simultaneity" defined a specific causal structure. A given event sits on an absolute horizontal plane. Events lying on a plane above this plane are future events, events lying on a plane below this plane are past events in relation to our given event. Events lying on the horizontal plane between the past and the future plane are events happening now, in other words, they are simultaneous.[11]

By contrast, the Minkowski light cone consists of an upper cone, the future light cone, representing the future history of a light flash emitted at that event, and the lower cone, the past light cone, representing all directions from which light flashes can be received at that event. According to the principle of relativity, all observers, regardless of their motions, must, following Maxwell's laws, measure the speed of light to be the same constant speed in all directions. The plane that Bergson places at the point of the cone of memory represents one inertial observer, and this observer will regard events on that plane as simultaneous with each other. Thus, my observation of the sugar melting in the glass of water is indeed simultaneous with my own observation. However, my observations are not simultaneous with those of another observer; another observer will occupy a distinct spacetime and will therefore exist on a different plane. Therefore my plane and hers will not be simultaneous with one another.[12]

Of course the spacetime of special relativity does not correspond to our ordinary experience of time. And perhaps due to the error on Bergson's part, his attempt to reconcile the absolute experience of a human observer with the relative spacetime of the the physicists, classical physicists have little positive to say about Bergson. Nevertheless, Bergson made an impact on some philosophers and natural scientists, who recognize that the "denial of becoming," or the denial of lived experience and common sense on the part of physics, significantly increased the rift between science and philosophy.[13] Looking to mend this rift, Stengers and Prigogine proposed a structure that takes its orientation from the point of view of a different observer, one "who measures coordinates and momenta and studies their change in time," leading to the discovery of unstable dynamic systems, intrinsic randomness, and irreversibility, proceeding to dissipative structures and from there back to the one-way time-oriented observer.[14] That this attempt was successful is still open to debate, but minimally, they raise again the question brought forth originally by Arendt, that is, what are we to do about earth alienation, the view of terrestrial life as governed by cosmic forces far removed from earthly affairs?

The argument they propose is that nonequilibrium thermodynamics, sometimes called open system thermodynamics, describes systems of flow, growth, or change that are not in equilibrium and that are characterized by gradients, that is, a difference in temperature, pressure, or chemical concentration across a distance. Gradients will be eliminated, sometimes spectacularly, by complex, growing systems. Although the second law of thermodynamics holds that systems lose their ability to do work and, reaching equilibrium, fade out and burn away, life appears to defy the second law, demonstrating opposite, evolutionary tendencies of complexity that increase with time.[15] According to Stengers and Prigogine, open, dynamic nonequilibrium systems import material and energy from beyond their system boundaries, they exhibit material and energy cycling, but they also degrade energy, making it less available to do work. But rather than simply burning away, they export or dissipate this entropy into their surroundings, thus the term *dissipative structures*.[16] The second law persists, but at a remove, allowing for increased complexity within the original system. In other words, the "low-entropy, more organized state within the dissipative structure, living or not, depends on increasing the entropy of the larger 'global' system in which the dissipative structure is embedded. The second law is not violated."[17]

Prigogine discovered that as systems open to new flows of material and energy are pushed farther from equilibrium, that is, farther from stability, they may undergo sudden transitions or bifurcations. The further from equilibrium, the more bifurcations are possible, yet following these bifurcations, the system reaches new stable states. Other scientists have discovered that living systems, such as human beings, are threatened by too-large entropy production that would destroy us. But in animal life, the chemical tendency for the hydrogen of bodies to react with the oxygen in the atmosphere, inherent in the second law, is channeled through the complex chemical systems called "metabolism," so *we burn "slowly," metabolizing rather than bursting into flames,* making possible the so-called survival of the past, our own past flows of material and energy. Insofar as all scientific activity is time-oriented, the scientist must come to see herself as part of the universe she describes. Irreversibility does not appear to be universal; it requires a minimum of complexity in the dynamical system, such that with an increase of complexity, the role of irreversibility increases.[18]

Stengers and Prigogine conclude that contrary to the model put forth by Thomas Kuhn, change in science does not occur as a result of a crisis, a near-violent disruption of an otherwise homogeneous and conservative scientific continuity.[19] Although they concede that crises do occur, science can also be characterized by problems that arise as the consequence of "deliberate and lucid questions asked by scientists who know that the questions had both scientific and philosophical aspects." In other words, change occurs as a result of both the "internal logic of science" and "the cultural and social context of our time."[20] Such a conclusion appears in strong contrast to the claim of Steven Weinberg that there is no correlation between science and social context.

We stated above that the "denial of becoming" on the part of physics significantly increased the rift between physics and philosophy, but that open-system thermodynamics formulates a structure for which, when there is increased complexity, the role of time irreversibility also increases. This view of nature seems to bring it closer to lived experience as formulated by Henri Bergson. Yet not all philosophers are interested in modeling nature on lived experience. This is especially the case for some postmodern philosophy, which, as we maintained in the preface, tends toward a formalist methodology and worldview. In particular, the philosophy of Gilles Deleuze is exemplary for its firm commitment to the Archimedean point of view, for the limits it places on the role of human experience, and for its concept of time.[21] Understanding this is critical to understanding the role of science and mathematics in the work of this philosopher whose ideas have gained a huge audience, but whose use of mathematical and scientific concepts remains largely misunderstood.

The Grand Style: The Interesting, the Remarkable, the Unusual

What makes something interesting, remarkable, or unusual for philosophy? What philosophy, according to Gilles Deleuze, is capable of creating and characterizing the interesting, the remarkable or the unusual? Such a philosophy, Deleuze has made clear, must set out a new image of thought, for no two great philosophers utilize the same image of thought, that is, every great philosopher changes what it means to think and has thought differently.[22] For example, although Descartes, Kant, Husserl, and Sartre all have an image of thought that may be characterized as a field of consciousness, each field is constituted as a unique type of universal: the eidetic, the critical, the phenomenological, and that of radical empiricism.[23] Each of these philosophers establishes a new image of thought that distinguishes them from the philosophical functionaries who enjoy the use of "ready-made thought," lacking even awareness of the efforts of the great philosophers who have devised the images they use.[24]

This account is echoed by Alain Badiou, who also argues that philosophers must resist the comfort of what he calls "the little style," a philosophy that makes the interesting, remarkable, or unusual an *object* of study, something that can be relegated to the pre-existing philosophical specializations of epistemology or ethics or politics, there to be managed by the academic bureaucracy of teachers and researchers.[25] For Badiou, a typical exemplar of the little style grasps its object through historicization, classification, and endless commentary rather than through direct and dramatic affirmation of the ontological sovereignty of mathematics.[26]

By contrast, there is a kind of philosophy carried out in the grand style. The grand style, according to Badiou, is the style of doing philosophy exemplified by Descartes, Spinoza, Kant, Hegel, and Comte de Lautréamont.[27] What these apparently disparate figures have in common, Badiou claims, is something that Badiou himself has in common with Gilles Deleuze. "In each case," Badiou writes, "it is a question of giving thanks to *rigorous mathematics*. It doesn't matter whether the philosophy is conceived of as a rationalism tied to transcendence, as it is from Descartes to Lacan; [or] as a vitalist immanence, as it is from Spinoza to Deleuze."[28] What matters is that each of these philosophies proposes that mathematics directly illuminates philosophy and that it does so through a *forced* or even *violent* intervention. Thus Descartes is credited with finding, in arithmetic and geometry, the very model of philosophical certainty, while Spinoza confirms that "to know is to be absolutely and universally convinced."[29] Kant's contribution is the a priori, Hegel's a true conception of the infinite, and Lautréamont's the undoing of all the categories of humanism.[30] Badiou's own contribution is proclaimed by the philosopher to be the idea that mathematics is ontology.

And Deleuze, what of Deleuze? Insofar as Badiou believes that Deleuze's contribution, grand as it may be, is too limited to satisfy his own demands for a mathematics that is fundamental ontology, Badiou focuses on critique and mostly evades a positive elaboration of this question.[31] This leaves it to those of us who are interested in Deleuze's contribution to discover for ourselves. Thus, we will inquire, in what manner and to what end does Deleuze create a philosophy in the grand style, a philosophy directly illuminated by mathematics through a forced if not violent intervention? In carrying out this project, we will attempt to follow Badiou's prescription, that is, rather than exerting a grip on our object through "historicization and classification. . . . [thereby to] characterize this object as a neutered mathematics," we will seek a direct encounter with Deleuze's mathematical formalism.[32] In doing so, we must acknowledge the difficulty of proceeding in this manner. Deleuze's grand style, his new image of thought, rests on what he refers to as the "unlimited One-All," which includes all the concepts of his thought on one plane.[33] He calls this a plane of concepts or a plane of consistency, a single wave embracing multiple waves that are concepts, but concepts that must move at infinite speeds, thus faster than the speed of light, something physically impossible but something that is, in the realm of thought, thinkable.

Rethinking the Second Law of Thermodynamics

Deleuze formulates his philosophy from the notion of a plane of immanence that arises from some consequences of the second law of thermodynamics. Recall that the second law of thermodynamics states that in a *closed* system, where no new matter or energy enters, disorder must increase, so for the classical mapping of gas particles distributed in two chambers, there are far more disordered states (mixtures of particles in various states) than ordered states (mixtures of particles in a limited number of states). So we noted that when there are many more ways for particles to be distributed evenly (in various states) than lopsidedly, the probable state of particles is one in which their energy–once unconcentrated–is *of little use.*

For example, heat follows the arrow of time, meaning it is of little use relative to the sunlight that generates it, a potentially depressing conclusion. In the world of time asymmetry, classical thermodynamics studies structures whose complexity decreases, machines that lose the capacity to do work–closed and isolated systems sealed to incoming matter.[34] Moreover, at equilibrium, when molecules are most disordered, that is, unstructured, then everything is homogeneous and *nothing interesting, remarkable, or unusual* can happen. In this state, what is often called "complexity," meaning the tendency toward order, is matched equally by the tendency toward disorder–meaning heat and entropy. What interests us now is the examination of the philosophical import of these ideas for Deleuze. What image of thought, what plane of immanence do they entail?

From a philosophical perspective, Deleuze takes up these developments in the natural sciences and mathematics. Turning away from open-system thermodynamics, he conceptualizes an immanent, therefore relatively closed and still deterministic, atomistic, and reversible system that is not immediately reduced to entropic equilibrium because its processes take place on the molecular level at speeds he hypothesizes are beyond the speed of light. He postulates a manifold, a sphere of immanence that is the entire universe and not merely Earth or our solar system. In spite of being closed or immanent, it develops into the idea of a system governed by sensitivity to initial starting points and unstable boundaries, thus it is chaotic as well as probabilistic, but still a *deterministic* philosophy, where deterministic means that once established, the rules governing the field of thought do not alter.

Deleuze proposes that such a system can be formalized mathematically by means of differential calculus and vector fields. Motion and change are particularly difficult to study mathematically, as the tools of mathematics, numbers, points, lines, equations, are themselves static. Calculus, "a collection of methods to describe and handle patterns of infinity–the infinitely large and the infinitely small," made possible the use of mathematical tools to study motion and change without falling into paradoxes.[35] "The basic operation of differential calculus is the process known as differentiation [whose aim is] . . . to obtain the rate of change of some changing quantity. In order to do this, the 'value' or 'position' or 'path' of that quantity has to be given by means of an appropriate formula."[36]

Newton and Leibniz developed the rules for differentiating complicated functions by starting from the formula for a curve and calculating the formula for the gradient (or steepness) of that curve. The method involves using a grid defined by Cartesian coordinates, then taking minute differences in the x and y directions and computing the gradients of the resultant straight lines–the gradient function is called the *derivative* of the original function.[37] "The crucial step . . . was to shift attention from the essentially *static* situation concerning a gradient at a particular point P to the *dynamic* process of successive approximation of the gradient [of the curve] by gradients of straight lines starting at P."[38] Nevertheless, it is crucial to remember that the apparently dynamic motion can only be captured, mathematically, by a static function and likewise, the dynamic process of closer and closer approximation to the gradient must also be captured in a static manner known as a *limit,* a sequence of approximations.[39]

To utilize and expand on the possibilities offered by differential calculus, Deleuze proposes what may be called a sublime Idea, an Idea in the Kantian sense.[40] As we will see below, Deleuze turns away from the possibility of an experience of the sublime in nature. He reformulates the sublime as a formal event, an event occurring in three-dimensional abstract space rather than the space of experience. Such an event has a formal mathematical name. In that context, it may be called a catastrophe.[41] Mathematically, on an abstract surface, the fixed point governing the system's behavior shifts from being a stable attractor with smooth transitions to a temporarily unstable one with discontinuous transitions.[42] However, "the change of stability forces the system to move abruptly to the region of a new stable fixed point."[43] Imagination moves from the harmony of free play of the faculties to the violence of inadequacy, and finally to the stability of its suprasensible destination, the Ideas of Reason. But it does so, as Deleuze emphasizes, by first approaching its limit, then experiencing a radical break, a discontinuous transition, finally restabilizing beyond the sensible, in an accord with Reason, as it awakens Reason to the rational Idea that arises from and regulates its field immanently.[44]

However, many phenomena in motion do not involve sublime insta-bilities. Most motion appears to be continuous, in smooth, homogeneous space. Utilizing mathematics, "Leibniz had shown that calculus . . . expressed problems which could not hitherto be solved or, indeed, even posed (tran-scendent problems)," problems such as the complete determination of a species of curve, or problems characterized by the paradox of Achilles and the tortoise.[45] But what if we wish to make determinations beyond a single curve? Is there a means to make "a complete determination with regard to the existence and distribution of . . . [regular and singular] points which depends upon a completely different instance," an instance characterized in terms of a *field of vectors*?[46] The goal here is to explicitly link differential equations and vector fields.

A vector field is defined by Deleuze in *Difference and Repetition* as the complete determination of a problem given in terms of the existence, num-ber, and distribution of points that are its condition.[47] This corresponds fair-ly well to the more or less standard mathematical definition where a vector field is defined as associating a vector to every point in the field space. Vector fields are used in physics to model observations, such as the movement of a fluid, that include a direction for each point of the observed space. Let us try to flesh this out.

The Idea and the Rules:
Association, Commutation, Distribution

If, as Deleuze claimed, it is the condition of a problem that it would be the object of a synthesis of the Idea, then what is this Idea? The problem, as it has been set out here by Deleuze, is that of the existence, number, and distribution of points. This problem would be the object of a certain Idea, initially no more than the abstract Idea of a plane of immanence, a vector field, a model consisting of vectors (in physics, an abstract entity that has magnitude and direction in a plane or in three-dimensional space, or in a space of four or more dimensions) in vector space, from which may be pro-jected an infinity of possible trajectories in spacetime.[48]

In mathematics (specifically linear algebra), the rules of *association, commutation, and distribution* define vector space without reference to magnitude or direction, thus they may be utilized in a variety of fields whose terms are not material or physical. The rules of association, commutation, and distribution are the least restrictive set of linear rules that remain commutative, that is, for binary operations any order is possible.[49] They are also the name given to the transcendental Ideas governing Kantian practical reason, which tell us what actions are universal in their application.[50]

These rules have their equivalents in logic, where association is an expression of logical equivalence permitting the valid regrouping of simple propositions; it governs the relations, which is to say, the connections between subject and predicate in the categorical proposition. In syllogistic terms, this would be expressed as the categorical relation "S is P."[51] Commutation permits the valid reordering of disjunctive (either/or) statements, which, using the logical rules of transformation, can logically be recast as hypothetical (if/then) propositions without a change of truth value.[52] The rule of generation of a vector field is commutative. In logic, this means that statements may initially be combined in any order. Given a hypothetical proposition, "If there is a perfect justice, the obstinately wicked are punished," it consists of a relation between two propositions, "There is a perfect justice" and "The obstinately wicked are punished," and can be understood as intrinsically commutative.[53] Reformulated using truth tables, we arrive at its logical equivalent, "There is *no* perfect justice *or* the obstinately wicked are punished," a proposition to which commutativity now applies ("The obstinately wicked are punished *or* there is *no* perfect justice").[54]

This reformulation separates, tears apart, the causal order of the inference, making it possible to reorder the propositions, to *disturb their causal linearity*. This appears to be the basis of the Deleuzean claim that causal connections are broken. The success of this move may be debated, and we will look at this later, but that will not be the most important consideration at this point. A third element of vector space is distribution. In deductive arguments, distribution permits the mutual replacement of specified pairs of symbolic expressions. In categorical propositions, it permits the distribution of a term if it refers to all members of a class.[55] In syllogistic logic, this would be expressed as *conjunction* or *connection*.

Deleuze is clearly irritated with Kant's failure to maintain the purity of these relations. "Of all philosophers, Kant is the one who discovers the prodigious domain of the transcendental. He is the analogue of a great explorer-not of another world but of the upper or lower reaches of this one.

However, what does he do?"[56] The irritation is palpable. What Kant does is correlate transcendental structures with the empirical acts of an "I think," a psychological consciousness. He does this because, as we discussed this in the preface, Kant believes that something extra-logical must be the pre-condition of all such knowledge. Otherwise something that is logically possible could end up as an empty concept leading to antinomies, incompatible assertions.[57] This appears to be why the schematism of the understanding operates in Kant's philosophy. Schema synthesize or temporalize concepts so that concepts may represent objects.[58] Such representation is anathema for Deleuze, on the grounds that representation arises as the effect of the "I think," which instantiates common sense, and the schematism, which instantiates good sense, so that together they enforce orthodoxy.

The identity of the Self in the "I think" grounds the harmony of the faculties and creates agreement as to the form of their object. This is common sense, the unity of the faculties. And good sense is the norm of distribution that qualifies objects as this or that kind of thing; it is the form of the Same.[59] Thus, for Deleuze, the object of this kind of thinking is something we always already recognize, a repetition of the Same, an impediment to thinking anything new. And furthermore, Deleuze complains that for Kant, the faculties and their object are always attached to a set of values that return us to the Ideas of God, World and Self, the transcendental Ideas, not in their character as illusions, not as broken up and disordered, but as harmonizing with one another to produce logical, moral, and even aesthetic forms of common sense.[60] In place of the sensible being referred to an object that may be harmonized with other faculties in a common sense, Deleuze raises up the *being* of the sensible, the *sign*, that by which the given is given in a purely transcendental exercise.[61]

Thus, unlike Kant, who "induces" the transcendental from empirical forms under the determination of common sense and good sense, Deleuze insists that he has access to a "superior empiricism," which is really not an empiricism at all but rather its dissolution, a radical skepticism if you will.[62] In this way, each faculty, even those yet undiscovered, must be forced by an extreme violence to the point where common sense and good sense are ungraspable and each faculty dissolves, pushing thought to the supersensible transcendental Ideas.[63] Once this is accomplished, Deleuze can make use of the transcendental Ideas, not for harmony and recognition, but to ensure the continuing destabilization/deterritorialization of all that we think we know and the destabilization-deterritorialization of the Self. The harmony of the faculties dissolves in violence, each communicating to the other only difference and discord, on the order of that catastrophic discord between imagination and thought in Kant's conception of the sublime.[64] Deleuze will then employ the transcendental Ideas in their unique logical capacity. He will affirm only their logical function, taking up and utilizing the transcendental Ideas insofar as they tell us what we can do, what actions are universal in their application.

What is significant about Deleuze's use of these rules is that Deleuze argues that once freed from empirical forms, these rules are the rules for what he refers to as vector space, and, as Kant insisted, they do indeed apply to nature. This is not to say that they are empty without a corresponding sensible intuition. What Deleuze means is that the rules have ontological effects and that ontologically nature is associative, commutative, and distributive. This is, indeed, the core of Deleuze's mathematical intervention in philosophy. Deleuze will utilize the rules to carry out the project he believes Kant abandoned.

Beginning with simple association $[(x+y)+z = x+(y+z)]$, as opposed to unity or totality, means that the laws of nature distribute parts which cannot be totalized, and that nature is conjunctive, expressing itself as this *and* that, this *or* that, rather than as Being, One or Whole. Following Kant's transcendental Ideas, the claim is that we can never have knowledge of nature as a whole. *Divine* power is manifest in the relation of disjunction, in diverse parts (places, species, lands, and waters) organized in a system in relation to an Idea; each *self* is not identical to any other but is represented by the categorical relation of that self with an Idea; and every body comprising the *world* consists of diverse matter, manifest in the hypothetical or causal relation between an Idea and that diversity.[65]

As such, nature is associative, commutative, and distributive, and our knowledge of nature is limited to its immanent, regulative functions. If nature's immanent, regulative functions are associative, commutative, and distributive, each of these, as mathematical or logical operations, reflects a view of nature as the power of things to exist one by one without any possibility of them being gathered together in a unity.[66] Following these rules, whatever has been added together can be taken apart and reformulated. Thus becoming seems to be everywhere, and nowhere is anything gathered together into a totality. How then, if nothing is gathered together, is it possible to have a world or a concept of a world? Insofar as we are still in the realm of classical thought, the answer may be clarified using Hume's radical empiricism, the method of association of ideas.

That things exist one by one without the possibility of being gathered together is the expression of purely external relations of association within an immanent field, relations of proximity that thermodynamics came to characterize in terms of the chance collisions of particles. However, the key to thinking through this aspect of the model Deleuze proposes is that at this point, the things that exist one by one are, in fact, gathered, not into a whole or a totality governed by a divine or transcendental principle of unity. Rather they are gathered by means of a transcendental principle of differential relations. Not surprisingly, the rules of vector space and the construction of vector fields are connected to the functions of differential calculus. That is, given a complete set of functions in a given space in differential calculus, each function in that space can be expressed as a combination of that complete set of functions, and functions with the property of completeness can form a vector space under binary operations.

Deleuze's task throughout his work, but especially in *Logic of Sense,* is to connect these mathematical concepts to nature, that is, to the physical world. He does not do this as Kant does, meaning by reference to sensible intuitions. Referring both to Lucretius and to classical physics, Deleuze argues that although the sum of atoms (or particles in physics) is infinite, they do not form a totality in the Kantian sense, an absolute and unconditioned totality for the series. Rather, atoms, which it is said *are not sensible objects but objects of thought* (since due to their size they are below the level of human perception), fall in the void and collide with one another. The result of these collisions produces motion. In the void, "all atoms fall with equal velocity . . . the velocity of the atom is equal to its movement *in a unique direction in a minimum of time* . . . [expressing] the smallest possible term during which an atom moves in a given direction, before being able to take another direction as the result of a collision with another atom."[67]

Rather than a highly structured principle of causality, Deleuze argues, this collision, insofar as it takes place in a time smaller than the minimum of continuous time, a limit that approaches but never reaches *zero,* must be something else. Following Lucretius, Deleuze calls it a *clinamen,* the original determination of the direction of movement of the atom.[68] The clinamen expresses the idea of looking for numerical and geometric patterns in a process of successive approximation. Long after Lucretius, the notation dx and dy came to be used to refer to infinitely small quantities or "the velocities of evanescent increments," once called "fluxions," ultimately "a dynamic process of successive approximations."[69] Differential calculus, we noted, allows one to begin with a differential relation (dx / dy), the expression of the infinitesimally small limits of motion in a specific direction, then, taking the derivative, to derive the formula for a curve, and then to calculate the formula for the gradient (slope or steepness) of that curve by taking small (infinitesimal) differences in the x and y directions, and computing the gradients of the resultant straight lines.[70]

Each derivative of a differential relation takes place each time in a minimum of time. No doubt, this is the ultimate, subtle form of disjunction/conjunction, which in the physical world may be mistaken for causality, as each collision determines the next direction of the atoms, and if we were to look at patterns, rather than individual atoms, clear patterns do in fact emerge. "In general, a differential equation arises whenever you have a quantity subject to change. . . . Strictly speaking, the changing quantity should be one that changes continuously. . . . However, change in many real life situations consists of a large number of individual, discrete changes, that are miniscule compared with the overall scale of the problem, and in such cases there is no harm in simply assuming that the whole changes continuously."[71] Defining a problem is thus inseparable from recognizing its ideal, objective nature.[72] This is why "the ideal connections constitutive of the problematic (dialectical) Idea are incarnated in the real relations which are constituted by *mathematical theories* and carried over into problems in the form of solutions . . . the solutions are like the discontinuities compatible with differential equations."[73]

In other words, differential calculus is a mathematical instrument, but the solutions or projections, the fields of operation of the mathematical instrument, may be mathematical, or they may be physical, biological, psychical, or sociological. One begins with the abstract mathematical structure, then one projects it into physical or psychical reality or onto different aspects of reality. So there are different orders of problem where each different order is a different expression, a different realization or projection of the mathematical schema.

What Deleuze claims, however, is that one does not simply apply mathematics to other domains; rather, each domain in which Ideas are incarnated possesses its own calculus, its own quantitability, qualitability, potentiality, processes of determinability, reciprocal determination, distributions of distinct and ordinary points. This, he argues, is the true *mathesis universalis*, a system of multiple, nonlocalizable, ideal connections, a differential calculus corresponding to each Idea, where each Idea differentiates the field, becomes the universal for individuals, differentiating each and every element.[74] The question that arises then is, how does this occur and what are its effects?

This position is not realism, which would amount to the claim that mathematical entities are thinglike but abstract entities. Formalists, who do not want to commit to this, remain tied to the position that mathematical symbols are not abstract entities but merely figures on paper or a screen or board.[75] The emphasis on structure or syntax is an expression of the idea that mathematical entities are not self-subsistent as material objects are; they are not independent of one another.[76] They are connected in patterns that cannot be denied without denying still other patterns . . . without end. But when we are thinking about the status of mathematics and how it correlates with the physical world, the question of what grounds our axioms comes into view as well as the question of their relation to physical reality. Perhaps we might consider what Frege has written on this matter. "The laws of number . . . are not really applicable to external things: they are not the laws of nature. What they do apply to are judgments about things in the external world, they are the laws of the laws of nature."[77]

The Persistence of Binaries

In *Difference and Repetition*, Deleuze provides several examples of Ideas differentiating a field. Ancient atomism as a physical Idea, the organism as a biological Idea, Marxism as a social Idea, but it seems as if it is not until much much later in his work that he provides a structural solution to his own question, in fact, a structural solution that is mathematical.[78] In *What Is Philosophy?* Deleuze, along with Félix Guattari, argues that every trajectory in a vector field is an assemblage of affects and percepts connecting, disjoining, and conjoining with one another. For living beings, affects and percepts are real, physical, and effective sensations that bypass Imagination and Understanding and directly encounter the nervous system. No sensible intuitions or categories of the understanding are called for to apprehend them and none are needed.

The contingency of assemblages lies in particles; every assemblage of particles produces a different world, a different and unpredictable entity, but within the range of a particular pattern oriented by an attractor. An attractor is defined in mathematics as a set of states, invariant under the dynamics, which neighboring states in a given basin or arena approach asymptotically in the course of dynamic evolution.[79] Attractors are key components of dynamical systems. A dynamical system may be conceptualized as consisting of a manifold, something like a field of play, a stage upon which action takes place, along with rules that tell the players how to move on that stage.[80] In mathematics, these rules are called a vector field. The end point of the action is the attractor. Attractors orient the orbits, meaning the motion of a system, the way players in a game are oriented by the goal of winning. Importantly, once a system is oriented by an attractor, it remains there, either stopping its motion because it has reached the end of its game or repeating itself in a cyclic manner in an endless repetition of the game.[81] Thus the importance of so-called strange attractors, whose periodic orbits are unstable. If the actor's motion is even minutely perturbed, minutely off its pathway, the strange attractor pushes the actors even further away from the pathway or orbit they are following.[82] The rules governing the system do not alter; they are and remain deterministic. Yet the motions resulting from strange attractors are unpredictable, contingent, random.[83]

This model of a system in motion governed by immanent rules underscores the difficulty, if not impossibility, of distinguishing object and world or subject and object. For this reason, Deleuze proposes that every subject or object is an event, nothing but the result of the contingent encounters of affects and percepts, which are themselves independent of and exceeding any living being, standing on their own, simply expressing a pure sensation–freeing it from objects and from states of a subject.[84] In addition, every event is an effect of concepts, prospects, and functives (the objects of logic and mathematics), that is, forms of content (structured materializations) and their forms of expression (structures) that constitute and define one another. Were the world not an ongoing process of trajectories differentiating themselves by means of predictable motions and unpredictable perturbations, there would be no events and no intelligence either.

It seems, then, that with the idea of dynamical system, the binary thinking that arose most powerfully with the conception of an *ego cogito* has possibly been overcome. And one of the most significant implications of this structure could be that all binaries, including those powerful cultural signs such as male-female, heterosexual-homosexual, rational-emotional, active-passive, etc., have come undone. Deleuze, in particular, is quite specific about the mechanism by which this seems to occur. But as we will see, even for Deleuze, in mathematics and in philosophy, *binaries persist.* What has changed is only that a layer of microstructures is conceptualized and differentiated from macro or molar structures. Ultimately, however, the microstructures give way to binaries and so remain within the logic and mathematics governing binaries.

In order to distinguish the micro and macro structures of his system with respect to the thinker, Deleuze begins by citing the Cartesian will to distinguish doubt from certitude. Deleuze argued previously that making this distinction presupposes the good will of the thinker and the good nature of thought, that is, the expectation that identity, analogy, opposition, and resemblance will be accompanied by the "I think," such that I conceive, I judge, I imagine, I remember, and I perceive become branches of the cogito and "difference becomes an object of representation always in relation to a conceived identity, a judged analogy with other genera, an imagined opposition of predicates or a perceived similitude."[85] In this scheme, difference, differentiation, and even repetition are impossible to think, and so are lost to recognition in a concept, distribution through analogy, reproduction in imagination, and resemblance through perception.[86]

It appears that Descartes did not yet possess the conceptual apparatus necessary to do without the *cogito* and to develop the idea of differentiation. Although Zeno of Elea (450 BC) gave a number of problems that were based on the infinite, and Archimedes used the method of exhaustion to find an approximation to the area of a circle, an early example of integration, no further progress in the development of mathematical differentiation was made until the sixteenth century. Descartes was aware of the development of a method for calculating maxima and minima when the derivative of the function was zero, but it was Newton who first mathematically represented a particle tracing out a curve with two moving lines that were the coordinates. And it was Leibniz who thought of the variables x and y as ranging over sequences of infinitely close values. He introduced dx and dy as differences between successive values of these sequences.[87] Lacking the full power of differential calculus, it would have been impossible for Descartes to think difference and differentiation in the manner made possible by Leibniz and

Newton. Moreover, breaking away from the science and the worldview of the ancient Greeks and many medieval thinkers meant breaking away from a world in which the Earth is the center of the universe and material entities were conceived of in terms of a substance or genus that is the same as itself (identical) and the attributes of that substance, where there is and must be something identical from which those attributes differ.[88] This, according to Deleuze, is something Descartes did not fully achieve.

Descartes's partial success accounts for the critique levied against him regarding the various aspects of the *cogito*. This is that the I conceive, I judge, I imagine, I remember, I perceive, do nothing to disturb thought; they are clearly objects of recognition whereby thought recognizes itself in things and in the comfortable certainties of the cogito when it thinks clearly and distinctly in the immediacy of a now moment. What is problematic is that truths generated in this manner are, in fact, no more than hypothetical. They assume or presuppose exactly what is in question and therefore lack certainty, or what Deleuze calls absolute necessity.[89] But something, Deleuze maintains, forces us to think differently, meaning that some event leads us to ask about what conditions Cartesian recognition and certainty, that is, what makes recognition and certainty possible? What forces us to think differently is possible through a *violent disjunction* in the strong, exclusive logical sense of this term, where disjunction refers to a logical proposition in the form of "either x or not-x, but not both," a proposition that, following logical rules of transformation, may be reformulated.

Deleuze points out that in *Republic,* amidst the violence of Socrates's encounter with the sophist Thrasymachus, Socrates recalls the Idea of justice, an Idea that is not able to be remembered on the empirical level. Yet, influenced by empirical, moral motives, Plato is said to miss the opportunity to cast aside common sense and the empirical, and thereby, Plato clouds thought. Faced with the claim that something is both just and unjust, a logical contradiction, Plato insists on making sense of the empirical realm and therefore insists on the law of noncontradiction and the law of the excluded middle. The former establishes that for any proposition, that proposition and its negation are never both true, only one may be true, and the latter establishes that for a given proposition and its negation, at least one must be true *and* they cannot both be true.[90]

Within the logical order the asymmetry of true or positive propositions is symbolized by the representation of negation through the addition of a negation symbol to the positively expressed proposition "P," thus "P" and

"~P." Although for some logicians such as Göttlob Frege, "P" and "~P" co-emerge and are thus logically equivalent, for others, such as Ludwig Wittgenstein, "the sense of ~P *cannot* be understood unless one understands the sense of P."[91] In other words, when the negative is thought through strictly, it cannot appear as an object of thought. This would leave us with the strange ontological notion that somehow, non-Being (~P) *is*.

For this reason, some philosophers interpret logical contradiction as constituting a structural relation of dominance and erasure because it constructs difference or otherness in terms of exclusion or by denial.[92] Other types of opposition such as contrariety seem to be less hierarchical insofar as a single term may have a variety of contraries that need not indicate the lack of a specific property, so that if both contraries are asserted, the system does not collapse. Yet Plato, like Aristotle, generally presumes that the contrary of a term is not a pluralistic set (such as bad, sad, or unrepentant, for the term good), but that the contrary of good is nongood, which, if it is to mean anything, seems to reinstate privilege and hierarchical unity without admitting overtly to it.[93]

Deleuze, as such, seems to use the idea of contrariety in this latter sense, as commensurate with *noncontradiction*. He finds that for Socrates, contrariety disrupts common sense and compels even the Socratic soul to probe, to problematize, "arousing thought in itself."[94] But in the end, the sensible discordant encounter with contrariety must be harmonized. Coaxing Thrasymachus to become gentle, to give up his anger, Socrates upholds the law of noncontradiction and the law of the excluded middle, thereby affirming binaries and their seemingly hierarchical structures. Seeking to escape the fate of binaries, of exclusive disjunction (either x or not-x), although caught up in the same logical system, Deleuze proposes an alternative. As we noted above, he proposes a Kantian solution, a solution possible only after Plato and Aristotle, and even after Descartes, whose system of coordinates makes the new solution possible but does not yet completely abandon the Greek view. Deleuze proposes a spacetime manifold according to which *nature,* meaning physical reality, is associative, commutative, and distributive, where association $[(x+y)+z = x+(y+z)]$, is opposed to the Aristotelean conception of unity in a genus.

In this manifold the laws of nature distribute parts that cannot be totalized, so that, as Kant argued, nature is conjunctive, expressing itself in the logical forms of this *and* that, this *or* that, rather than as Being, One, or Whole. As we have noted, that things exist one by one without the possibility of being gathered together is the expression of purely external relations of association within this spacetime field, which is an immanent field, a plane of immanence. It is in this sense self-regulating, governed by its immanent laws. In this field, relations between things can be further characterized in terms of the subatomic particles that are their conditions, the chance collisions of particles that exist one by one and are not unified or governed by a divine or transcendental principle of unification. Instead they are connected by means of a transcendental principle of differential relations where the construction of vector fields is organized by the functions of differential calculus. In other words, Deleuze appears to propose a formal structure, a structure that allows him to bypass empirical and commonsensical arguments.

According to this formal structure, the condition of the possibility of those substances, those molar existences, those objects of recognition and representation, lies in the molecular. "Molecular desiring-machines are in themselves the investment of the large molar machines or of the configurations that the desiring-*machines form according to the laws of large numbers,* in either or both senses of subordination. . . . Desiring-machines in one sense, but organic, technical, or social machines in the other: these are *the same machines under determinate conditions.*"[95] Every physical entity is a "molar" individual, an investment made by formal desiring machines whose atomistic individuality, meaning discernible particles, are invested with absolute properties. Possessing internal unity, inscribed in a part of space, resisting external influences through circular causality and thus immanent, the molar physical entity is taken to be an individual.[96]

However, the molar is posited as the limit of physical knowledge. Molar structures are not real, that is, they are not physical, causal forces. They are instead an Idea, a signification common to an ensemble of molecular facts, expressed by all the facts but not contained in any one.[97] This striking formulation is found in Deleuze, for whom the Idea provides, in general, an indication of the signification of what mathematics refers to as a dynamical system. A dynamical system, we noted above, consists of two elements: first, a playing space on which the motion of the system takes place, and second, a rule or rules (a vector field) determining what moves are possible. In addition, every dynamical system is also oriented by an attractor that fixes the overall behavior of the system.[98] For Deleuze, each dynamical system is governed by a vector field and an Idea (attractor) that organizes the realm it constitutes, whether the attractor is biological, political, or any other realm.

The rules (the vector field) that govern dynamical systems are the same for all of them, and, for Deleuze, the rules governing the physical field take on ontological status.

Deleuze ontologizes the formal structure so that all realms of existence are governed by its laws. This is his grand style. This becomes the basis of the claim, coming from Deleuze, that below, or as the condition of the possibility of Oedipus, we find a molecular unconscious; beneath stable forms, there is functionalism; under familialism, polymorphous perversity. We are in the same system, the same classical molar structure, and every molar entity is an effect of molecular interactions in a dynamical system. So the molecular is simply the same entities or events removed one level to a smaller scale, which, Deleuze claims, makes possible our everyday molar and representational world. If we are to understand this we might want to ask, what is the distinction between the molecular and the molar, the microphysical and the statistical?

The Molecular and the Molar

In the most formal, mathematical sense of the term, the molecular refers to Avogadro's number, the number of atoms needed such that the number of grams of a substance equals the atomic mass of the substance; an Avogadro's number of substance is called a mole.[99] Avogadro's hypothesis was key to solving many problems in the chemical sciences in the 1800s. For chemistry, molecules and moles are a matter of physical relations, ascertaining that equal volumes of gases with the same pressure and temperature contain the same number of molecules. By analogy, these terms reveal several possibilities. The first is that "the machine taken in its structural unity, the living taken in its specific and even personal unity, are mass phenomena or molar aggregates . . . merely two paths in the same statistical direction."[100] From the point of view of molar or statistic aggregates in physical relations, molar machines may be social machines, technical machines, or organic machines. Physically, statistically, they are machines that appear as single objects and living organisms that appear as single subjects.

And what of the molecular? Desiring machines are of the molecular order. What does this imply? In the language of Deleuze and Félix Guattari, "desiring-machines work according to regimes of syntheses that have no equivalent in the large aggregates . . . the indifferent nature of the chemical signals, the indifference to the substrate, and the indirect character of the interactions."[101] Deleuze states that what he calls the "regimes" of molar aggregates, their coded organization, is one with recognition and representation. In other words, these regimes were defined by Aristotle in terms of substance and its attributes, and by Descartes as representations.

By contrast, molecular desiring machines work according to regimes of synthesis, but not those of the large aggregates. Their syntheses have functional properties—properties such as heightened coherence and efficiency that affect their operations—so that only on the level of fundamental structure does one discern the so-called play of blind or chance combinations. The key feature here is that the organization of molecules occurs independently; they are not structured "from above," by the large aggregates, the molar formations. Quite the opposite. Molecular syntheses are the condition of the possibility of molar life. That particular molecular syntheses give rise to specific forms of molar life may certainly be a matter of chance, that is, a chance meeting of environmental factors that in turn gives rise to highly organized molar living structures.

Formalism

In the grand style, this system involves violent interventions. The characterization of proteins as the ultimate molecular elements in the arrangement of desiring machines reveals the method at work here. The method requires that one go beyond the molar to the molecular. How to reach this level, the level of analysis where all aggregates are broken down and reduced to their most fundamental components? If we begin with the regimes of recognition and representation, regimes encompassing thinkers from Plato and Aristotle to Descartes, regimes built on the identity of a genus or the identity of a *cogito*, then there is, for Deleuze, only one solution. "Destroy, destroy. This is the task of schizoanalysis, which goes by way of destruction—a whole scouring of the unconscious, a complete curettage."[102] A harsh solution, for by means of the latter, by means of destruction-reduction, we end up standing before the gates of a pure functionalism: formalism, structure without context, pure structural differentiation.[103] Perhaps this is the ultimate equality a molar individual can achieve, the reduction of each and every one to molecules, nothing more abstract or more equal in the universe.

Like Spinoza, who set out his philosophy as a series of propositions, each one following from the previous proposition, Deleuze's mathematical formalism constitutes his grand style. Mathematical formalism has been characterized as not merely "Plato playing pleasantly with yesful youths . . . and getting them to say that they see lovely patterns laid up in heaven, but a tough game played against a tough opponent who is as skeptical as it is possible to be and will not let anything pass unless he absolutely has to."[104] Formalization allows one to abstract the fundamental shape of a system in order to to discern patterns without superficial and messy flesh.[105] Formalization is built upon a frame of maximum cogency, meaning that at every step the premises are true and the conclusion is undeniable, to the point where no alternative arguments can even be considered. "Formal systems minimize the demand made on both the intelligence and the cooperativeness of the opponent. The stock of symbols is small and the rules for manipulating them explicit," such that the *average sensual man* can recognize the pattern.[106] Recall Deleuze's words cited above, that ideal connections constitutive of the problematic, that is, of the dialectical Idea, are incarnated in the real relations that are constituted by mathematical theories.

Deleuze's disdain of half measures is palpable and brings to the fore the idea of his philosophy as philosophy in the grand style. His insistence on requiring the constitution of real relations in mathematical theories is manifest in what he takes to be the failure of Plato's dialogues. "In his development of the idea of dialectic, he [Plato] came to think of the respondent as utterly bloody-minded, who would not be persuaded by anything less than the fear of inconsistency, since the one sanction capable of coercing every recalcitrant reasoner into conceding the validity of each step was self-contradiction."[107] Plato was driven to this extreme, Deleuze implies, because he did not cast aside common sense and the empirical. Deleuze will not make this mistake, but will put into play his version of the dialectical or problematic Idea, with its ideal rather than empirical connections.

Formalists, it is said, are prepared to respond to challenges, to respond to end games, and to reach metamathematical conclusions based on what appears to be possible. For this reason, dialectical argumentation remains essential in order to extend cogent arguments to what exceeds finite demonstrations. In other words, dialectic allows one to respond to disputes, to examine claims about invalid steps in an argument, and to prove that they are valid. Moreover, if a challenger cannot find counterinstances, there is no need to justify claims about an infinite number of instances. "Instead of having to go on forever, waving our hand implausibly over an infinite number of instances, we can get our teeth into a definite, finite case, and chew through it to incontrovertible refutations."[108] Dialectical justifications enable us to demonstrate the validity of transfinite formalist arguments without appeal to only the law of noncontradiction.

In order to overcome the limitation of Socrates's giving into sensation, thereby, strictly speaking, violating the law of noncontradiction, Deleuze proposes an image of thought *unsullied by the opacity of physical existence,* that is, an image set free from recognition, similarity, identity, and analogy; it is, therefore, a molecular, insensible image. Qualitative opposition within the sensible is quickly tamed by common sense, which knows that contraries cannot coexist in the sensible object. The simultaneity of contraries violates the logical law of the excluded middle. But if we leave aside the sensible, if we merely think, if there is only thought unsullied by physical existence, then what is that thought? It is the thought that arises with Newton and Leibniz. It is a thought made possible by the calculus of infinitesimals. It is thought that is pure difference, differentiating itself in a continuous spacetime trajectory. It will be the same for memory, imagination, language, for all so-called faculties. This transcendental empiricism is empirical only insofar as it designates as imperceptible and unthinkable that which takes place at the empirical level and thereby immediately transcends it.[109] Opposition (contrariety), resemblance, identity, and analogy are effects of this thinking in the empirical realm where common sense and the law of noncontradiction prevail. For the faculties, there is only violence, the violence of not harmonizing or unifying one another, instead, disjoining all that they encounter. Disjunction of the faculties is their *discordant harmony.* This is how its elements exist one by one without the possibility of being gathered together.

First, thought undergoes its clash with the unrecognizable sign, the *being* of the sensible, not with sensibility itself. The sign defies common sense and good sense, which is the "coexistence of contraries, the coexistence of more and less in an unlimited qualitative becoming," which, for Deleuze, in order not to violate the law of noncontradiction, can never be sensible, which is always only given as a sign.[110] Then, in place of one's own sensibilities, all that is left is a violated "soul," no longer a *cogito* but the fractured I that is forced to pose a problem. In the trauma of this violence the fractured I forgets anything that can be recalled, anything seen, heard, imagined, or thought, in order to think and recall that which has never been empirical, which is transcendental with respect to both sensibility and memory, thus what is essentially nonsense and forgetfulness. In the midst of this original violence, the faculties themselves are forced to their limits, meaning they are forced into discordant harmony, their disjunction, the open-ended disorder of the faculties, so that each may pursue its own "essential" projects, the transcendental projects of thinking, willing, or imagining.[111] If a faculty is forced to its limit, this does not imply that it reaches some end, but rather that it moves on a trajectory, forever, closer and closer, toward some point, some Idea attractor, without ever crossing it.

Transcendentally, in a purely formal sense, in the realm of thought, binaries continue to exist, but the formal Idea, rather than determining that something is male or female, animal or vegetable, can be left indeterminate, replicating the Kantian free play of all the faculties "where each goes to its own limit and nevertheless shows the possibility of some sort of harmony with the others."[112] For Deleuze, outside of the formal transcendental realm of thinking, willing, and judging, we admit contradiction into our faculties and fail to adhere to the law of the excluded middle. Although the conception of the problematic Idea that undergoes continuous differentiation/differenciation is a conception that undermines the recognition, representation, habituation, equalization nexus of classical, modern thought, replacing it with the Idea of difference and the diverse, an important question remains. Does it it contribute to conceptions beyond the formal and external description of particles? Does it characterize sensible existence?[113] Let us briefly examine this.

Classical physics, the work of Galileo, Kepler, Newton, Leibniz, first gave us the laws according to which particles move and interact with one another. Given any arrangement of the particles that make up the universe, and any choices for their initial motions, these laws can be used to predict the future. Different worlds are arrived at by starting with the particles in different positions.[114] Every trajectory in each universe is defined by laws that specify the movement and interaction of particles. But even for dynamical differential systems, the rules of motion are given. What may be contingent are the particular particles themselves, that is, which particles enter into any given trajectory and in what order? Which affects, percepts, concepts, prospects, and functives?

In an immanent system, such as that proposed by Deleuze, a system sensitive to initial conditions and with unstable boundaries, as opposed to Newton's closed and certain universe, some of this cannot be predicted, thus every configuration of particles produces a deterministically chaotic world. This is because once the rules that specify the movement and interaction of particles are set in place, they do not alter; this is what makes them deterministic. These rules, we have stated, are connection, conjunction, and disjunction. Moreover, in the deterministically chaotic world, space and time are given, not emergent. They are, as Kant posited, the pregiven, pre-existent manifold, and time is simply a parameter of *any space whatever,* a fourth dimension, a means for differentiating different spaces, but not an emergent and unpredictable reality. Where the spacetime manifold is always already given, creation per se disappears insofar as predictability is the goal of the system, if not a requirement. The implication of this is that as revolutionary as Deleuze's grand style may be, insofar as it is a projection of mathematical and physical structures, it can do no more than what they do. One can idealize, as Deleuze certainly does. One can imagine speeds beyond the speed of light that would interfere with the organizing power of the rules governing the spacetime manifold, but there remain physical constraints on such ideas and limits, even for the grand style of philosophy.

Philosophy and Cosmological Concepts

How are we to understand all of this? Why does Deleuze pursue this line of thought? Perhaps it makes the most sense to think of it in terms of the problematic set out by Kant, a problematic so difficult to find a solution for that contemporary philosophy still struggles with it. This is the problematic cast, by Kant, in terms of the antinomy between transcendental idealism and empiricist skepticism. The question Kant raises is, is the I that thinks a simple substance that is independent of outer experience or is all knowledge the product of experience? This is the point of the second antinomy, which appears to be key to Kant's understanding of nature and to the conflicting views of nature that have arisen between philosophy and the natural sciences, with which we are concerned throughout this book.

The second antinomy explores the cosmological concept of the absolute totality of reality in space.[115] Human reason, according to Kant, is naturally inclined to extend the categories of understanding beyond the limit that the fragmented nature of finite human cognition establishes for them. Human cognition is fragmented because it relies on sensible intuitions and cannot create its own objectively valid objects. Possibly to compensate for the fragmentation of cognition, reason extends its categories beyond the conditions of possibility of experience, resulting in antinomies, a simple linear series whereby a finite series of experience is expanded to an infinite series of pure reason, the unconditioned unity of the objective synthesis of appearances. This is why antinomies are called cosmological concepts; they yield a concept of the world.

The second antinomy argues that with respect to our representations of external objects, space and matter correspond to one another. Space is defined, first, as an infinite given magnitude and so as the necessary condition of all external phenomenon, in other words, the form of external phenomena. Matter appears in space as reality and individual spaces are limitations of the infinite given magnitude.[116] If reason extends this category, it extends spatial reality or material space to an absolute concept of the world. In what does this world consist? The antinomy's thesis claims that it consists of simple parts and that all composites are composed of simples.[117] A simple is defined as the unconditioned first member of the absolutely total series of the synthesis of appearances. This is the regressive limit in the division of the whole into atomistic parts.

But the thesis appears to be impossible if space is an infinite given magnitude, a whole intuited prior to its parts, therefore not composed of atomistic entities. If space is an infinite given magnitude, then material forms appear in space only as limitations of the a priori form of external intuition. Space may be represented as a synthesis of spaces external to one another, but individual spaces are actually possible only as limitations of the one original, a priori space. This means that space is not a substance, something that might be constructed out of simples, for we have no intuition of such simples. Material space would have to be a noumenal thing-in-itself in order to be able to be atomistically constituted, and therefore it could not be the form of experience and what is represented through that form.[118]

Thus the antithesis of the second antinomy states that no composite is made up of simples, and it further states that no simple exists anywhere in the world. This means that matter is infinitely divisible or infinitesimal, as in mathematics, a limitation of the originally given intuition of space, and the absolute totality of infinitely divisible matter is what we call the world. Space, in the antithesis, is understood to be the formal condition of the possibility of all matter and the original intuition of space is that of an infinitely given unity, such that what is given in space (matter) must conform to the unity of space. It is important to keep in mind, then, that material, physical, or mathematical points are simply delimitations of this original unity of space.[119]

The second antinomy shows that we can conceive of space as consisting of either atomic simples or as infinitely continuous. Neither idea corresponds to anything in our experience, that is, to the objects of our representations organized in accordance with our good sense and common sense in the manner of the harmony of the faculties. The antinomy posits either the empirical idealism of self-subsistent composites derived from experience or the transcendental reality of space. Kant's solution (his transcendental idealism) is to point out that the objects of our experience are determinable only in relation to a subject whose unity of apperception is the form of their unity, and so they are not determinable in relation to the cosmological concept of the absolute totality of appearances. In other words, nature is not to be conceived of as an absolute totality, but as the order and regularity of appearances in relation to a subject.

But things are not so simple. Even if nature is the order and regularity of appearances in conformity with the categories of a thinking subject, it is still nature as physics conceives of it, conforming to a priori laws. The laws of the manifold are the laws of classical physics, consisting, in general, of a grammar, axioms, and rules of inference.[120] Considering the mere form of understanding, "all relations of thought in judgments" are relations of the predicate to the subject (the categorical relation), the ground to its consequence (the hypothetical relation), and the relation of divided knowledge (the disjunctive relation).[121] In other words, "all we know in matter is merely relations . . . [and] if I abstract from these relations, there is nothing more left for me to think."[122]

If nature is a phenomenal unity consisting of relations, space as the form of these relations, a priori, is a system of relations, and mathematics, physics, natural science in general, and philosophy are then all theories of relations. What is crucial here is that if we remove the specific and determining categorical relations from our representations, we are left with bare extension and figure. "In space, shape, magnitude, and relation to one another are determined or determinable."[123] Space is the a priori intuition that makes it possible to represent any thing as in the world or alongside something else or in different places, or in any relation. So we should not be surprised that mathematics in the form of geometry is the schema of Kant's concepts that are prior to all other aspects of knowledge. "The mathematics of space (geometry) is based upon this successive synthesis of the productive imagination in the generation of figures. This is the basis of the axioms which formulate the conditions of sensible a priori intuition, under which alone the schema of a pure concept of outer appearance can arise."[124] The axioms of intuition are extensive magnitudes, thus geometric; they are a priori synthetic propositions, and they are spontaneous and active judgments; thus they are axiomatic. In other words, they are postulates of thought, essential intuitions of the nature of space given a priori and confirmed by outer intuition.

That the axioms of intuition must be confirmed by outer intuition represents a limitation, a limitation that Deleuze, along with modern mathematics, does away with. What limits Kant's science of relations is that its axioms must have a possible object in outer intuition. Out of all logically possible geometrical relations, only those which may actually be constructed can be such an object. This requirement limits Kant to Euclidean geometry, the one space we can experience. Our human intuition of spatial relations reveals the finitude of human understanding when it is limited by sensibility, for only spatial axioms tied to sensibility are objectively valid. This limitation was overcome by mathematicians who proved that there are geometries that are different than Euclid's, geometries that do not apply to the physical world and physical space.[125] This led eventually to the development of Riemannian geometry, applicable to the surface of a sphere where the straight line of its axioms refers to the endless (because circular) but finite (because circular) circles on the circumference of that sphere.[126]

Most importantly, for our purposes here, "the creation of non-Euclidean geometry brought into clear light a distinction that had always been implicit but never recognized–the distinction between a mathematical space and physical space."[127] Mathematical space is the space of scientific theory different from the physical space whose axioms are supported by sensation, as the latter are (as Kant's antinomies imply) purely subjective constructions as opposed to the objective constructions of mathematical space. The latter, objective constructions of Archimedean logic begin with the construction of a geometry in one's own mind, made out of the symbols found in one's own mind, only then putting that geometry to use.[128] Such axioms, moreover, cannot be determined to be true on a priori grounds. Their truth lies only in the extent to which they may be put to use, not to account for experience, but to provide an abstract and logical understanding of any question of interest, for which any interesting axioms might be proposed.[129]

This is the point of statements by Deleuze, referred to above, that Kant's failure is his empiricism insofar as Kant's transcendental idealism remains bound to empirical sensibility and empirical memory. This forces him to connect what for Deleuze is immanent, the spatial manifold, with what is transcendental, the concepts of the Understanding, utilizing schemata, a priori determinations of time in accordance with rules. "What the schematism of Understanding effects by means of the transcendental synthesis of imagination is simply the unity of all the manifold of intuition in inner sense."[130] As we have noted above, this may be a desirable goal for generating the manifold, but it is inappropriately achieved insofar as the route is external, a purely external harmony of intuitions and concepts. Thus, for Deleuze, Kant is unable to posit immanent, serial connections between the undetermined, the determinable, and the determination, and he is unable to conceptualize Ideas as problems whose immanent genesis is a solution to a problematic, thereby taking Ideas to be nothing but conditions for the possibility of knowledge and experience.[131]

In this way, Deleuze follows the lead of the post-Euclidean mathematicians whose objective constructions of mathematical space provide an abstract and logical understanding of any question that is interesting, remarkable, or unusual. Likewise, this is the orientation of Alain Badiou, whose grand style asserts that mathematics is ontology. In other words, what can be rationally asserted of being qua being, aside from any qualitative characteristics or predicates, but taken solely as the mathematicians take non-Euclidean geometries, as an entity exposed to thought, must be written in purely mathematical terms. "What's more, the actual history of ontology coincides exactly with the history of mathematics."[132] In other words, the abstract and logical understanding of being qua being can only be ascertained mathematically. And although Badiou characterizes Kant as being among those philosophers whose philosophy represents the grand style, he more or less agrees with Deleuze that Kant restricts his own thinking by binding ontological intuitions to judgments about experience, the lowest degree of thinking, as well as to a subject who is the "operational unity of a multiplicity."[133] In what follows, we will be concerned with the implications of this way of characterizing ontology in particular and philosophy in general. In other words, when mathematics is ontology, as Deleuze implies and Badiou openly asserts, we will ask, what are its limits as it engages in problematizing philosophical questions? Does Archimedean ontology give us clues as to how to speak and act in the context of the *vita activa*? These are the questions to which we now turn.

5

PHILOSOPHY'S
EXTRA-SCIENTIFIC MESSAGES

The Culture of Extinction?

We began chapter 1 with the admonition of physicist Steven Weinberg that those philosophers who seek extra-scientific messages in what they "think" they understand about modern physics are making a grave error. And yet we also saw that philosophers, historians, and social scientists have linked changes in natural scientific methods and theories to changes in worldview, a system of intertwined, interrelated, interconnected beliefs. Recent events have brought conflicting positions regarding worldviews to the fore once again. The Large Hadron Collider, situated outside of Geneva, Switzerland, and funded by an international consortium of nations, was constructed to aid scientists in verifying the existence of the Higgs boson and other subatomic particles. Ultimately, the point is to explain the origin of mass and the origin of the universe itself. Scientists engaged in this experiment suffered an unexpected setback when an electrical short caused extensive damage to the accelerator and revealed problems with the experiment itself.[1] The accelerator was constructed over fifteen years at a cost of approximately $9 billion. Weinberg acknowledges the unhappiness this event produced among teams of scientists, but takes it only as a delay and not as a failure, unlike an earlier project of his, the Superconducting Super Collider that was supposed to have been built in Texas but was abandoned due to excessive costs.

An alternative view comes forth, however, from Richard M. Leventhal, an anthropologist who has led many archeological digs at the Mayan pyramid at Xunantunich, Belize. Leventhal implies that the Large Hadron Collider is similar in some respects to the pyramid. "All of these multigenerational projects are based upon a strong and ongoing belief system in how the world works."[2] In other words, for the anthropologist, a worldview is at work and he believes that cultural and scientific projects are abandoned when the worldview crumbles, leaving unanswered the question of how and under what circumstances a worldview would simply crumble. The physicist cites no worldviews. He sees the electrical short in the collider's colossal magnets and the experimental errors as causing frustration but certainly not abandonment of the project. Witnessing all this, historian of science Allan Franklin, also a former particle physicist, nevertheless cautions that if the project fails, it is "almost a disaster for an entire field."[3] Whether or not the development of a worldview based on a dominant scientific paradigm is an error, we can ask ourselves what the consequences of each worldview might be. Thus we have begun with the classical model of nature, which arose along with classical physics. As the previous chapters have indicated, not all the effects of the classical worldview have been benevolent. Some philosophers have, in fact, read the history of the influence of modern science in society as extremely harmful.

Western cultural and philosophical development has been analyzed in order to argue that culturally and philosophically, Western ideas promoted and justified the ecological destruction of the planet.[4] This historical analysis points beyond philosophy and culture to what became, by the seventeenth and eighteenth centuries, the dominant source of truth and knowledge, that is, classical science. Similarly, the point of our examination of natural science throughout this book is not to demonize or relativize the sciences in order to dismiss the truth of their discoveries, but instead to bring to light the limitations of classical science for science, and especially for philosophy and ethics. That is, what, if any, is the correlation between the worldviews we construct on the basis of natural science and our own human actions? Is their correlation related to the difficulties we encounter in constructing an ontology that does not exclude ethics and an account of human affectivity, extending to our ideas about love? Can we examine these relationships without calling for an end to science, to science's objectivist stance, or an end to the long-term relationship between philosophy and science?

In carrying out this aspect of our analysis, we shall look, in particular, to the politically oriented philosophy of Hannah Arendt and the ethically oriented philosophy of Simone de Beauvoir. Arendt has already drawn our attention to the invention of the telescope, which gave rise to what she calls (following Descartes) the Archimedean point of view, the mathematical view of human and earthly life, a statistical view of reality. We will examine how, although she has suggested that this statistical view is the most banal view of all, Arendt maintains that potentially, under certain conditions, it gives rise to unethical behavior as extreme as the most evil of crimes, genocide. From her point of view, Beauvoir addresses the mathematical view of classical science in its most radical form, the clinamen, where this term represents what mathematicians now call deterministic chaos. She asks if such a structure, which gives rise to "being and nothingness," is appropriate for human life and ethics, and why it does nothing to put an end to gulags and death camps.

Beyond these critiques, we will maintain that both philosophers inaugurate a new way of thinking that does not reject scientific objectivity and mathematical-logical precision, but which pinpoints the inability of classical science to address temporality, past, present, and future, in a manner adequate to human existence, to human ontology, ethics, and love. It is in the interests of bringing temporality into the scientific and philosophical picture that we examine these questions.

Previous chapters have emphasized the role of Sir Isaac Newton, the first scientist able to prove that the motions of bodies on Earth and the motions of heavenly bodies are governed by the same set of natural laws. Describing the three laws of motion and universal gravitation, Newton made possible classical mechanics, the science of predicting the motion of bodies deterministically (according to unchanging rules) and with certainty. Using the calculus of infinitesimals, a new mathematics developed simultaneously by Newton and Gottfried Leibniz, it was possible to track instantaneous changes in the motions of bodies. Thus Newton was thought to have demonstrated that the orbits of the planets circling around the sun, as well as those of comets, are stable ellipses because the system of bodies, of which each of them is a part, is in dynamic equilibrium. In other words, the tendency of a planet to fly off on a tangent is restrained and balanced, placed in equilibrium by the gravitational pull of other bodies in its neighborhood.[5] This was conceivable insofar as Newton founded classical mechanics on the view that space does not shrink or grow if an object is in motion, and equally that time is something that passes uniformly without regard to whatever happens in the world.[6] For this reason he referred to space and time as absolute, so as to distinguish these entities from the various ways by which we measure them (which he called relative spaces and relative times).

We made the point in chapter 2 that Newton's system ideally conforms to a set of idealized presuppositions, that Newtonian systems are closed, deterministic, reversible, and strongly decomposable or atomistic. And we argued that the unifying and deterministic certainty of these laws was integral to the development of modern science and to the predictive power of modern science, a power closely tied to the role of science in progress. But such advances in human scientific knowledge, especially advances advocating a view of life or the universe that anticipates or predicts the future, seem to have simultaneously revealed what may well be a substantial residue of uncertainty lying on the borders of their proper sphere of application.

Given the inevitability of this residue, it is understandable that every attempt might have been made to apply newly forming scientific knowledge outside the sphere of its original intended applications. And so the reach of Newtonian science did not stop with predictions concerning the motions of earthly and heavenly bodies. As we have maintained, Newtonian principles became the basis of a general worldview, which we defined as "an intertwined, interrelated, interconnected system of beliefs."[7] The rationale for such a worldview is not difficult to imagine. Western European philosophers and intellectuals, many of whom were also scientists, were emerging from the dark ages of divine right monarchies and aristocrats whose privilege came not from their intelligence but from a universal teleology that was never wholly abandoned by the educational, religious, and political establishment.[8]

When nature's laws were taken as the ultimate authority regarding human actions, political equality could be derived from the equality of human faculties and opportunities, where each "man" is an atomistic individual, possessing the same rights and duties. What is crucial here is that when men embraced reason and self-interest, they became individuals, each one statistically more or less like the next, with the same duties and rights. This is the point of so-called universal moral law. In view of the natural equality of atomistic individuals and universal natural law, the only moral law thinkable is one that maintains universality. In order for any act to be moral, it must be universal, universally applicable. Without this, the natural order of the universe is violated.

Life and the Human Condition

As Arendt reminds us, Karl Marx also understood the idea of growing wealth to be a natural process following its own laws, a process the functioning of which cannot be checked.[9] Marx conceptualizes labor in terms of production; labor is a pure process of production, producing both itself and surplus labor. As we have seen, for Arendt labor's production is simply for the sake of life and life's necessities. But when all activities are reduced to a form of labor and labor is identified with pure processes of production, this can be considered a revaluation of all values. Glorification of the life process, the pure process of production, eliminates the idea of making durable objects that exist and are not simply for consumption; it does away with the existence of noble speech or actions that exist separately from nature's cycles and laws.[10] This, for Arendt, is what makes philosophies of life problematic. For philosophers, beginning with Hume, Locke, and Smith, but continuing with Marx and with twentieth-century philosophers such as Sartre, Serres, and Deleuze–though Arendt could not have anticipated the work of the latter two, they appear to have utilized many of her concepts–nature is sublimely indifferent to human beings and to language. The growth of wealth for society as a whole appears to be a natural process that follows its own laws, and accumulation can, in principle, go on infinitely.

Arendt's objection, which we will examine more closely, is that the deterministic certainty or even the probability and randomness of natural processes can still be challenged by the finitude of individuals, by the temporality of their lives. However, ours is not an era of freedom, and her objection appears to have been shouted down, since statistically, as a species, production and reproduction, accumulation and consumption, continue without limits as long as humans continue to find the means to live this way.[11] Liberated by man-made technologies from the pain and effort of physical labor, human beings are now able to produce and consume the entire world. Things that were once made by human hands that were durable, lasting beyond an individual life, are being used up, consumed at a faster and faster rate. Nothing is safe from human consumption, and from this point of view, truly we exist in a culture of extinction.[12] Lacking any distinction between the private realm of nature's necessity and the public realm of the *vita activa,* of persuasion through speech, of change through deeds, all private activities are now on public display, resulting in the near domination of mass culture.[13] Much more could be said about mass culture, but it is not the focus of our concerns here. What we wish to consider is whether there is a need to reconceptualize the border between classical nature and ethics, between the necessities of life, the ability to make things that are not immediately consumed, to speak noble words, and to perform deeds that stabilize and give value to human life.

For Arendt *the vita activa* is the life of speech and action, without which life ceases to be human life: "With word and deed we insert ourselves into the human world and this insertion is like a second birth."[14] She calls this second birth "natality," an insertion that does not arise out of the natural necessity of labor nor the utility of work. Indeed, is it not the case that to act is to begin; to act is to set something in motion, something whose effects can be completely unexpected and improbable, yet something humanly disclosed in words, such that "in acting and speaking, men show who they are, reveal actively their unique personal identities, thus make their appearance in the human world"?[15]

What makes human action unique is the boundlessness of its consequences. It is shocking to realize that every consequence stemming from an act is itself part of a mutually intersecting and mutually influencing structure of human interactions that will bring about new and unknown outcomes as well as new and unknown structures of human interactions. Thus each and every human act is not just deterministically probable, but actually *unpredictable*; interactions are started whose outcomes are unpredictable, making uncertainty decisive in human affairs.[16]

Peg Birmingham defends Arendt's conception of natality from critics who argue that this concept reduces the political to the natural.[17] She emphasizes the temporal structure of natality, which, in mathematics and physics, is called "the parallelogram of forces," as when two noncolinear forces act on an object.[18] In Arendt's case, it is the infinite past and the unlimited future that converge and provide a perfect metaphor for thought bound to and rooted in the present wherein one "would have discovered . . . what had come into being only with his own, self-inserting appearance."[19] Birmingham argues effectively that Arendt's distinction between the immortal life of the species and the mortality of human beings separates cyclical, biological life from the event of natality. As we saw previously, the biological foundation of human life is fundamentally the same for all. It is only through speech and action that humans manifest their self-inserting appearance, their unique self, the birth of the unexpected and new.[20] Simply because one cannot give birth to speech and action without a body does not necessitate reduction to the physical body and to the classical view of nature.

This conclusion is further amplified by Arendt's observation that what philosophies of nature and philosophies of life do not openly acknowledge is that the conception of nature as a process of production is a human invention. Scientific experimentation, so integral to modern science, completely changes the relation of human beings to nature. For rather than merely observing, modern science demands experiments. As we are seeing with the Large Hadron Collider, in devising experiments, humans have opened up elemental processes, essentially "'making' nature . . . creating 'natural' processes, which without men would never exist and which earthly nature by herself seems incapable of accomplishing."[21] Earth, left to its own devices, does not reveal subatomic particle collisions or fractals or relativity. This is a difficult idea and it should not be misunderstood as commensurate with the cultural relativist's claim that science is just another interpretation of reality that lacks objectivity. Nature and nature's processes are real; human beings are part of this world, their brains evolved along with the rest of nature, so it is not accidental that human beings are able to create ideas that open nature to knowledge.

Hume's skepticism concerning the source of our perceptions may have led to the conclusion that although we may not know the truth of nature as something given to our senses, humans can know what their mind's make, and what human minds make are relations, the relations between ideas. This leads Hume to assert that mathematical knowledge is the only certain knowledge that humans possess. Whatever certainty there is in our knowledge can only arise from the comparison of ideas and the discovery of some unchanging relations between these ideas, as long as the ideas don't change. For this reason, only arithmetic and algebra seem to offer the assurance of exactness and certainty in the chain of reasoning.[22] But as Arendt makes clear, "this permits the replacement of what is sensuously given by a system of mathematical equations where all real relationships are dissolved into logical relations between man-made symbols."[23] In other words, it invites formalism and functionalism. What ensures the objectivity and therefore the power of mathematics is that its truths can be fully translated into spatial relationships, projected onto physical reality to produce technological achievements previously unthinkable.[24]

Since the invention and use of the telescope, science has been tied to tools and instruments. Making is decisive in the experiment because the experiment produces its own objects of observation and leads to the idea that if one can imitate the processes by which things come into being, even things humans did not make can be reproduced. The question, "What is nature?" thereby shifts to questioning how something came into being. The experiment was developed in order to repeat or imitate the natural process of coming into being. Humans came to trust scientific instruments, like the telescope, the work of their hands, for such instruments forced the universe to yield its secrets. But, as we will see below, these methods meant that scientific and philosophical truth parted ways because the capacity to imitate natural processes does not mean that human beings understand what they are imitating or even how it works.[25] Asking how something comes into being implies processes, the history or story of coming into being. As the object of science has become the history of life or the universe, so nature has become a process in place of Being.[26]

However, processes remain invisible as fabrication disappears into the product. This occurs when our philosophy as well as our science place near-exclusive emphasis on the process. The reason for both is the same: science makes only to know, philosophy thinks only to know. In other words, as important as technological products and practical reason are to human commercial, political, and ethical development, for the scientist as for the philosopher, technical and practical applications are a mere side effect, a by-product of scientific and philosophical activity. The goal of scientific and philosophical activity is knowledge, not applications. Thus if nature is the model for philosophies of life, but natural processes are the effect of human intervention, then it seems that it is the human political and ethical ability to speak and act, to start "new unprecedented processes whose outcome remains uncertain and unpredictable," that should be understood to be the real source of nature understood as process.[27]

So perhaps we should not be too surprised when a physicist tells us that although Newton's laws of gravitation are only approximations of the general theory of relativity, mathematical models use the laws of gravitation to predict the motion of real particles or planets. For example, complete mathematical solutions are available only for two-particle or two-body systems. However, physicist Xhihong Xia has shown that a system of five or more point-masses behaves so unpredictably that if each is influenced by the gravitational attraction of the others, they all fly off into infinity.[28] So much for prediction.

Arendt would like to remind us that it is only because we humans are capable of acting, of starting processes, that we can conceive of nature as a process as well. In other words, our political and ethical acts serve as the model for the structure of our pursuit of knowledge even in the sciences. Simultaneously, because deterministically certain nature and reason, which is one with nature, have been our models, it is truly unreasonable, even irrational, for human beings to expect the unexpected, thus we make every attempt to predict the outcome of the processes we put into place.[29] Given this situation, the question seems to be, how can human life and thought be rescued from itself, from the endless necessity of the life process, the cyclicity of nature, and the processes of production to which it has condemned itself?

Mathematical and Logical Formalization

For Arendt, speech and action separate the public life of the *vita activa* from the private sphere of necessity, but the active life of noble words and deeds does not exist without others. Without other human beings to witness and affirm our speech and action, we are nothing but laborers and consumers, toiling away in accordance with nature's processes, with no special human qualities or attributes. If it is possible for others to witness our actions, we must ask what structure makes it possible for each of us to recognize and be recognized by others, for in the classical view it appears that nature's laws govern necessity, and if they govern human communication as well, then recognition may be extremely difficult to achieve.

Earlier we noted that Newton made use of differential equations to show that the same laws of planetary motion apply to, and so unify, the motions of heavenly and earthly bodies. The power of this discovery has been irresistible. Humankind has come to realize that the laws of physics can be expressed in the language of differential equations. This is true for the equations governing the flow of heat, air, and water; for the laws of electricity and magnetism; even for the unfamiliar and often counterintuitive atomic realm where quantum mechanics reigns.[30]

The laws of physics are expressed as differential equations, and physicists are engaged in the creative and constructive search for the right differential equations for every process, for every flow. One mathematician has even used differential equations to plot the physical laws of human attraction. This works insofar as his ideal lovers, appropriately named Romeo and Juliet, in another version of the two-body system, behave like simple harmonic oscillators. In the equation, Romeo's love increases in direct, linear proportion to how much Juliet loves him. As the mathematician points out, because we are dealing with human beings and human nature, the assumption of linearity is not emotionally realistic, but he assumes it because it makes the analysis much easier. Juliet's behavior, on the other hand, reflects the tendency to cool off when Romeo expresses his love for her.

Given these equations and an assumption about how the lovers felt about each other initially, one can use calculus to move Romeo and Juliet forward, instant by instant. In this way, we can predict how much Romeo and Juliet love (or repel) one another at any future time. According to this model, Romeo and Juliet love one another simultaneously one-quarter of the time. If this is the case, if emotional attachments are so predictable, then it seems that human behavior is not free but that it is entirely circumscribed by nature and nature's processes. But there is a caveat here. At first the lovers follow this simple mechanical process, rules of push and pull. But then, at a certain point, the differential equations could and usually do break down. A third person or entity enters the picture—Juliet's old boyfriend, Romeo's new love interest, Juliet's mother—or Juliet goes away to graduate school, leaving Romeo behind.

Alternatively, perhaps Romeo suffers from a personality disorder, an unconscious third body, as so many might prove to be. Either totally aggrandized, or denied approval or love from a key figure in his childhood (another third person), he obscures his true self, a painful, hurt self, which he renders unconscious with an inflated and emotionless false self that seeks only to be recognized for its uniqueness. As a result, he is cruel and abusive, shallow and deceitful, under a façade of modesty, co-opting others by making use of social conventions of conduct.[31] Given enough power (elevated to a leadership role) and resources (the approval and/or adoration of a chosen few that gather around him), Romeo could become a tyrant; he might carry out or order the punishment or deaths of numerous individuals for the sake of a grand scheme, proving thereby his uniqueness and value, and giving rise to the banality of evil.

This may help to explain why, for example, Arendt insists on taking Adolf Eichmann at his word when no one else involved in his trial was able to do so. Ascribing his own birth to the "movement of the universe," a "higher Bearer of Meaning," with the implication that the burden of responsibility for carrying out orders from this source fell upon himself, Eichmann was otherwise the totally undistinguished, first-born child, unable to complete a course in even vocational school and undoubtedly a great disappointment to his father and/or mother, setting the stage for his later actions.[32] Eichmann distorted and aggrandized his life story at every turn, and when he joined in the military in 1932, quite arbitrarily, after drifting from job to job or being fired, he was as bored as ever until the opportunity arose to join the S.S.[33] Thus launched into "History" as an "expert" on emigration, he took matters into his own hands. This meant, to Eichmann, an apparently pathological narcissist, that he acted on purpose but that the base motives attributed to him and the horrifying outcomes of his actions were not criminal deeds on his part, because he would have had a bad conscience only if he had not done what he had been ordered to do. Rather, as Arendt maintains, he was simply unable to distinguish right from wrong, an effect, possibly, of his narcissistic grandiosity.[34]

This situation, like that of Romeo and Juliet above, might be said to exemplify what mathematicians and physicists call the "three body problem," at this point unsolvable utilizing differential equations, making prediction impossible.[35] "The essence of the three-body problem resides somehow in the linkages between all three bodies," and complicated behavior arises out of the interactions of relatively simple inputs.[36] In physics, the three-body problem is complex and difficult to understand, but a correlated problem arises when mathematicians try to account for language. For example, the anthropologist-linguist Derek Bickerton states that the sciences of human behavior have not achieved anything like the success of the natural sciences in understanding the processes of matter and how matter comes into existence. He suggests that social scientists have been looking in all the wrong places and that language alone underlies all human behaviors (as differentiated from other species), thereby returning human behavior to the realm of two bodies, language and speech.[37]

It is precisely this idea that has led linguists, starting with Noam Chomsky, to pursue the science of language using mathematical methods, that is, to describe rules that allow for an infinite collection of sentences to be generated from even a finite collection of words. Just as mathematicians use the rule that allows them to add $1 + 1 + 1$ infinitely to generate the series of natural numbers, so linguists use the rules of propositional and predicate logic to generate infinite collections of syntactically correct sentences.[38]

As the logicians of the early twentieth century observed, when syntax is separated from semantics as in the case of formal languages, the result is a universal grammar. The grammatical rules of predicate logic provide a universal grammar that can be applied to the language used in any branch of mathematics–arithmetic, geometry, calculus, chaos theory, any branch you like.[39] In other words, just as mathematical logicians had formulated rules for combining propositions into valid proofs, so Chomsky formulated rules describing how words are combined to form grammatical sentences, a universal grammar.

Much apparent evidence was garnered to support this position. First, it was claimed that all people, regardless of education, learn to speak their native language correctly, indicative of an "instinctive tendency" to speak.[40] Second, even more speculatively, it was claimed that many sentences are new combinations of words never previously uttered but that follow universal rules.[41] Third, it was posited that children unconsciously recognize abstract patterns that allow them to form correct sentences before the age of four.[42] What is central to Chomsky's approach to language is that it is objective, rational, dispassionate, and context-free. Even if all three claims above turn out to be perfectly valid, there are limits to Chomsky's generative linguistics. Although this theory addresses grammatical structure in a useful and creative way, useful especially to persons in the computing fields where the parameters of language use can be well-defined and static, it does not address meaning. Meaning is not addressed insofar as it remains "unamenable" to mathematics.[43]

Nevertheless, even meaning (semantics) has been taken up as something that is, ultimately, mathematically approachable, bringing meaning into logic. So the sentence, "Romeo loves Juliet, but Juliet loves someone else," can easily be expressed in predicate logic, which when translated into

English appears as: R loves J and there is an individual X who is not R such that J loves X.[44] However, the logical form of even many simple sentences is overwhelmingly complex. Logical form assumes that words have fixed and definite meanings, but meaning depends on context and context is like the third body in physics: it is precisely what stymies the mathematization and logicization of language. Attempts to describe situations in formalist or functionalist mathematical language must, in the end, rely on claims about what is true or false, something that is often problematic in this type of system.[45] As was pointed out in the preface, formalist systems do not make truth claims, they simply strive for consistency. Furthermore, unlike Arendt's conception of natality, the temporal structure for formal mathematical and logical languages is one in which the past and future do not influence the present and therefore events have no causes and no consequences. Let us look at this in more detail. In order to carry out an assessment of the limits of formal languages, let us examine this in a familiar context, that of the logician Lewis Carroll's tale of formalist linguistics, otherwise known as *Alice in Wonderland*.

Alice in Wonderland has been described as the paradigm for releasing thought from the constraints of reference, signification, identity, and causation.[46] Yet it seems that we probably do not quite understand what this implies with respect to postmodern philosophy and the scientific turn. With this in mind, let us reread the story of Alice's adventures and examine the logic and linguistics of her fantastic journey down the rabbit hole and into the world of Wonderland. Why, we might ask, is this story so preoccupied with certain kinds of questions that belong to logic and to philosophy of language? Why is the underground world called Wonderland? How is Alice's strange adventure related to her own discoveries and realizations about making sense as narrated in the story? How does the tale of Alice relate to the project of postmodern philosophy and to that of philosophers like Arendt who do not make the postmodern turn to formalism and functionalism?

The Long Fall

On a very hot day, raised out of her sleepy state by the astonishing sight of a rabbit removing a watch from the pocket of the waistcoat it was wearing, a little girl named Alice runs after the creature.[47] She races across a field and, without hesitation, follows it down a large rabbit hole hidden under a hedge. She falls from the surface of the earth into the depths, seemingly end-lessly, into the rabbit's hole, "Down, down, down. Would the fall never come to an end?"[48] The fall takes so long that Alice starts to get sleepy again and she shakes herself out of it, perhaps not surprisingly, by talking to herself, and perhaps somewhat surprisingly, by beginning to engage with the con-ventions of logic: Does "All A are B" convert, she asks, to "All B are A" as in the questions, "Do cats eat bats?" and "Do bats eat cats?"[49] But because she is unable to provide a solid empirical answer for herself regarding the dietary habits of the creatures in question, she forgets about this problem the mo-ment she finally lands upon a heap of dry leaves. However, on her feet once again but now deep underground, she begins exploring this place in which she finds herself, and she continues articulating her discoveries in terms of logical rules.

Perhaps this is startling, for the underground world has been strongly associated with animality and embodiment. Only animals, it has been said, are deep, and depth is no compliment. "The entire first half of Alice still seeks the secret of events . . . in the depths of the earth, in dugout shafts and holes which plunge beneath, and in the mixture of bodies which interpenetrate and coexist."[50] This leads, we are told, to Alice's eventual climb to the surface and her disavowal of false depth, her discovery that everything linguistic happens at that border. Yet strangely, in spite of the claim (coming from Gilles Deleuze) that Alice disavows false depth and returns to the surface, it seems that it is precisely in the depths that she finally wakes from her sleepy, stupefied surface state and investigates the deep structures, the rules of logic. In this investigation, Alice questions many formal structures, such as causal-ity, identity, reference, and the logical rules of replacement, and as we shall see, she discovers that as wonderful as unleashing these formal structures might be, nevertheless Wonderland does not generate consequential con-duct. In fact it generates no conduct whatsoever! In other words, when it comes to consequences, Wonderland may not be all that wonderful.

Finding herself in a long hallway of locked doors and spotting a tiny gold key on a table, Alice again talks to herself, this time addressing herself with a disjunctive proposition. Either the locks are too large or the key she finds is too small to open any of the doors in the great hall. This is fol-lowed by a set of hypotheticals. If eating the little cake she finds under the table makes her larger, then she can reach the key that she left on the table. However, if it makes her smaller, then she can creep under the door lead-ing into the lovely garden. Having begun her musings with these disjunctive and hypothetical propositions, Alice alerts the reader to the possibility of putting into play the so-called "rules of replacement": rules governing logically equivalent expressions that permit an inference from any statement that results from replacing any component of that statement with a logically equivalent statement.[51]

Therefore, given any hypothetical statement, "if p, then q," which consists of a relation between two propositions, "p" and "q," and which invokes a causal relation between "p" and "q," the statement can be reformulated using the rule of material implication to arrive at its logical equivalent, "not p or q."[52] In this way, Alice can be said to create a series of disjunctive terms, beginning with "either the locks are too large or the key she finds is too small to open any of the doors in the great hall." From there we proceed to the next set of disjunctions in the series. Either it is not the case that the bottle named "DRINK ME" will make her smaller or she can go through the little door.

So we are led to the discovery, with Alice, that propositions that might have been stated as linear and causal hypotheticals can be transformed into a series of disjunctions bearing no causal relation to one another. This is the reason why *anything is possible*. By evading causality, one may evade consequences. Evading consequences implies that actions are mere events with no before and no after, no causes and no effects, no actors and no one or no thing responsible. In other words, Alice discovers a world without what we have been referring to as good sense.

Of course, even after opening our and her eyes to the replacement of the series of causal relations that would have allowed her to proceed in the manner of good sense, Alice remains cognizant of causality. In other words, using good sense, the sense of temporal or causal relations, she remains cognizant of the arrow of time and thus constitutes the relation between what is most differentiated (poison, which might be the contents of the bottle named "DRINK ME") and so fixed in the past, and what is less differentiated and oriented as the future (the disagreeable results of drinking poison).[53] She does this with the aid of memory. Alice remembers that a red-hot poker will burn you if you hold it too long, that cutting one's finger very deeply with a knife usually results in bleeding, and that drinking from a bottle marked "poison" will indeed have disagreeable results.[54]

But it must be stressed that these relations are all things she merely remembers and that her current adventures continue along a disjointed trajectory. In this sense, she is correct, as she puts it, to "think that very few things indeed were really impossible," at least while she is underground.[55]

Drinking from the bottle named "DRINK ME," she shrinks to a mere ten inches, but having forgotten the key on the table, she is still unable to get through the door into the lovely garden. (Either she will not shrink any further or she will go out like the flame of a candle.) Upon finding a very small cake named "EAT ME" under the table, she states the following: *Either* it is not the case that eating the cake will make her larger *or* she can reach the key. And, *either* it is not the case that the cake will make her smaller *or* she can creep under the door.[56]

It seems that it is the power of disjunction, as much as, if not more than, the things she drinks and eats that convince Alice, at least at this point, that it would be dull and stupid for life to go on in the common way. Yet memory supplies her with the recollection of little children who suffered burns, had been eaten by beasts, or suffered other disagreeable outcomes because they did not remember the simple rules about these sorts of things.

However, insofar as eating the cake is disjoined from its effects, then it cannot provide Alice with any causal information she might apply to drinking from the bottle. Disjunction convinces Alice that as long as the bottle is not named "poison" (something she merely remembers) she need not concern herself with the arrow of time. Alas. For when she drinks from the bottle, tasting as it does of a very nice concoction of flavors, not only does Alice grow so large that she can barely even see her own feet, but more: she begins talking what she refers to as nonsense, carrying on speaking to herself about her feet as if they were not part of her and might walk off in a different direction if she is not kind to them, so that her feet need to be convinced not to do this.

It seems that her ability to proceed according to disjunctive statements leads her to what logicians call the "vicious circle principle," which is that "no entity can be defined in terms of a totality of which it is itself a possible member."[57] In other words, if a name is taken to be a label for an empirically given object, it is a logically proper name with reference but no sense. If it is a descriptive expression, it identifies an object in terms of its relations to other objects or as constructed out of previously given objects. The logical problem here is that no entity can be constructed out of itself and no verbal expression can be defined in terms of itself.[58] Yet this is precisely what Alice tries to do. And so, speaking to herself concerning her feet has taken her to the point of speaking nonsense. Her problem is that insofar as "an element cannot be part of the sub-sets which it determines" (for example, Alice and her feet), nor a part of the set whose existence it presupposes (thus, her feet and Alice), logically, she is engaged in a vicious circle. Either way, she is not making sense![59]

Not only does Alice begin speaking nonsense, but additionally, while fanning herself with a fan dropped by the White Rabbit, whom she frightens (as she is now nine feet high), Alice begins asking questions about her own identity: "Was I the same as when I got up this morning? I almost think I can remember feeling a little different. But if I'm not the same, the next question is, 'Who in the world am I?'"[60] As we can see, this is not just pretend angst. Poor Alice has changed so much that she can no longer recite her multiplication tables, nor can she remember geography or recite a short verse correctly. In other words, the past is not carrying into the present; good sense is not functioning, and this is having an effect on her identity. So it may be that having forgone good sense, Alice is now faced with the loss of common sense as well, if common sense is in fact what "subsumes under itself the various faculties of the soul, or the differentiated organs of the body, and brings them to bear upon a unity which is capable of saying 'I.'"[61] "Let me think," she asks herself, "was I the same as when I got up this morning? I almost think I can remember feeling a little different. But if I'm not the same, the next question is, 'Who in the world am I?'"[62]

And she resolves not to return above ground until her identity is resolved to her satisfaction. Postmodern philosophers and formalists may take this turn of events to be a positive development. The disappearance of the author or of the self is celebrated as an encouraging step away from the concept of a centered, egoistic subject. But for Alice, it could have serious consequences: she could in fact go out like a flame! Fortunately, just before shrinking completely out of sight, Alice realizes that there is a causal relation between fanning herself and growing small again and she stops fanning just in time.

A Dry Tail

Good sense at least partially restored, Alice nonetheless falls into the pool of tears that she herself has cried. Suddenly and inexplicably surrounded by strange creatures (a Duck and a Dodo, a Lory and an Eaglet, a Mouse and others) who simply appear without any cause and fall into the water, then follow her to shore, Alice is once again faced with logical and linguistic problems.[63] In particular, the Mouse has trouble with the sense of words. The Mouse tells the driest story it knows in order to dry off the company, who are all wet from falling into the pool of tears, and when it offers to tell a long tale, Alice can only imagine a long tail.[64]

The problem that interferes with communication here seems to be related to the question of distinguishing sense and reference. Sense and reference have been defined most notably by the philosopher Göttlob Frege. For Frege, a sign or a name represents a proper name that must have a definite object as its reference. Moreover, although a definite sense corresponds to the sign, certain signs (the extinct Dodo) have sense yet no reference. The reference of a sign is an object able to be perceived by the senses (the long tale that we hear or the long tail that we see) of which we may form an internal image, an idea, arising from memories of sense impressions.[65] What this means is that sense does not assure that there is a reference, and therefore the same sense is not always connected with the same idea.[66]

The Mouse and Alice connect different ideas to the name "dry." Alice wants to dry off because she is wet, cold, and shivering. The Mouse wants to tell a dry story; thus the importance of reference. The reference of tale, tail, or dry is an object we designate, but the idea is wholly subjective (to dry off or to tell a dry tale). "In between lies the sense, which is indeed no longer subjective like the idea, but is yet not the object itself."[67] "A proper name (word, sign, sign combination, expression) expresses its sense, stands for or designates its reference. By means of a sign we express its sense and designate its reference."[68] And, just like the Duck, who demands to know what "it" means when the mouse dryly relates that "Stigand, the patriotic archbishop of Canterbury, found it advisable," Frege also finds that when we say something we presuppose not just a grammatical dummy but a reference, and preferably something with a proper name.[69]

For the Duck, it refers to a frog or a worm that the Duck has actually found (and not simply thought about) and so it must have both a sense and a reference in order for saying it to matter to us at all. We want the proper name to have a reference, Frege states, because of our concern with truth value. Poems and stories that convey only sense and feeling through their images do not lend themselves to truth. Thus the dry tale is not meant to delight but to convey something true. Truth value is identified with reference and all true sentences must have the referent "true" and all false sentences have the referent "false." This allows the Duck to replace frog or worm with the name "it," but still seems to undermine the Mouse, who wished to tell a dry story, a story with truth value.[70] For the Mouse's "it" may have sense, yet it appears to be without reference.

And so one might argue that Alice is beginning to recognize the limits of undoing causality and the relation of causality to the problems associated with sense and reference and so to truth. It is this growing recognition, we propose, that eventually sends her fleeing back to the surface. When the White Rabbit abruptly orders her to find his gloves and fan, taking her to be the maid (she is a girl after all), Alice also finds a bottle named "DRINK ME." She seems to take this name to be an imperative, even though this time she knows, as she puts it, that something interesting (as she also puts it) will happen each time she eats or drinks anything.[71] She does not just remember that there have been causal relations between eating and drinking and something interesting in the past, but she claims to know that causal relations are operating in her present as well.

Moreover, Alice's identity is not the only one in question. Little pebbles are thrown at her in an unsuccessful effort to kill her or drive her out, as she sits despondently in the White Rabbit's house where she has gone to fetch the gloves and fan. As they hit her, the pebbles turn into little cakes; fortunately, she anticipates that by eating them, she will shrink again.[72] Indeed, this is exactly what happens. Good sense seems to be once again operating even though Alice's identity remains uncertain and problematic.

Thus the question "Who are you?" when posed by the hookah-smoking Caterpillar is more than appropriate, even though, as the story makes clear, "This was not an encouraging opening for a conversation."[73] Alice cannot explain herself but the Caterpillar does not understand this at all and continues to speak to Alice with some contempt, prodding her eventually to try to recite a verse correctly. She of course completely fails, offering instead an irreverent parody of the original, in which the old and corpulent father threatens to kick the inquisitive son down the stairs, a story that is "wrong from beginning to end."[74]

It is just such a story, Gilles Deleuze asserts, that shows that Lewis Carroll detests boys in general. After all, the male baby in *Alice* turns into a pig. Boys, it is claimed, are associated with animality, with organs, with the objects of smell, taste, and touch that are perceived, imagined, or remembered. And boys are associated with the self that breathes, sleeps, and walks following the laws of a determined system.[75] In *Silvie and Bruno*, Deleuze claims, the little boy is the inventive thinker only by becoming a little girl, passing from reality to dream, from bodies to the incorporeal, bringing to language becoming and its paradoxes.[76] By contrast, the little girl is said to eagerly abandon good sense and common sense, to undo causality and identity, and it is implied that this is laudable. Indeed, it ends (in Deleuze) with the girl or the woman being characterized as the molecular becoming of the molar boy or man.

Yet Alice does not necessarily associate boys with animality and with the senses. She is concerned when the baby is nearly hit in the nose by the shower of pans, plates, and dishes thrown by the cook. "'Oh please mind what you're doing!' cried Alice in an agony of terror. 'Oh, there goes his precious nose'; as an unusually large saucepan flew close by it, and very nearly carried it off."[77] Certainly the Duchess seems to abuse the little boy, violently shaking and tossing him and recommending (in her so-called lullaby) speaking roughly and beating him. But then she speaks roughly to Alice as well, ordering the cook to chop off her head, and the cook is throwing pans at the Duchess, Alice, and the baby![78] The Duchess finally throws the child at Alice, who reflects, "If I don't take this child away with me, . . . they're sure to kill it in a day or two: wouldn't it be murder to leave it behind?"[79] And upon hearing the baby grunt, she looks at it anxiously while "the poor little thing sobbed again."[80]

It is only when it finally transforms completely into what she calls a rather handsome pig that she lets it go, thinking about other children she knows who might also be pigs. And such transformations, as we have seen, are entirely possible in a world of disjunction, where causal chains have been torn apart. Perhaps it is the Cheshire Cat who provides the best explanation of what is going on, claiming that everyone there is mad, including itself. And it too invokes the vicious circle principle, appearing and vanishing so that only its grin remains: how can the grin be defined as belonging to, as part of the cat? If it does belong to the cat, then it cannot be distinguished from the cat. To do so might not be madness, but it is certainly nonsense.

Tea and No Sympathy

Reaching the Mad Hatter's, Alice is again met with considerable rudeness. She is offered wine when there is none. She is told that she needs a haircut. She is told she is stupid and generally treated badly. She is given a riddle to guess, but it has no answer. She is tricked into making logical errors. Hoping to guess the answer to the riddle, she is asked, "'Do you think that you can find out the answer to it?' . . . 'Exactly so,' said Alice. 'Then you should say what you mean.' . . . 'I do,' Alice hastily replied—'at least I mean what I say—that's the same thing, you know.'"[81] Of course, logically it's not the same thing at all. The problem still involves the relation between sense and reference. Alice *means* that she can solve the riddle, but she also *says* that she means that she can solve the riddle. For her, there are two different references, so in fact, it's not the same thing. She must sort this out for herself so as not to be caught in a logical error, such as that of declaring that the referent of the name "Time" is a "he" and that the sense of the expression "killing time" can result in a murder and a permanent 6 o'clock, which just happens to be teatime.[82]

In his analysis of the significance of sentences, Bertrand Russell argues that there are three sorts of sentence: those that are true, those that are false, and those that are nonsensical.[83] The latter are clearly not true, but they are also not false; when a sentence is nonsense, or meaningless as Russell calls it, then so is its negation. Paradox arises from sentences that seem to signify something but really do not. Still it is not clear how to distinguish sentences that signify something and those that do not. Significance, according to Russell, must be propositional, able to be true or false.[84] This, in turn, relies on perceptual experiences that can be imagined or that actually occur, making us use a phrase as an assertion.

The phrase uttered during tea by the Dormouse, "They were learning to draw . . . everything that begins with an M—," can be significant if it is true.[85] However, what is *expressed* must be distinguished from what makes a statement true. Expression is a state of mind, a belief or even a desire that others should have this belief.[86] For Alice, since the drawing lesson is supposed to be taking place at the bottom of a treacle well, this claim strains her credulity; she does not believe it. Assertion, however, is not the same as expression. One does not assert the belief that is being expressed, rather *one asserts that the object of the belief is true or false.* Thus, asserting that three little girls are sitting in the bottom of a treacle well learning to draw things that begin with the letter M (things such as mousetraps, moon, memory, and muchness) truly confuses Alice! No wonder she declares, "It's the stupidest tea-party I ever was at in all my life!"[87] Lacking significance, the Dormouse's story is pure nonsense. That Alice's credulity is challenged and that she slips away is evidence that her identity is less in question, even if she does not yet notice this.

The order of language just set out is severely questioned by Deleuze. Addressing Russell's assertion that denotation, manifestation (the statement of beliefs or desires), and signification are the three accepted relations holding for a proposition, Deleuze brings the proposition back to nonsense.[88] That is, manifestation, the statement of beliefs or desires, is precisely the relation that Alice comes to expect, and when it does not occur; what she hears she takes for nonsense. At the tea party, she expects that beliefs or desires are causal inferences that correspond to the proposition.[89] Following Russell, Deleuze states that desire is an inference between the internal causality of an image and the existence of an object or state of affairs. Belief is also an inference; it is the anticipation of an object or state of affairs produced by external causality.[90]

Manifestation, the statement of beliefs or desires, always involves the "I," so that, for example, what Alice believes–her belief–grounds her judgment regarding denotation. Denotation is the relation of the proposition to an external state of affairs. Alice has a hard time believing the Dormouse's story that three little girls are living in a treacle-well. "True," would signify that the denotation is fulfilled by a particular state of affairs; "false" signifies that the denotation is not fulfilled. But Deleuze reads this differently from Russell.

Russell, we noted above, demands that significance be propositional (meaning true or false) and that truth and falsity, in turn, require a perceptual ground, something Deleuze's formalism clearly does not require. Referring not to significance but to signification, Deleuze never mentions perception or experience. Instead, he states that signification is the relation of a word to universal or general concepts.[91] It seems that Deleuze departs from Russell and returns here to the same ideas as those asserted by Frege who, we have noted, states that sense does not assure that there is a reference, thereby doing away with the necessity of empirical verification.[92] Since the sense is no longer subjective like the idea, but is also not the object, it must be something else.[93] Sense is, it seems, a fourth dimension. Specifically, as Frege has stated, a proper name (word, sign, sign combination, expression) expresses its sense and stands for or designates its reference.

To make sense of sense, Frege asks that we consider a sentence and not merely proper names. Sentences contain thoughts, that is, objective content, something capable of being the common property of several thinkers.[94] This objective content is the sense of the sentence, but it seems possible that sentences may have sense but no reference at all. "The Dodo fell into the pool of tears" seems to be one such sentence. And if one wanted to go no further than this thought, there would be no need to assign a reference. The thought remains the same whether "Dodo" has a reference or not. The problem with looking for truth is that it forces us to abandon certain affects, particularly those such as aesthetic delight.[95] Truth also forces language away from the "idea" or the "Idea" and back to the perceptual, the phenomenological. Still, if we are not concerned about truth, we need not be concerned about reference.

Thus we can understand why, strictly speaking, if we are not concerned about reference, sense does not exist outside of the proposition that expresses it.[96] Sense is therefore a logical attribute, but one that does not and is not compelled to describe a physical state of affairs; it does not require a referent; it is the event that is no longer causally linked to what came before or what comes after: "The event belongs essentially to language."[97] With this, Deleuze pushes a bit, revising the arguments of the logicians: "It seems difficult to say . . . that the fantastic work [of Lewis Carroll] presents simply the traps and difficulties into which we fall when we do not observe the rules and laws formulated by the logical work."[98] Admittedly, Carroll's work is about signification, implication, and conclusions, but to what end? Is it, as Deleuze argues, to introduce paradoxes that signification does not resolve and even creates, or is it to raise other, still unanswered question?

The Making of a Philosopher

Escaping the tea party through a door that she notices in a tree, Alice finds herself back in the long hall, a curious return. Spying the little golden key on the glass table, she recalls her previous experience and puts into play her newly acquired causal knowledge. First she takes the key and unlocks the garden door, then she nibbles carefully a bit of the mushroom she had saved, a feat of memory regarding causation! Now only a foot high, she can at last walk through the door and go into the beautiful garden with its bright flowerbeds and cool fountains.[99] There she finds gardeners who are nothing but playing cards (two, five, and seven of hearts are painting the white flowers red), as well as soldiers, courtiers, kings and queens, and finally "THE KING AND QUEEN OF HEARTS."[100]

Although she is very small, Alice does realize that "they're only a pack of cards, after all. I needn't be afraid of them."[101] And even when the Queen, in a fury, screams, "Off with her head!" meaning Alice's head, nothing unfortunate happens. In Wonderland, where words do not signify and causality is disjoined, such statements have no consequences. Invited to play a very odd sort of croquet with playing cards for wires, flamingos for mallets, and hedgehogs for balls, Alice remains concerned about the Queen's constant demand for beheadings, and she notices that no one plays fairly, that the game has no rules, and that it is very confusing with everything alive and moving all the time. Moreover, during the entire game, the Queen never stops quarreling with the players, till Alice feels quite frightened again.

The Duchess appears (released from prison, where she was placed for boxing the Queen's ears). Informing Alice that "Everything's got a moral, if only you can find it," she squeezes herself up unpleasantly close to Alice, putting her sharp chin on the little girl's shoulder.[102] And the Duchess does have a moral for everything; but in Wonderland it is no surprise that the moral has nothing to do with the event for which it is supposed to be the moral. When Alice timidly states that the game is going better, the Duchess responds that the moral of that is "'tis love, 'tis love that makes the world go round!"[103]

With almost all the players in prison for various faults, Alice is taken by the Queen for one final adventure, the Mock Turtle's story. There she listens to the Mock Turtle's sad tale, which is that he had once been a real turtle who had studied a wild list of courses from the master Turtle called "Tortoise" (because he taught them).[104] They teach her to dance the lobster quadrille, and although Alice is bored by much of this, she struggles to be polite. They do not notice the extreme nonsense of their own stories, school subjects such as "the different branches of Arithmetic—Ambition, Distraction, Uglification, and Derision," as well as "—Mystery, ancient and modern, with Seaography; then Drawling—."[105] But when Alice tells them her own story, they readily agree that her recollection of the poem "Father William" is seriously flawed, uncommon nonsense. Alice "sat down with her face in her hands and wondered if anything would ever happen in a natural way again."[106]

The final episode erupts when the Gryphon hears the call to come to the trial of the Knave of Hearts, accused of stealing tarts that sit on the table in front of all in the courtroom. At the trial, Alice is pleased to have the common sense to be able to identify the judge and the jury, but she forgets her manners and cries out that the jurors are stupid because they must write down even their names, lest they forget them. Problems with identity such as those Alice initially experienced are spread far and wide. During the trial Alice begins to grow again, physically, and seeing the tarts makes her feel quite hungry. It is as if embodiment and growth are having an effect. She also grows impatient with the illogicality of the court. The judge (who is the King) does not seem to be able to discern what is and what is not evidence and commands the jurors to write down nearly everything said, no matter how foolish. When witnesses are called, the King threatens to execute them if they act nervous or if they cannot remember. Of course, given that causality and reference have been abandoned, it would be surprising if any witness could remember anything, let alone anything true. When an unsigned letter is introduced as evidence, the King takes its lack of signature as evidence that the Knave must be guilty or he would have signed it. And even though the letter contains no names, no references whatsoever, the King believes it points in the direction of the Knave's guilt. Taken to its limit, in a world without reference, anything can signify anything else.

As Alice begins to grow, she also grows up, physically and intellectually. When the King announces, "Rule Forty-two, All persons more than a mile high to leave the court" and proclaims it to be the oldest rule in the book, Alice is quick to assert the truth, that she is not a mile high and that anyway, if "Forty-two" were the oldest rule it would be number one.[107] Nor is she afraid of stating that there's not an atom of meaning (that is, reference) in the nonsensical anonymous letter read to the courts. When, following the well-established convention of Wonderland, the Queen calls for the sentence before the verdict, Alice loudly objects to this failure of good sense: "Stuff and nonsense!" she scoffs. "The idea of having the sentence first!"[108] Enraged, the Queen orders Alice to hold her tongue and when Alice refuses, the Queen commands, "Off with her head!" which only incites Alice to angrily proclaim the lot of them to be nothing but a pack of cards, which indeed is all that they are.[109] And when the cards rise up and attack her, she fearlessly beats them off and then finds herself once again lying on the bank with her sister, waking as if from a dream.

Feminist philosophers have noted the unusual role that Alice, in particular, and the little girl, in general, play in Gilles Deleuze's work. Catherine Driscoll asserts that "Deleuze frequently aligns Alice with becoming, and through Alice insists that becoming is a paradox defined as 'the affirmation of both senses or directions at the same time.'"[110] She adds that becoming as transformative process is not necessarily opposed to standard models of development, "But becoming seems to be strictly opposed to any linear conception of time."[111] Rosi Braidotti notes that Deleuze complains that "feminists refuse to dissolve the subject 'woman' into a series of transformative processes that pertain to a generalized and 'postgender' becoming," and that although politically correct, this is conceptually mistaken.[112]

Clearly, Deleuze and Félix Guattari recognize this. Their assertions were previously noted that below Oedipus, they discover a molecular unconscious; beneath the stable forms, functionalism; under familialism, polymorphous perversity.[113] And so beneath woman, or even man, the little girl, *Alice in Wonderland*, releases language from the constraints of reference, signification, identity, and causation, making it possible to take apart whatever has been joined together and to reverse direction and deny the arrow of time. Underlying all this is the distinction between the molecular and the molar, the microphysical and the statistical.

From the point of view of molar or statistical aggregates in physical relations, there is no difference between machine and life; molar machines may be social machines, technical machines, or organic machines. As such, they may be language machines. And all becomings are molecular. So the becoming-woman and becoming-child do not resemble the woman or the child, which are the molar forms arising with language that signifies and refers, enacts causality and identity (good sense and common sense). But what is quite curious is that the woman has to become-woman in order for the man to become-woman. In writing, atoms of womanhood, particles, sweep across the social field and contaminate even men![114] Society steals the girl's becoming and imposes a history on her, makes her an object of desire, an example, and a trap. Is the entire history of men's writing then nothing more than an escape from this "trap"? Because if so, then it seems to be an escape from truth, from consequences, and from the arrow of time.[115]

Carroll points to the idea that in Wonderland, where causality and reference no longer reign, anything is possible. Causal links of any kind are dissolved. But in fact what occurs is that nothing happens. A tea party is eternal. The Queen orders beheadings all day long and not a single one occurs. A trial is seemingly held but no evidence is gathered. And in any case, if something does happen, accidentally or without any cause one can discern, it's a simple matter to undo it; the pig could just as well turn back into a baby. By implication, therefore, no one is responsible for anything because nothing takes place and, in any case, lacking reference to real objects, all is Idea, nothing but Idea. This is, Deleuze and Guattari state, the only way to get outside of dualisms, by producing an Idea, the universal girl, the key to all becoming.

Yet we do not live in Wonderland, and therefore our actions have consequences. That Deleuze and Guattari choose the little girl as the origin of all becomings evinces a fundamental binarism at the heart of their philosophy. Molecules are neither male nor female; such a determination is purely molar. Why choose girls, unless their molar existence is already in question? Why organize language so as to escape causal relations, unless to eliminate the possibility that a little girl might grow up and that words and deeds have unpredictable effects?

Let us not forget Alice's older sister, "sitting just as she left her, leaning her head on her hand, watching the setting sun, and thinking of little Alice and all her wonderful Adventures."[116] Her surface world comes alive with all the creatures of Alice's adventures, but the older sister knows that these creatures and events are versions of the reality around her. Carroll calls it "dull reality," but he describes something quite different. He describes grass rustling in the wind, a pool rippling to the wave of reeds, tinkling sheep bells, the shepherd boy's voice, the confused clamor of the busy farmyard. Truly, are these dull realities or are they part of the beauty and joy of life? And Alice? It seems that through all her years, she would keep the simple and loving heart of her childhood, gathering other children about her to tell them her tales. She would feel their sorrows and find pleasure in their simple joys. But Carroll leaves out one thing. He forgets to say that Alice will also understand the limits of language and logic, the limits of a limitless world of Wonderland where anything is possible but nothing really happens—a world without causality and identity, without the arrow of time, without signification or reference. And in understanding this, Alice will be not just a woman with a simple and pure heart but a woman who understands: a thinker . . . a philosopher.

Information Comes From the Past

Perhaps we can now see that a significant problem for *Alice in Wonderland* was correlated with time and memory. It takes Alice a while to remember that eating and drinking in Wonderland cause her to grow or to shrink. She cannot recall even simple children's rhymes that she had once memorized and, until the final episodes, logical reasoning and causal thinking appear to be beyond her capacity. These failures, which perturb Alice quite a bit, appear to be closely correlated with her experience that time, in Wonderland, stands still or is reversible. The tea party is eternal, no one's head comes off, the Cheshire Cat appears and disappears and appears again out of nothing. The lack of temporal connections, of memory, and the undoing of anything that has been done, all are correlated with the disappearance of objects of reference and the elimination of causal relations, eliminating even the need for ethical conduct. But for those of us who do not reside in Wonderland, a different temporality prevails. In fact, for human beings on Earth, all our communication arises out of the past; it is part of the endless stream of prior knowledge.

Henri Bergson, whose meditations on time address both its ontological and its sensory aspects, argues that perception never consists of a simple representation produced when the mind comes into contact with an object. Every perception requires memory-images drawn from the past, materialized out of a pure memory, and embodied in the actual perception.[117] Sensory information comes to us necessarily out of the past. Light from the sun and stars travels at approximately 300,000,000 meters per second. Given the great distances between Earth and even our nearest neighbors, it is surprising that we are not more cognizant of and thoughtful about the past that influences us.

> We're also in a place surrounded by the past. . . . All this light is dead, . . . All this light was emitted thousands and millions of years ago. It's the past, do you see? When these stars cast their light, we didn't exist, life on Earth didn't exist, even Earth didn't exist. This light was cast a long time ago. It's the past, we're surrounded by the past, everything that no longer exists or exists only in memory or guesswork is there, above us shining on the mountains and the snow and we can't do anything to stop it."[118]

The speed of sound in air at 20 degrees Celsius is 343.599 meters per second; the speed of odors and scents is as much as 200 meters per second, the speed of touch and taste are perhaps unmeasurable, but not instantaneous. If memory and sensory information come out of the past, the same cannot be said for information provided by logical and mathematical models. Logic and mathematics do not implicate the past in a way that carries the stream of memory into the present in order to allow us to understand the present and to make decisions about the future. The differential equations of calculus measure quantities subject to change, where the quantity changes continuously.[119] Differential equations describe growth, development, and decay; when processes in the physical world are translated into mathematical terms, they form a continuum, "a set of 'points'–real numbers–arranged in a line that stretches out to infinity in both directions," and "numerical measurements of time and of physical quantities, such as length, temperature, weight, velocity, are assumed to be 'points' on the continuum."[120] Processes taking place along the continuum can move forward or backward, as the calculations hold in either direction.

The real-number continuum is organized by axioms governing rational numbers with one important addition, the axiom of the limit.

> Suppose that $a_1, a_2, a_3, \ldots$ is an infinite sequence of real numbers that get closer together (in the sense that the further along the sequence you go, the closer to 0 the differences between the numbers becomes). Then there must be a real number, call it l, such that the numbers in the sequence get closer and closer to l (in the sense that the further along the sequence you go, the closer to 0 the differences between the numbers a_n, and l become).[121]

The "number" l is the limit. Each point in the continuum of real numbers is a limit, each approaching the next by smaller and smaller margins until they are an infinitesimally small distance away, but they never actually reach the 0 point. Moving from point to point or number to number in the sequence produces a situation such as that described by Simone de Beauvoir in the opening pages of *The Ethics of Ambiguity*. Referring to the continuous work of our life, Beauvoir says of "man" that "at every moment he can grasp the non-temporal truth of his existence. But between the past which no longer is and the future which is not yet, this moment when he exists is nothing."[122] What can this mean? Can the axioms governing continuous transition on a real-number continuum be utilized to make sense of the human condition?

Philosophers, Beauvoir argues, have tended to address the dualism of matter and mind either by absorbing matter into mind (idealism) or by absorbing mind into matter (naturalism/materialism). Ethically, this transpires as either an escape from the sensible world into pure mental inwardness, the realm of thought, or as being engulfed by matter in the pure moment.[123] Both positions have been connected to the modern mathematical conception of motion and change. The pure moment is the mathematical point on the continuum that approaches but never reaches 0. This can be understood as the mathematical foundation of Jean-Paul Sartre's axiom that man is "that being whose being is not to be, that subjectivity which realizes itself only as a presence in the world, that engaged freedom, that surging of the for-oneself which is immediately given to others."[124]

According to Sartre, when "man" makes himself lack in order that there might be being, he does it by affirming the moment independently of what came before, actually by denying the past as nothingness, as inconsequential for the present. Mathematically, this is a simple operation. We have discussed above how the notation dx and dy came to be used to refer to infinitely small quantities or "the velocities of evanescent increments," or *limits*, "a dynamic process of successive approximations," but let us repeat what we said there in order to remind ourselves of how these symbols operate.[125]

Differential calculus allows one to begin with a differential relation (dx/dy) on an x/y axis in an abstract (conceptual) space, then, taking the derivative, to derive the formula for a curve, and then to calculate the formula for the gradient (slope) of that curve by taking small (infinitesimal) differences in the x and y directions and computing the gradients of the resultant straight lines. Each derivative of a differential relation takes place each time in a minimum of time. We noted also that in logic, this is the ultimate and perhaps the most subtle form of logical disjunction/conjunction, which in the physical world may be taken for causality, as each collision determines the next direction of the atoms. And significantly, if we were to look at patterns rather than individual atoms, clear patterns do in fact emerge, for example in economics, where differential equations are used to predict growth and decay.[126]

Dynamical Systems and Human Existence

But what happens when such patterns are taken to describe human existence? Physicist John Casti has given us the simple example of a treasure hunt played in a park, where the game exemplifies what mathematicians call a dynamical system. The playing space is a spatial manifold governed by a rule of motion called a vector field, supplied in this instance by lists of instructions telling a player how to move from her current position to the next one. As the players move from point to point, their motion follows a trajectory from their initial state or starting point. If the players follow the rules correctly, their trajectory is completely fixed and they reach the end point of the game, called the attractor, the winning prize. The end point truly governs the motion of the game. In fact, "the overall behavior of a dynamical system is for the most part fixed by the number and character of its attractors."[127] We noted previously that several different types of attractors govern dynamical systems. They may be fixed points, where the rules direct motion to one particular place, or they may be limit cycles, where the rules result in a cyclical pattern of repetition, or they may be strange attractors, which are unstable because they are extremely sensitive to initial and boundary conditions and their trajectories are therefore difficult to predict.[128]

One of the interesting characteristics of dynamical systems is that by following perfectly deterministic (mathematical or logical) rules, one can end up with essentially random results.[129] What matters is not the past course of events, but the rule that one follows, in other words, the attractor of the trajectory. What characterizes a dynamical system is that each step on the trajectory can be said to negate whatever came before it. This means that each past point is a unique, infinitesimal position on an x/y axis, and nothing more; *it does not enter into the present.*

Existentially, for Sartre, each small difference in the x and y directions can be understood to be a choice, a project that discloses being by declaring the previous position to be a lack of being. But as Beauvoir points out, if man is nature, if the acts of men follow purely natural patterns, then there is no ethics, there is only nature in the sense of classical science. Natural patterns preclude choice. They are cyclical and rule-following, thus deterministic and certain, or rule-following (deterministic) and probable.[130] Natural patterns are probable because even though individual steps are uncertain, statistically, overall patterns do emerge. However, following natural patterns, there are no principles for making choices; a choice will be made from nothingness. Insofar as each choice is a limit, an infinitesimally small difference approaching zero, then that choice is itself nothing with respect to the next choice, and so on, infinitely. The past is a position, a point, but it does not influence the present; it is merely the limit of what was possible in that moment.

Yet, as Beauvoir argues, the Sartrean claim is that we "choose" to make ourselves a lack in order that there might be being; it does not just happen to us.[131] "Choice" means that we act, in effect negating mere negation; we acknowledge and assume our failure, and the act that failed is still valid as an effort to exist. In this way, choice re-establishes our positive existence, and ethical existence does not masquerade as a purely formal freedom without content or context.[132] If freedom were natural or mathematical, a thing or a point in abstract space, then it would be given; it could not be chosen. "To will oneself free is to effect the transition from nature to morality by establishing a genuine freedom on the original upsurge of our existence."[133] Now we are able to distinguish between choice and contingency, "an upsurging as stupid as the Epicurean atom [the clinamen] which turned up at any moment whatsoever from any direction whatsoever."[134] The clinamen is a physical concept, but the Epicurean, Lucretius, conceives of the clinamen in relation to free will or change. Rather than following a determinate path prescribed by a causal sequence of events, atoms swerve, thereby originating a new movement that appears to "snap the bonds of fate, the everlasting sequence of cause and effect."[135]

In mathematical and physical terms, the clinamen corresponds to deterministic chaos, the dynamical system governed by fixed rules but oriented by a strange attractor. On this model, to exist is to escape the causal determination of the past; it is to deviate moment by moment, from nothingness to nothingness, where each new moment is an effect of the past but breaks completely with that past, which can then be defined as nothingness. The future we freely chose turns into a fact; our own past is an otherness and our projects are frozen in that past. Yet for Beauvoir, this view fails to be an ethical view insofar as it corresponds to a purely physical view of nature.

For humans, the world, objects, bodies, are finite, physically destined to wear down and wear out, to fall apart and die so that, as Lucretius saw it, it appears that nature is in decline. This purely physical decline is also purely outside of one's choices; it is an effect of external forces, nature's laws, driving atomistic entities to collide with one another. But for Beauvoir, human freedom must project itself in a specific direction and we must choose to found that direction.[136] No existence can found itself moment by moment. Moral freedom requires a past and a future, temporal moments that are organized into behavior. In order to keep the accomplished act from being just an opaque and stupid fact, I must justify it as belonging to the temporal unity of my current project.

This raises a number of important questions that will be our focus for the remainder of this book. Beginning with the problem of temporality, what coherent ontological structure allows for the continuing influence of the past in the present and even into the future? Given the limits of post-modern formalist mathematical and philosophical structures, what hope is there of finding a mathematics, a logic, or a linguistics that acknowledges the human reality of the arrow of time, the causal relation between past and present and the unpredictability of the future? Can we retrieve refer-ence along with sense, truth along with signification? Although each of these problems potentially gives rise to other sets of issues, the extent to which we are able to address these preliminary questions indicates, at least, the extent to which we may correlate what are now seemingly separate realms: that of mathematics and the natural sciences and that of the humanities and social sciences.

Philosophically, let us begin looking for solutions to these problems precisely where we might least expect to look, in the sphere of logic. From there we will move on to explore a potential mathematical and physical structure and rethink the very definition of human and nonhuman enti-ties. For, as we have tried to make clear, we need not restrict ourselves to the classical modern worldview of atomistic life forms following nature's laws. Although Newton's laws of motion govern bodies on the human scale, we can now see that we exist on a variety of scales and we can conceive of our existence and our acts in accordance with the possibilities of those alterna-tive scales of existence.

6

LOVE'S ONTOLOGY

ETHICS BEYOND THE LIMITS OF CLASSICAL SCIENCE

If we are willing to throw out space, we can keep time and the trade is worth it.

—Fotini Markopoulou

The Excluded Middle

We concluded the previous chapter with a discussion of dynamical systems theory and made the claim that this is the structure exemplified by the Sartrean concept of being and nothingness. Let us continue this discussion by reference to the logical presuppositions of this same Sartrean concept. Being and nothingness rests on the law of noncontradiction, which claims that for any proposition, that proposition and its negation are never both true, only one may be true. It also seems to require the law of the excluded middle, namely, that for a given proposition and its negation, at least one must be true *and* they cannot both be true. This means, of course, that for Sartre, Being cannot be both some x and its negation, only one can be true and at least some position x is true until superseded by its negation. By negating the being that we have been, we declare the past to be false and the present to be true.

With the exception of mathematical and phenomenological intuition-ism, discussed briefly in the preface, all the mathematical and logical struc-tures we have examined rigorously follow the law of noncontradiction and the law of the excluded middle. Not so surprisingly, it appears that Beauvoir, a phenomenological philosopher, does not. The very title of her treatise on ethics, *The Ethics of Ambiguity*, provides an invitation and incentive to think past the binaries of noncontradiction and the excluded middle. Minimally, by name alone, Beauvoir can be said to put into play a logic of ambiguity, one that makes possible an ethics of ambiguity. We would like to correlate Beauvoir's conception of ambiguity with certain aspects of intuitionism.

Philosophically, intuitionism can be traced back to Descartes, who claimed that knowing requires acts of immediate mental apprehension, in-tuitions, the sole source of true and new knowledge.[1] Intuitionists also claim Henri Bergson among their number for his distinction between duration and formalist moment-by-moment notions of time, such that utilized by Sartre. For Bergson, duration is the form the succession of our conscious states assumes when our ego lets itself live–not separating its present from its former states–but forming an organic whole, and so, for example we can perceive the notes of a melody floating, each one in and through the other.[2] In mathematics, intuitionism was brought to full flower by L. E. J. Brouwer and in algebra by Brouwer's student Arend Heyting. Our use of intuitionist principles here will not follow the strict formalism of Heyting nor the gen-eral principles expressing an intuitionistically correct construction of logic in the work of Michael Dummett, who claims to be the foremost contem-porary philosopher of intuitionism.[3] We will, however, adhere to the basic framework of intuitionism in order to understand how it is correlated with the ethical views of Beauvoir and Arendt.

"The mathematical nature of causality and the Primordial Intuition of Time as the fundamental creative act of mathematics are the central theses of Brouwer's analysis of science and language."[4] Brouwer refers to intuition as a process of building (*bouwen* in Dutch), a time-bound process beginning in the past, existing in the present, and evolving into an open future. But unlike in Descartes, once constructed, mathematical formulations remain alive in mind or memory. It follows from this that the scientific observation of nature's regu-larity (causality) is an effect of linking things and events in time sequences and that causality is a mind-made structure derived from the time relations of subjects and not an objective characteristic embedded in the natural world.[5]

And as for causality, so also for truth. "The whole of the Subject's constructive thought-activity, past and present, constitutes mathematical reality and mathematical truth."[6] From this follows what is perhaps the most radical aspect of Brouwer's thought for the postmodern, formalist perspective: his insistence on freeing mathematics from theoretical logic. Theoretical logic neither carries common objective concepts nor, as in Hilbert's account, does it consist in symbols with no meaning. The "truth" and the "noncontradictory" nature of mathematical formulations are found solely in constructions that are the result of temporal, intuited thought activities.[7] Thus logic will never generate new mathematical truths, a position the formalists find highly irritating.

Among logical axioms, the principle of the excluded middle is called the most flawed and obvious misstatement of fact. The principle of the excluded middle, we recall, states that for a given proposition "P," either "P" or "not-P" *must be true,* thus it affirms the fundamental principle of binary thinking and the logic of identity.[8] However, since for the intuitionist, mathematical statements, whether affirmative or negative, express the completion in a temporality that "flows with the flux" of the mathematician's own inner time, with an open future and unpredictable free choices, there is no a priori fixed determination of the elements of that proof.[9] Given the temporal nature of mathematical thinking, a negative statement that expresses the incompatibility of two mathematical constructions that are represented by the subject and predicate of a sentence is, for Brouwer, absurd.[10] Time is nonatomic, it does not consist of infinitesimally divisible points but is more like a "fluid paste from which points cannot be picked out with atomist accuracy."[11] The mathematician is always able to choose how to construct any given sequence, thus every element in a construction has an *indeterminate future.*

Of course, and this is the point of introducing intuitionist concepts, these ideas are strongly opposed to formalist, postmodern theories. Recalling our discussion of this in the preface, we noted that although postmoderns participate in communities whose cultural conventions are given to them, what this means is that words perform certain functions in this system and users are trained to observe these conventions. So-called unidentifiable subjective contributions remain external to language and its conventions. In functionalist systems, semantics is given in the cultural syntax, and so syntax alone yields semantics.[12]

The chief intuitionist objection to this is that mathematics is a mental *activity*. Its languages, including formalism, are tools for communication, a system of formulas, none of which are equivalent to the mental processes because the possibilities of thought are open and unpredictable and cannot be reduced to a finite set of rules laid out in advance.[13] As the creative act of an individual will, mathematics cannot be reduced to an a priori language. Language is a product of consensus, making social organization possible, but no one can halt the ability of any language user to reinterpret language. In direct opposition to the formalist postmodern position, the social and cultural context are formative but never determining. The unexpected is always possible.[14]

For intuitionist mathematicians, as for Simone de Beauvoir and Hannah Arendt, choosing and willing take time. As Beauvoir argues, it is not the moment of choice, the atomistic point, but the course of time that creates freedom. Only in the course of time can a genuine goal be pursued and only in the course of time can freedom confirm itself, manifesting itself in its outcomes. We escape the absurdity of the clinamen, the limit, negation, by escaping the absurdity of a pure moment, for as Beauvoir makes clear throughout her explicitly temporal philosophy, novels, and memoirs (the point of a memoir is to bring the past into the present), no existence can really found itself moment by moment, that is, point by point.[15] If moral freedom requires a past and a future, then in order to keep the accomplished act from being just an opaque and stupid fact, we may justify it, not as a unique, atomistic decision, but as belonging to the temporal unity of our current project. When a project is complete, the value of this provisional end will be confirmed indefinitely only insofar as it too is acted upon, thereby becoming the starting point for another project. This is how creative freedom develops without congealing into facticity.[16] Leaning on anterior creations, embracing the past, one creates the possibility of new creations, placing one's confidence in future freedom.

Temporality and Narrative

Perhaps we can now see how this structure, anticipated by Bergson and intuitionistic mathematics, operates in Arendt's conception of ethical behavior as well. Arendt calls for differentiating labor and necessity from making and duration, speech and action. Speech about action is a kind of birth; it is the natality that is capable of producing meaningful stories about human beings. These narrations reveal the uniqueness and distinctness of human actors to other human beings. But also, and significantly, once actions are begun, they cannot simply be negated, stopped, turned into nothingness. Rather, they are unpredictable, irreversible, and in principle immortal. One can only imagine how such narrative temporalization would have altered the course of events in history.

In Arendt's philosophical reflections on the trial of Adolf Eichmann, she recounts how the Nazis exempted some Jews with important connections and acquaintances in the outside world from deportation and almost certain extermination.[17] What made these persons special was precisely the recognition of them as unique and distinctive human beings with significant stories. This is a recognition that had to come from someone who could influence the Nazis, someone the Nazis recognized in the same way as unique and distinctive. Had all Jewish persons, along with the many exterminated Central and Eastern European intelligentsia and minorities, Jewish and other, been recognized as the subjects of meaningful stories that immortalized their actions, perhaps there would have been much less killing and murder, even in the midst of war.

But of course, this did not happen, and it is for this reason that human beings must also be able to exercise their capacity to forgive. Certainly, not everything can be forgiven. Arendt clearly condemns Eichmann, rejecting his argument that his role was accidental, that he was simply following the law given to him by his lord and master, as anyone in his place would have done. In other words, Eichmann's explanation seems to be that his actions were determined by laws akin to nature's classical laws, understood as deterministic (rule-following), laws governing physical forces, and that he was simply a part of nature, pushed this way and that by nature's laws. It was nature, in the end, he implies, that brought about the Final Solution, where nature might just as well have pushed the man in some other direction, and he would not be appearing in a criminal court.[18] Of course Arendt rejects this argument, and in its place suggests something like Beauvoir's notion of ethics. The past, the choice to carry out the law, brings the consequences of this murderous act into the present and the future, obliterating the narration of the lives of millions of human beings. This cannot be forgiven. Forgiveness undoes deeds by releasing the doer only from the unknowable consequences of her deeds and so from nature's unforgiving processes.

Eichmann evaded the consequences of his actions by refusing to acknowledge what he knew, for example that the Jews he claimed to have sent to Lødz, Poland were instead headed to their deaths elsewhere. And certainly, given the contrariety and uncertainty of human nature, humans must allow themselves to be bound to the fulfillment of promises in the public realm. Neither forgiveness nor promises are solitary activities nor are they mere effects of nature's life processes. They depend entirely on the presence of others, for no one can either forgive herself or make a promise in solitude.[19] In the end, this is the manner in which the spontaneity and unpredictability of both nature and other humans can be addressed. It is an aspect of humanity and nature reflected by the intuitionistic view.

The act that brings and keeps people together is not the force of deterministic laws of nature, but the choice to recognize past, present, and future, to engage in noble words that narrate the stories of others, and noble deeds that are the context and meaning of life. Given the possibility of choice, personal as much as political, we then have the choice to make promises and to forgive, all in the presence of other human beings. It is the ability to undo what has been done and to rein in the processes we have set in motion. Recently, Seyla Benhabib suggests that this was the hope behind the Berlin salons of Rahel Varnhagen that Arendt wrote about in her biography.[20] Varnhagen created a place where friends could meet and interact, a place unlike the Greek *polis*, which excluded women, a place that could have given rise to the possibility of action and choices, but ultimately did not. Rahel's typical female life and assimilation into gentile society were not the result of free choice.

For Arendt, to act (*archein*) is to begin, to take the initiative, to lead and to rule, to set something into motion (*agere*). This, she maintains, is the beginning of somebody. To act is to begin and the principle of beginning is the principle of freedom, created only through human temporality.[21] Action that is the new happens against the overwhelming odds of statistical laws and their probability. That humans can act means that the unexpected can be expected, the infinitely improbable is probable because each being is unique. With each birth, there is something unique before which there was nobody. This is not simply the birth of a human being; this is action. Action is the beginning that corresponds to birth, the actualization of the human condition of natality.[22] It is this natality, this birth of action and the promise of the birth of new human beings, that, as Arendt proposes, might ultimately save humans from themselves and from their ongoing drive to produce processes that they do not yet understand.

From Classical Nature to Intuitionistic Ethics

Throughout this book, we have been asking about how to go from a classical or formalist view of nature to the intuitionist framework of the primordial intuition of time. Like the mathematician who is always able to choose how to construct any given sequence, and for whom every element in a construction has an *indeterminate future,* the ethical philosopher must choose and must accept the consequences of choice. Beginning with modern classical science and classical physics, we have examined the presuppositions that this theory and its subsequent incarnations entail. We have looked specifically at the formalist, postmodern treatment of the classical view. We began with the idea that classical physics requires a manifold that is closed, determinate, atomistic, and reversible, that the questions it asks are about processes, that its language or toolbox is mathematical–specifically algebraic geometry or differential calculus which is then projected onto material, physical reality–that its view of reality is Archimedean, a view from far out into the universe where only very general, statistical patterns can be observed. We have seen that this structure is valued for its predictive power, that its predictions are deterministic (rule-following) and certain, unless sensitive initial conditions and unstable boundaries lead to predictions that are deterministic but merely probable. And we have seen that this structure has given rise to a particular worldview, one only mildly disrupted by thermodynamics, a science that accounts for systems that range from being isolated and out of contact with events outside itself, to closed systems that allow energy but not matter to be exchanged, to open systems, ranging from heavenly stars to terrestrial cities, which trade both energy and matter across their borders.[23]

These systems, we have also noted, correlate roughly with questions about equilibrium. Isolated systems generally possess the greatest equilibrium, meaning that large numbers of molecules are distributed randomly, without structure, and without further changes. Closed systems are probably merely slightly out of equilibrium and will generally return to equilibrium.[24]

Near-equilibrium systems feed off of gradients, heat, electricity, chemical reactants, diffuse matter, all of which are processes, flows, allowing new particles to be added and subtracted. Surprisingly, such "metastable" states, as they are called, do become structured; flows of matter, for example, stand in reciprocal relations with force or pressure, so that power is conserved and minimum entropy is produced. The system stays alive by maintaining its flows and its processes, and most of what is called life is near-equilibrium.[25]

Far-from-equilibrium systems exhibit strong nonlinear behavior and maintain stable states after a first bifurcation. Even these systems involve "sufficient but not excessive" energy that materially cycles, as well as entropy, which is reduced only by exporting the excessive entropy into the surrounding environment in forms such as pollution and garbage.[26] These are the dissipative systems of Stengers and Prigogine. And it is not irrelevant to note that in nature, there is a relatively unlimited amount of energy, but a much more limited amount of matter, so that when an organism comes to total equilibrium, its matter is immediately taken up by other organisms and made use of.[27] It is important to reiterate these theories because as we saw in chapter 1, they have become the basis of numerous claims in the humanities that have been hotly disputed by many in the scientific community.

These presuppositions about the nature of physical reality have been associated with the creation of what we have referred to as worldviews, defined as a system of beliefs that are intertwined, interrelated, and interconnected. The assumption on the part of natural scientists seems to be that sudden and dramatic shifts in paradigms in the natural sciences have given rise to sudden and dramatic shifts in worldviews, yet philosopher of science Isabelle Stengers has given us reason to believe otherwise. Changes in natural scientific and philosophical paradigms are not sudden but are prepared over long periods of time. Sometimes a new insight or discovery can propel these shifts, but sometimes a new philosophical or scientific model emerges gradually due to dissatisfaction with the limits of current models and efforts on the part of all thinkers to construct new ones.

Yet certainly the scientific method holds a distinct advantage, for even the most innovative philosophical shifts require either the power of pure thinking, logic or mathematics, or experimental verification coming from the sciences. Nevertheless, we will state in general terms that the classical or Newtonian worldview, which emerged out of the work of philosophers and scientists in the sixteenth and seventeenth centuries, is strongly correlated with the ideas of Hobbes, Locke, Hume, Smith, Marx, and others. These ideas made possible and justified the notion of an atomistic individual, a notion that continues to the present day in philosophy, politics, economics, and other social and human sciences. Even Gilles Deleuze does not substantially alter this model; rather, he fragments it by insisting that atomistic individuals are still too molar, too representational, and must be reconceived on the molecular level. But his is not a new model except with respect to the pointed critique of representationalism in Aristotle and Descartes.

Additionally, Deleuze, like other continental or postmodern philosophers, does not abandon the law of noncontradiction and the law of the excluded middle. "On the contrary, it [postmodern philosophy] is among many other things, a case of Formalism taken to unfathomable extremes."[28] In other words, in place of the awkwardness and ambiguity of sensuous, physical reality, we have pure thought, formalism, the statistical view from far, far away, whose advantages we have accounted for in chapter 4. Simply restated, formalization allows one to abstract the fundamental shape of a system in order to to discern patterns without superficial and messy flesh.[29] Formalization allows maximum cogency, since the premises must be true and the conclusion undeniable, so that no alternative arguments can even be considered. And finally, "the stock of symbols is small and the rules for manipulating them explicit," such that even the average sensual man can recognize the pattern.[30]

With the advent of formalism, the careful and cautious Cartesian method of doubt is no longer necessary. The *ego cogito*, the idea that "I" am a thinking thing, that identity, analogy, opposition and resemblance will be accompanied by the "I think," fades away. With formalization, there is no I that is thinking, no I conceive, I judge, I imagine, I remember. The ontological substance, genus, or common sense that served as the substrate of the Aristotelean "being" around which differences gathered without loss of identity has been transformed into process, pure processes that give way to endless production and consumption of the same forms, over and over. The universe, not merely the Earth, but the entire universe, is now understood to consist of processes undergoing differentiation according to the deterministic rules of dynamical systems, patterns that even the ordinary, average sensual man can recognize. Everything, every single thing undergoes processes, and every single thing proceeds according to some deterministic set of calculations–many still awaiting discovery–but in the view of this ontology, they surely will be found.

The ancient Greek ontology does seem to have revolved around human sensibility, around Aristotle's common sense and the representations to which it gives rise. From this point of view, logic and mathematics are derivative from human sensibility, and the identity of substance was guaranteed by the laws of noncontradiction and the excluded middle. With the advent of modern classical physics, the invention of the infinitesimal calculus, the creation of dynamical systems theory, and eventually the creation of mathematical algorithms, computations for problem solving, the formalization of thinking becomes more and more complete, permeating all aspects of theoretical science and all branches of philosophy, analytic and continental philosophies alike.[31] If the ancient Greek's ontology extolled "Being," or "substance," the moderns have perfected the ontology of becoming, of processes and change, theories of life, where life describes nature's necessities in the most formal terms available.

Yet far from celebrating this release into processes, we have seen that Arendt is deeply worried about it. She is worried not over the loss of Being (perhaps a uniquely Heideggerian concern), but because distinctions between modes of life, between what is necessary, what is enduring, and what is noble have been obscured, if not totally abandoned, in the rush to uncover processes. The classical scientist values the Archimedean point of view, the distance that allows pursuit of the process of discovery for its own sake, and claims proudly that the results of research in physics have no legitimate implications whatever for culture or politics or philosophy. The formalist philosopher sets epistemology above all other philosophical pursuits with the claim that "there is thinking." For each, the realm of noble words and deeds, the realm of human relations is a matter for others, for those who do not pursue the pure discovery of what can be thought clearly and distinctly, those who do not, first and foremost, think formally and statistically, from far, far away. Yet it is precisely this realm that we wish to advance in this work, the realm of noble words and deeds, the realm of human relations, the view from "inside," as we will call it.

We have done this first of all by taking up the critiques of classical natural science and its epistemological counterpart in philosophy, the accounts of the limits of formalist mathematics and postmodern formal philosophical structures, as well as concerns raised by Hannah Arendt and Simone de Beauvoir regarding both formalism and temporality. We have suggested that the philosophy of natality and the philosophy of ambiguity do, in fact, operate on the basis of a coherent structure, but one that eschews binaries for the ambiguity of an open future. The logic of ambiguity, which does not insist on binary notions of truth in the framework of atomic determinable points, allows for unpredictable futures, the simultaneous existence of several possible outcomes, that is, something may or may not be true or false today and may or may not turn out to be true or false in the future. However, in asserting this, we do not deny the possibility of truth. Additionally, in asserting this, we maintain that the logic of ambiguity also brings the past, even several pasts, into the present and the future. Temporality, as we will see again below, enters for the first "time" into our logic since the advent of modern science.

But if the logic of ambiguity, which we are correlating with "intuitionistic logic," provides intelligibility for temporal phenomena, is there a correlative physical structure that makes it possible for human beings to be other than atomistic individuals blindly following universal natural laws? Perhaps caution is called for here. Philosophers like Daniel Dennett have proposed that even an evolutionary process like natural selection is a mindless, automatic, step-by-step process that a computer can simulate. The limitation of such simulation is that it is a method unsuited to predicting particular cases of statistical evolution; it is capable only of predicting general tendencies over large numbers, given enough time. If any process can be an algorithm or can be defined using a differential equation, then all that would be necessary to understand the process is to discover the algorithm or differential equation appropriate to it, thereby removing any notions of the accidental or the unexpected, as well as any notion of temporality, the past entering into and influencing the present and the future.

Yet as we saw with the case of Romeo and Juliet, many differential equations are completely mundane or uninteresting and banal. They tell us nothing about why something happens; they merely predict statistical outcomes. It is no different for algorithmic computations. This is not, however, only because they imply the reinterpretation (perhaps a better term than "reduction") of an ongoing process as a step-by-step procedure, but also because, once again, the processes they organize are too general to be interesting. Moreover, there are many ways to explain or make sense of any particular phenomenon or set of phenomena. Looking to the sciences, no one demands conformity to a single theory or method simply because it is the most abstract formulation possible. Why should we do this in philosophy? And, as we have seen in Arendt's work on the banality of evil, tracking general tendencies does not assist in revealing or creating any ethical guidelines for words and deeds. It encourages solutions that are justifiable as rule-following regardless of how devastating their effects. The remainder of this work will specifically address this issue, the issue of what sort of thinking makes it possible for us to conceive of a human being who does not blindly and atomistically follow natural law? That is, how can we go from nature to ethics, from formalism to intuition?

The Universal and the Realm of the Sensible

Universal moral law follows naturally from universal laws that even God must follow. This version of moral law is freed of subjectively determined desires that are empirically conditioned and sensible, and which therefore are different for everyone, different because, unlike logic and formalist mathematics, sensibility arises individually. It is an aspect of our embodiment, and as such sensibility has been relegated to the realm of unknowable subjectivity. Subjectively determined desires are said to be private, part of life's necessities, perhaps the last feature of our existence that is still relegated to the private realm.

In addition, empirically conditioned, sensible desires are taken by Kant, the philosopher of universal moral law, to be entirely subject to necessity, meaning to nature's causality. They belong to the causal chain of nature's cycles. This is, for Arendt, the realm of necessity that should be part of the private sphere of life and not brought into the public sphere. However, once the private becomes public, the labor producing life's necessities becomes the model for all actions, and private desires as well as nature's causal necessity enter the public sphere. To manage this situation, one in which desire becomes universal, where it is one with the flow of near-equilibrium systems, we need to provide ourselves with a moral law, a rule that tells us what we ought to do, rather than what merely happens due to natural necessity. Given that we think we are natural beings, that we follow nature's laws, this cannot be easy. We can do this in only one way, by putting a check on sensibility and on causality.

First, we can abstract from empirical conditions. This is not the Platonic move of idealizing appearances. It is something different. It is a formal procedure in which we procure the form of giving a universal rule, that is, we procure the Archimedean point of view, a pure a priori commanding that legislates universal moral law.[32] We do this by procuring the symbols in our own minds, the pure logical form of relation derived only from syllogisms, from categorical, hypothetical and disjunctive syllogisms representing pure relations without content.[33] We procure their form not through idealization but through negation. One's current situation, one's subjective feelings and their objective natural causes, will both be negated; they will be nothing. We will, each of us, make choices, carry out acts that take us from act to act, point to point, along a trajectory toward an attractor, which is "freedom" or "transcendence."

Moral law, according to Kant, is a negative incentive; it is pure negation of feeling. It checks one's own sensibility so that the higher functions may take over the process of thought. And likewise, moral law negates nature's formal causal law, a law that governs empirical and material necessity. In its place, when subjective and objective motives are negated, there we find the pure laws of the logical category of relation: connection, conjunction, and disjunction, or immortality (self), freedom (world), and god (the a priori spacetime manifold). These are laws that cannot give us knowledge, but do tell us purely intelligible beings what we can do. They tell us how to think logically and they tell us what we can do, universally. They act as attractors, providing incentives for our autonomy.

In this model, only our intelligible self, a first cause with no prior cause, is free of both sensible existence and nature's necessity.[34] Just as we formulate differential equations and project them onto physical reality, so we formulate moral law and project it onto the physical world, which then is taken to be the effect of autonomous freedom.[35] What this means is that the effects of autonomous freedom in the physical realm do not interest us. We have no subjective, sensuous interest in them nor do we have even the interest of knowing beings, knowing what is or what exists. Our interest is only in the pure process, the pure form, which yields a disinterested aesthetic pleasure in the beautiful scientific theory, the beautiful moral rule. Certainly there is nothing physical or material here. Universal moral law yields pleasure in necessary and universal beauty, valid for all, completely indifferent to the existence of objects and persons.

In the face of this structure, we would like to once again propose an alternative, the alternative of a sensible universal. What would this mean? The physicist Fotini Markopoulou puts forth a theory that shakes up all we think we know. Like Bergson and Brouwer, like Beauvoir and Arendt, she argues that geometry, in other words space, is not fundamental in the universe. Keep in mind that in mathematics, the rules of association, commutation, and distribution define vector space. They are also the rules governing Kantian practical reason, that is, they tell us what actions are universal in their application. Thus, association governs the connections between subject and predicate in the categorical relation.[36] Commutation permits the valid reordering of disjunctive statements, which, using the logical rules of transformation, can logically be recast as conjunctive propositions without a change of truth value.[37] The point is that the rules governing logic are also those that govern algebraic geometry. Claiming that geometry is not fundamental is a daring move, one that brings into question all of our assumptions about nature and the sciences and logic that study nature.

What if, mathematically, we are able to make a distinction between two kinds of time, the geometric and the fundamental, and to posit the thesis that while the geometric time is symmetry, only the fundamental time is real? In other words, what if geometric time, the spacetime of the classical model, emerges out of the microscopic fundamental time of quantum gravity?[38] At the high-energy levels of the early universe, Markopoulou explains, there is no geometric locality. Matter and with it geometry only make an appearance when the universe starts to cool down, when the system as a whole starts to cool. Moreover, reversing the commonly accepted formulation, geometry can now be conceptualized as a property of matter and "geometry is nothing but the collective organization of emergent matter."[39]

In other words, the Kantian a priori manifold, which Kant calls "God," is derivative of temporalized matter and not the other way around. The shocking conclusion of this reversal is that physically and philosophically, we may have trapped ourselves inside a physical structure or a system of knowledge that we think organizes our behavior but in truth is the effect of the collective action of matter in nature as well as the collective action of those who feel, act, and think in culture. So, by analogy, Markopoulou argues that we cannot simply study the structure of society and ignore the actions of people in that society.[40] This would have been Arendt's point as well. The banality of evil could then be understood to be an unfortunate consequence of adhering to an a priori manifold that commands universal moral law while ignoring the actions of individual people in that society as well as the unpredictable consequences of those actions. Can we now conceptualize a philosophical point of view that does not assume the existence of an atomistic individual in a formal, statistical, geometrical manifold, proceeding from act to act by means of a process of negation, negating the previous act in order to carry out the next one?

The Sensible Universal

Many readers will be familiar with the image of a cone that the philosopher Henri Bergson used to characterize ontological memory, that memory created by the imperceptible influences of states in the universe on an individual sensibility. The cone describes a situation in which the entire past coexists with each new present in relation to which it is now past. We noted previously that Bergson describes the cone of memory relativistically as a process of time dilation and space contraction evolving to a single point of view. According to Bergson, this aspect of memory is ontological, not personal, because the information it carries comes to us from the entire universe, transported by the energy of light. Memory responds to the appeal of the present state by moving as a whole, contracting into a present perception so that we may act.

In this model, the past is not negated; negation does not enter into this movement. In this model, temporality is the fundamental structure, as the past of the universe, or as much of it as reaches us and therefore influences us, moves wholly into the present in order to participate in the future through that action.[41]

The light cone is a well-known structure in physics; its shape corresponds to information that arrives at a particular location at the speed of light. It assumes particular importance in the theory of general relativity. General relativity tells us that the speed of light is invariant and nothing (no causal effect and no information) travels faster than the speed of light. "The causal past of an event consists of all the events that could have influenced it. The influence must travel from some state in the past at the speed of light or less. So the light rays arriving at an event form the outer boundary of the past of an event and make up what we call the past light cone of an event."[42]

By drawing a light cone around every event, we may specify all the causal relations affecting it. Doing this with every event would yield the causal structure of the universe. This is significant insofar as "most of the story of our universe is the story of the causal relations among its events . . . [but crucially and unlike differential dynamical systems] the causal structure is not fixed. . . . it *evolves*, subject to laws."[43] The question is, of course, how? "How many events are contained in the passage of a signal from you to me. . . . How many events have there been in the whole history of the universe in the past of this particular moment?"[44] Or how many events constitute a point of view, making it not an atomistic individual subject to the law of noncontradiction, but a crowd? The answer to these questions depends on the nature of spacetime.

The classical model assumes that space and time are continuous. This means that they can be (at least in thought) divided infinitely, that there is no smallest possible unit of space or time. This implies that for any event, at least on the level of particles, it could always be faster and the number of events, being infinitely divisible, could be infinite. Such assumptions are nonphysical, since no physical person or thing can travel faster than the speed of light nor can they be infinitely divided. However, another emergent approach to this question is worth considering, and that is the idea that space and time are fundamental on the quantum scale, thus that they are discrete.[45] If space and time are discrete, they cannot be infinitely divided and the number of events or states may be very large but still finite. What this suggests is that continuous or smooth spacetime may be useful illusions but that the world consists of discrete sets of events that can be counted.[46] Referring back to the conception of light cones, rather than a single cone, a single event, let us think about a causal network of interconnected states for which every perspective and every state consists of a multiplicity of cones linked to one another, influencing one another, "combinatorial structures" that have been called "spin networks," networks giving rise to situationally organized, intra-active behavior?[47]

This conception is also part of the theory being created by Fotini Markopoulou, who is constructing a physical description of the universe, thus one that is not based on the physically impossible but mathematically conceivable notion of infinite divisibility of continuous spacetime. What Markopoulou proposes is a causal structure of spacetime that codes not the Archimedean view from outside that classical physics and dynamical systems utilize, but rather, what she refers to as *the view from inside*, what an observer inside the universe can observe.[48] Arguing against classical models precisely because they lead to uncertainty, Markopoulou suggests utilizing causal sets (large collections of causal relations), sets of events in discrete spacetime partially ordered by temporal causal relations. Moreover, Markopoulou proposes to work with evolving sets that bring the causal past of each event as well as the causal structure of each event into a causal set. She further suggests that evolving sets satisfy a particular algebra called Heyting algebra, which utilizes a nonstandard logic the historical development of which has been related to understanding the passage of time. This logic is precisely the intuitionistic logic we have traced from Brouwer and Heyting, which does not adhere to the law of the excluded middle. As we have noted, whereas the classical Boolean mathematician believes that a statement x is true or false whether or not she has proof for it, intuitionism does not allow proof by contradiction. Thus, from the onset, it does not consider x to be true or false unless there is a proof for it. In other words, if x may be true tomorrow or false tomorrow, without a proof the option is open. Thus intuitionistic logic is suited to time evolution, where certain physical statements become true at a certain time.[49]

In this manner, the logic used by observers in the universe to describe what they see has been modified. They must be able to construct proofs. Moreover, any single observer is able to know only a subset of true facts regarding their universe.[50] What is crucial here for my point is that "a theory with internal observables is fundamentally different than a theory describing a system external to the observers," as the former obey intuitionistic logic and the latter obey so-called Boolean logic and observe the law of the excluded middle.[51] Of equal importance is the idea of a theory that refers to observations made from "inside." For physicists, this means from one's temporal and spatial position inside the universe, and such observations can only be partial, that is, they contain information that is in the temporal causal past of an observer in a particular region of spacetime. They do not contain predictions, meaning information about the future, information that should be obtainable from a classical dynamical perspective. In terms of light cones, this means that information that constitutes a particular point of view intra-acts within the boundaries of any light cone where space and time are not taken to be infinitely divisible or infinitely extensible.

Even though this concept operates entirely within the realm of linear causality, there is no single wave function for the entire universe, that is, what is being measured or described is the evolution from one spacetime to another spacetime. Spin network graphs have been used to model quantum spatial geometry and events in a causal set that are evolving, yielding a quantum causal history.[52] One significant implication of this model is that unlike dynamical systems, the manifold of spacetime is not pregiven. Rather than a dynamically changing form of content and form of expression that takes place in a pre-established spacetime manifold and is produced or assembled from outside by the elements of that manifold, the model of quantum causal histories specifies that spacetime and the states that evolve, *the stage and the actors, evolve together*.[53] This is particularly useful for the exploration of states that occur at a scale where classical physics fails, the Planck scale of quantum states, and additionally it allows for the construction of a point of view that is not that of an atomistic individual but can only be called a crowd. A crowd is a point of view according to which different observers "see" or "live" partly different, partial views of the universe, partial views that nonetheless overlap. How can this be?

If the causal past of an event consists of all the events that could have influenced it, these influences travel from some state in the past at the speed of light or less. We have noted that the light rays arriving at an event form the outer boundary of the past of an event and make up the past light cone of an event. Under these conditions, the causal structure of states evolves and the motion of matter is a consequence of that evolution. So we have asked, following this model, what if continuous, differential spacetime (so-called smooth space) is just a useful illusion? Here we have the intuitionist conception according to which intuition is a process of building or constructing, a time-bound process beginning in the past, existing in the present, and evolving into an *open* future. Because the information from the past evolving as the present into an open future occurs on the quantum scale, the scale of photons, the world can be said to be composed of discrete states, states on a very small scale, but nevertheless states that are discrete in space and time. Under such conditions, what might be observed? Is it possible that this structure and these processes might involve the construction of vulnerable and sensitive beings in an ontological spatiotemporalization, an ever-changing perspective made up of a crowd of perspectives in the heterogeneity of space and time? Such a perspective, if it is thinkable, if it is real, could manifest itself as a sort of history, but it is more like a complex causality, layers and layers of states, always susceptible to realignment, its patterns and particles resolving in a point of view that is the effect of a crowd of influences and itself contributes to a crowd of influences. These overlapping conical flows of information, often imperceptible, influence one another and in this they influence the sensibility of all things.

Given that this is something extremely difficult to situate, it is much more likely to be overlooked. If it is the manner in which states (including very tiny states) influence and alter one another, the implication is that these states influence and alter sensibility, all sensibility. These influences are not the objects of perception nor of consciousness; they cannot be experienced as increases or decreases of power, as the raising or lowering of intensities. They are, at least, capable of receptivity. If they are noticed at all, it is usually only insofar as they are felt as pleasure and pain, discomfort and distress. Their influence on sensibility comes via a sensory system, thus they do not constitute a personal memory. This might be the way living beings evolve in relation to an ontological unconscious whose passive existence no longer refers to an individual or to a being but is unceasingly effected by the reflection, refraction, and dispersion of light in a spectrum.[54]

But how are we to study and understand such states? What is our access to this felt pleasure and pain and in what manner might it indicate the existence of states that influence and alter our sensibility? It has of course been well-noted that within the cognitive science tradition the "temptation to conflate emotional feelings and cognitive processes remains rather too prominent" and that scientifically important distinctions can be made between affects and cognitions.[55] Although the precise dividing line between affective sensations and cognitive processes is difficult to draw, there are credible ways to distinguish them.[56] The great question we wish to address is how sensibility and feeling manifest themselves and influence human choices. We can begin by providing a phenomenological description of these states and of the manner in which the past enters the present and opens up the future by means of sensibility. In order to do this, let us turn back to Beauvoir, whose philosophical reflections on love provide us with an opening onto an understanding of what we have referred to as the individual who is a crowd.

The Joy of Existence

A woman of sixty, possibly a philosopher, married, it seems, to André, a scientist, reflects on their life, past, present and future. "How many times had we sat there opposite one another at that little table with piping hot, very strong cups of tea in from of us? . . . The moment possessed the sweet gentleness of a memory and the gaiety of a promise. Were we thirty, or were we sixty?"[57] How many times had the couple sat in the sun-filled library in an ordinary, easy-flowing way? How sweet is the gentle present moment of this thought? How gay, the promise of future days, the very strong and very hot cups of tea to come?

The woman recognizes that together, she and André have had a long life filled, as she says, with laughter, tears, quarrels, embraces, confessions, silences, and sudden impulses of the heart, yet "sometimes it seems that time has not moved by at all. The future still stretches out to infinity."[58] And so it does, for the implication of these realizations will be that no existence founds itself only from moment to moment, that moral freedom requires a past and a future, a past and a future that belong to the temporal unity of one's current projects, projects that in turn may become the starting point for other projects to be carried out by other people, on and on into the infinite future, well beyond the strong cups of tea, the sun-filled library, and day's post.[59]

Soon, André will go off to the laboratory where he conducts scientific research and the woman will attend to the card indexes and blank paper that, sitting on her desk, urge her to work. For the woman and her husband, what matters is not falling into the paralysis of what Simone de Beauvoir has elsewhere described as a limited future and a frozen past, a situation that the aging and elderly often face.[60] The existential question Beauvoir fearlessly raises is precisely that of the weight of this past. Will the shortness of their future and the weight of the past necessarily close off all outlets to the woman and her husband? Will the process of aging lead them to cling to routine, to the advantages of their experience, to the point where they do not merely fall behind the times but stubbornly come into conflict with the present age because it endangers their economic or ideological interests?[61] But such circumstances, whereby one clings to the weight of the past, do not happen for an individual in isolation. The life of the individual takes place only in the context of the society, the life with others. Perpetually out of date, the woman or man must find a way to tear themselves free from a past that holds them in its grip, but even as they become, they seem to lose ground. The sciences grow more and more complex; the number of things one neither knows nor understands increases.

Given this situation, some individuals, unable to face the expanding and infinite future, begin to loathe novelty, to despise change, and even to deny what Beauvoir takes to be human nature itself, that is, the very fact of our transcendence.[62] The question she raises is obviously one of great importance. How are we to will ourselves free? All humans are mortal, all feel the tragic ambiguity of existing the past and the future in a moment that seems to be nothing, but if it is truly the case, as Beauvoir claims, that no existence founds itself moment by moment, on the model of the classical natural sciences, the dynamical system, for which each moment is exactly the same as any other and no moment has special significance, then we must ask ourselves: What structure and what ethical stand makes the gentleness of memory and the gaiety of future promises possible for mortals? How can we realize the joy of existence even as time passes? How are we to continue to effect the transition from nature to ethics?[63]

Let us begin with the question of nature. Human life, Beauvoir claims, is circumscribed by nature and natural laws. We have discussed at length the laws of classical physics that give an account of nature as it evolves from moment to moment in an open or closed system through which matter and energy flow.[64] In her novel *She Came to Stay,* each of Beauvoir's principal characters, Xavière, Françoise, and Pierre, exist as the embodiment of these laws. According to natural scientific principles, existence, as determined by the classical laws of dynamical systems, seeks to found itself moment to moment through the limit or negation of what has come before so as to remain absolutely free of the past. Beauvoir, we have stated previously, refers to this as "the absurdity of the clinamen," a concept attributed to Lucretius, who defines it as a type of atomic motion, a spontaneous and infinitely small change of direction in the course of an atom's downward fall resulting from the chance collision of one atom with another, without which nothing could be created in nature.

The clinamen is a physical concept, yet, as we have seen, Lucretius conceives of the clinamen in relation to free will or change, a common interpretation. Rather than following a determinate path prescribed by a causal sequence of events, atoms swerve, thereby originating a new movement that appears to "snap the bonds of fate, the everlasting sequence of cause and effect."[65] This is the clinamen. In this sense, to exist, to be a being, is to escape the causal determination of the past; it to deviate moment by moment, from nothingness to nothingness, where each new moment is an effect of the past but breaks completely with that past and so can be defined as nothingness. In this sense, to exist is to deviate from a state of equilibrium that is mute, motionless, and passive, governed wholly by natural forces outside of oneself. This means that existence or being, transcendence in Beauvoir's terms, denotes deviation from the position in which one has been fixed by external forces. "We do not exist . . . except through and by this deviation from equilibrium. Everything is deviation from equilibrium, except Nothing. That is to say, Identity."[66]

According to the theory of the clinamen, nature runs its course toward an equilibrium, but deviations appear stochastically. In chapter 4 we described this as the original determination of the direction of movement of the atom and noted that the clinamen expresses the idea of looking for numerical and geometric patterns in a process of successive approximation.[67] Unable to be predicted precisely, they swerve forth as minute, infinitesimal deviations from equilibrium, thereby producing something new in place of something that is identical with the past.[68] This description appears to conform to the very idea of transcendence, to the idea that we are beings who make ourselves a lack of being, a nothingness, in order that there might be being, in order that there might be something new. And yet Beauvoir objects to this. What is it for Beauvoir that makes this particular model of nature absurd for human existence? Crucially, it is that ethics does not correspond to the conception provided by classical physics and that we must find another way to proceed from nature to ethics.[69]

We have said that the characters Xavière, Françoise, and Pierre embrace and embody the climamen. Xavière, in particular, characterizes the world and other people as physical entities that attempt to resist her deviation, thereby limiting her power to exist, that is, to change course in infinitesimally small increments through chance collisions with other atomistic entities. It is the resistance of other entities, be they persons or events, to her changes of direction that are the negation of being that she wishes to overcome. "I'd like to live alone in the world and keep my freedom," declares Xavière. To which Françoise counters, "'You don't understand; to follow a more or less consistent line of conduct does not constitute slavery. . . .' 'You give them rights over you,' Xavière said scornfully."[70] Xavière disapproves of and is disgusted by the idea of other people to the extent that she takes any interaction with others to be equivalent to being bound by shackles that inhibit her spontaneous changes in direction, her deviations from consistency. As such, other people are nothing but what fix you, force you into equilibrium, the zero degree that is deterioration, ruin, and death.[71] In this sense, Xavière's life is completely unlike Eichmann's and we can see why it might appear to be a life freely chosen rather than the slavish adherence to fate. But, as we will see, this is not so.

It is not surprising that Xavière resents any others who take an interest in her well-being, including Françoise and Pierre, for she can only imagine that this is an attempt, like her own, at objectification, fixing her existence in a set trajectory, as certain as it is final. Nevertheless, her fear of being fixed does not keep Xavière from extending invitations to Françoise, but such invitations seem much more like "imperious orders," giving Françoise the feeling that one could never live with Xavière, but only beside her.[72] To live with Xavière, it would be necessary that she cease objectifying others, that she recognize them as existing independently, as free beings in relation to herself.

Alternating, as she says, between "brainstorms and lethargy," Xavière's determination to evade all consistency, to keep the past out of the present and the future, also prevents her from taking up a profession; she both denigrates any possible course of study offered to her and despairs of her own abilities.[73] Given the opportunity to study acting with the great professionals of Pierre's theater, Xavière ends by declaring the profession of acting and those who engage in it not worthy of her time or effort. In this manner, Xavière is even more insolent and full of pride than Pierre, who also rejects the idea of consistency and "with the fury of a renegade offered up his past in sacrifice to his present."[74] But each time Pierre negates the past and moves on, he deliberately places in Françoise's hands the dark responsibility for his former self that he now rejects and condemns, leaving Françoise in the cold and wondering, once Xavière and Pierre join forces, to what extent if any she is protected from the two of them.

Although it is Beauvoir who first realized and gave voice to the idea of the clinamen, an idea extensively adopted by Jean-Paul Sartre two years later in *Being and Nothingness,* Beauvoir came to reject the classical naturalism of this position, this transcendental position, in favor of an ontology and ethics of ambiguity that does not bury us in the weight of the past, insofar as that might well condemn the aging to the frozen past, but that also is not caught up in the arbitrary moment-by-moment destruction of the past and of other human beings. Let us try to see how she works this out.

The Other Within

In *The Coming of Age,* Beauvoir reaffirms the idea that life is based on self-transcendence, but it seems as though this has taken on a new meaning. The nihilistic self-transcendence of Xavière means that she avoids any commitments to persons or projects. The French title of *She Came to Stay, L'inviteé,* indicates clearly that Xavière is in Paris at the invitation of Pierre and Françoise. However, although Françoise and Pierre support her financially and mentor her professionally, she remains indifferent and without gratitude toward them. With Pierre, whose creative intelligence and life she admires and envies, Xavière seeks to make herself into a fascinating object, an "I" who puts herself beneath the look of the Other to make him look at her as a privileged and meaningful object, infinitely and unsurpassably deep. This is not, of course, love; it is the project of trying to make herself be loved to the exclusion of Françoise.

Once she has succeeded in being recognized by Pierre as a free subjectivity, Xavière refuses to recognize his own free, subjective existence, objectifying him as her admirer alone and driving to an end the intellectual and intimate relationship between Pierre and Françoise.[75] Offered friendship by Françoise, Xavière instead objectifies her and remains cold to friendship and oblique to Françoise's own subjectivity until, beaten down by Xavière's superiority and open contempt of her, Françoise becomes so ill that she must be hospitalized. Although she is only thirty, Françoise begins to see herself as a mature, meaning old, woman. Her illness reduces her to an inert mass such that "she was not even an organic body."[76] Xavière makes it clear that becoming ill is a serious fault, that the struggle for life is a humiliation and weakness that cannot be accepted. Like the adventurer, Xavière asserts her existence without taking into account that of others. Françoise, attuned to and infuriated by Xavière's objectification of her, can here find no solution but that of nature's contingency, the clinamen.

In order to go on with her own life, to open a new direction, Françoise negates and eliminates Xavière wholly. Without premeditation or reflection, Françoise spontaneously turns on the gas in Xavière's room, and Xavière dies. But this action is nature's clinamen; it arises contingently like nature's forces. Françoise does not plan to destroy Xavière, it simply happens in accordance with deterministic principles. It is the turbulent and unexpected negation of an otherwise objectified state of affairs that has the effect of freeing Françoise. It negates the objectification of Françoise by Xavière, but only by negating Xavière absolutely, an act in accordance with nature's contingent possibilities. But insofar as this act follows from the "absurd" law of the physical clinamen, it is not ethical, and so it seems that for Beauvoir, in *The Ethics of Ambiguity* and *The Coming of Age* as well as in other literary works, the concept of self-transcendence must take on a new meaning and a new structure.

In the latter text in particular, it is one's own life and not other people that set one up as "Another," as objectified; it is "the books I have written, which now outside me constitute my works, and define me as their author."[77] And as time passes, our own past weighs us down more and more. The future we had freely chosen for ourselves has turned into a fact, a necessity; our own past is an otherness and our projects are frozen in that past. Yet for Beauvoir, this view fails to be an ethical view insofar as it corresponds only to the physical view of nature as consisting of chance particles colliding according to deterministic laws and thermodynamic entropy. For human beings, the world, objects, and bodies are finite physically, physically destined to wear down and wear out, to fall apart and die in the "shifting aggregations of atoms," so that, following Lucretius, it appears that "the world, objects, bodies, my very soul are, at the moment of their birth, in decline. . . . Nature declines and this is its act of birth. . . . The past, the present, the future, the dawn of appearance and death, tenacious illusions, are only the declinations of matter."[78] This purely physical decline is also purely external, purely outside oneself, an effect of external forces and nature's deterministic laws, driving atomistic entities to collide with one another, to become less organized, and finally to become purely homogeneous.

But Beauvoir has already, in her ethics, discovered something more than the external and physical view according to which particles collide in accordance with deterministic laws. She accepts that one's own mortality is something only the outsider can see; it is something general, abstract, and assumed from without.[79] However, Beauvoir asks, is there not, in addition to this view, the ontological structure of being-for-itself, so that even if we were to live an additional hundred years, or forever, finitude would not be taken from us? Unlike the immortal Fosca in Beauvoir's novel *All Men Are Mortal*, who ceases to be human when he ceases taking up projects and turns away from all activities, when we make ourselves, when we take up a project in the world, that is how and when we make ourselves finite, and that is when we have only ourselves, our own past, our own skin to outstrip.[80] But it remains our own skin even as we evolve.

In other words, ontologically, our own finished projects fall back into the realm of our own Other, and we are left not negating ourselves but renewing ourselves, in order to be at all. Such a "passionate heroism," is precisely what the aging can embrace, "delighting in a progress that must soon be cut short by death . . . carrying on, the attempt to outdo oneself in full knowledge and acceptance of one's finitude."[81] This ontological view, it appears, is not the abstract and universal physical view, which is an external view of objects in motion following deterministic laws, nor is it pure inwardness, matter reduced to mind. In what does it consist? How is such a view possible? It is discoverable, we have seen, in a philosophy of ambiguity, a philosophy for which human beings are neither purely the effects of deterministic albeit chaotic external relations nor relations of pure mind and inwardness, nor a synthesis of the two.

Beauvoir states that humans feel their tragic ambiguity; they exist the past and the future in a moment that is itself nothing. This is the meaning of the claim that they are the beings that make themselves lack in order that there might be being, but in doing this, they do not follow the Kantian law, which prescribes that they must negate the feeling. To deny this feeling would be to deny ambiguity, to deny that subjectivity realizes itself only as a presence in the world, a surging for-oneself, but one that is always and immediately given for others. If this were a purely deterministic natural process, there would be no ethics. When Françoise unexpectedly opens the gas valve in Xavière's room, she does so impulsively, driven by Xavière's brutal collision with and intrusion into Françoise's attempts to be free, to free herself from Xavière's objectification of her. But ethics implies intentionality; it implies choice. It implies that we make ourselves lack, we quiet ourselves, stepping back as in an *epoché*, not to destroy but in order to disclose the being of the world and the being of others.[82] "I should like this sky, this quiet water to think themselves *within me,* that it might be I whom they express in flesh and bone," says Beauvoir, while "I" joyfully remain at a distance so that sky and water may exist before me.[83]

In *Being and Nothingness,* Sartre argues that we humans are encompassed by nothingness, the permanent possibility of nonbeing, such that what being will be arises on the basis of what it is not. Logically, we may formulate this by saying that being is x and outside of x it is nothing, but that this nonbeing is real.[84] Of course, given the law of conservation of mass in a closed system, it might be argued that being-in-itself is fully positive and according to nature's laws can contain no negation, that negation and nothingness only imply failed expectations, thereby making the proposition "x is not" only a judgment, nothing real. So it seems that it is only for humans that a storm or earthquake destroys and not for the Earth. But for Sartre, we must come to understand that the proposition "x is not" presupposes a comprehension of nothingness as such and conduct in the face of nothingness that is a human fact.

The ground of human perception is for this reason said to be an original nihilation necessary for a figure to appear but into which it melts like unwanted faces in a cafe when one is searching for one who is not there, and who thereby appears, but only as a nothingness on a ground of nihilation that is the cafe, a nothingness that is real for the searcher and not merely a thought. Such negation, Sartre claimed, is an abrupt break in continuity, an original, irreducible event, but also a perpetual presence in and outside us.[85] It is, in short, the clinamen that swerve in nature, originating new movement, and that appears, as we said above, to snap the bonds of fate, the everlasting sequence of cause and effect.

It seems, however, that Beauvoir denies this. Transcendence cannot be just a formal mathematical or Stoic freedom. It is, she claims, a double negation in which we first make ourselves lack, but then we go on to negate the lack so that it can be filled by the Other expressing itself *in* me, even as I remain distant from my "I." As my lack is filled by the Other in me, I may affirm both of our positive existences. But this may not work logically the way Beauvoir imagines. For intuitionistic mathematics and logic, for which the past influences the present and the future is open, double negation does not hold. Regarding any current proposition, intuitionist logic objects to the assertion that even if "we do not at present know whether it is in fact true or whether it is in fact false, . . . it must be one or the other."[86] This assertion presupposes that the future is actual, that we have a God's eye view of it, whereas for the intuitionist, the future–which mathematically is interpreted as an infinity–is always only potential. The idea of an infinite totality is profoundly mistaken. It fails to refer to anything, thus the double negative fails to refer to anything. If there is no object that my term "not P" refers to, then I cannot continue by negating this nothing.[87]

We may, however, take up Beauvoir's conception that the other influences me, and so is in some sense within, like mutually influencing light cones constructing the individual as a crowd. But we must reformulate her logic. In place of the binary logic of the excluded middle of the Sartrean clinamen, we have argued that Beauvoir puts into play a logic of ambiguity. This implies that to undo her objectification by Xavière, Françoise does not have to nihilate her. Were Xavière not to have embraced the classical model of the atomistic individual, she might well have come to recognize Françoise as the Other within and each mutually influencing the other, and not as the obstacle to be negated. After all Xavière seems to have been related to Françoise, and even in this sense she is part of her past. Although she may be able to do nothing about Xavière's actions, Françoise can search for a solution that evokes the birth or rebirth of her own narrative. She does this, in part, by giving up her intimate relation with Pierre and embarking on new personal relationships. But she can do more; she can accept that neither she nor Xavière is an atomistic entity, neither exists without influencing and being influenced by others.

Every One a Crowd

Utilizing this structure, it seems to us that each person, each individual, is not an atom, but every one is a crowd. In this way, Xavière's insecurity and failure or Françoise's relationship to Pierre are not to be simply events that are negated by new events, but can be taken up and lived as ambiguity, the ambiguity of existence that each human must accept and realize as the passage from nature to ethics. We rejoin ourselves to the extent we agree to this distance from ourselves, which means that we *feel*, we are sensible of and accept the others within. As time passes, this distance becomes all the more crucial as the growing weight of our own past projects defines and influences us, and similarly, it becomes an aspect of the other within.

Beauvoir argues that a mathematician or a scientist, like André in her story "The Age of Discretion," has already done away with his subjectivity, but in his case, it is in order to think along the lines of a universally valid rational system. But this is not the whole picture. As a scientist, he has been fortunate to have never worked alone but to have always taken part in a collaborative effort. He has always been part of a mutually influencing group, so that his work is the work of a crowd. But the evolution of science relentlessly demands the new, and that does involve an intellectual break with what has come before, with habits of mind, out-of-date methods, and seemingly self-evident ideas. To accomplish this the scientist may find it necessary to create new scientific narratives, perhaps by following the lecture courses offered to students, expertise to make room for something new. Or the scientist may have to follow out the implications of contraries, ideas that are not entirely commensurate with his own earlier work.[88] Euler, Galileo, and Laplace carried out important mathematical work in their seventies. Michelson published his experiments on the speed of light in his eighties, yet there is no denying that these accomplishments were quite unusual.[89]

Beauvoir's character André takes the route that is most likely. He carries out his research in a group with other younger scientists. His project will continue into the future with or without him as long as he does not atomize his past and negate it in the present, as long as he does not build his accomplishments on the negation of others, failing to feel and acknowledge the crowd nature of his own and other's existence and interactions. He is fortunate to have a "fine team" that is the source of "fresh ideas," but as the chief investigator, he must allow these fresh ideas to be asserted even if they are ambiguous. And, as we have noted, the ambiguity may arise because other types of opposition such as contrariety seem to be less hierarchical insofar as a single term may have a variety of contraries that need not indicate the lack of a specific property. If contraries are asserted, for example, a pluralistic set such as bad, sad, or unrepentant may be asserted for the term good, and the system does not collapse.[90] They make the future possible since at some stage one or another of them may be shown to be true in a manner that leads to other new ideas.

Unlike the scientist, who, classically, describes the world from outside, the intuitionist philosopher "wishes to understand the relationship between the world and man posited as a subject."[91] She wishes to understand it from the point of view that we have just called the inside. And given that it may take a lifetime to grasp all the implications of her original philosophical intuition, the philosopher's task proceeds well according to a logic of ambiguity. Having arrived at a philosophical intuition, the philosopher must lay out a system, but then, stand back, distance herself from it, criticize it, and allow it to be the site of fresh problems. The philosophical system must remain open, open to its own ambiguities.[92] So when the scientist, André, decides to go back to being a student and the philosopher-writer reluctantly discovers her own resistances to altering her habits of mind, they are both, in their own way, plunging back into ambiguity.

Therefore, unlike Françoise in *She Came to Stay*, the narrator does not resolve her conflicts with others naturalistically, which is to say atomistically, nihilistically, but resolves them ethically, in agreement with a new understanding of nature. Extremely disappointed and suffering from her son's decision not to pursue the intellectual life but instead, and with his father-in-law's assistance, to go into government service, the woman cuts off all contact with him. She objectifies her son Philippe and his wife Irène, calling them "half-wits" mired in bad faith, seeking only success and dishonoring themselves by this choice.[93] In her fury, she objectifies André, accusing him of being a plotter, plotting against her, behind her back, with their son, until she is carried away "thousands of miles from him and from ... [herself], into a desert that is *both* scorching and freezing cold."[94] And she wonders if she and André will simply end their days together, but this time, living only side by side, two atoms in chain.

Even worse, it is just at this moment that the first harsh criticisms of the woman's new book appear. Shocked, she characterizes her critic as an old fool and bitterly decides that she herself is no longer capable of writing. In her fury, she sends André off to visit his mother in the countryside without her. Yet by existing under conditions that can only be characterized as contraries, both scorching and freezing in the desert, the woman finally begins to act ethically. She follows André and walks with him under the moon, feeling both the influence of André and that of the moonlight. "Little star that I see, Drawn by the moon. The old words, just as they were first written, were there on my lips. They were the link joining me to the past centuries, when the stars shone exactly as they do today."[95]

And listening to André's familiar voice, finally her anger dissipates as she admits to the feeling of the Other within. For her sake, he will quit playing at being old, pitying himself and viewing himself as finished as a scientist. Thus he decides to stop his current research in order to bring his knowledge up to date in his field. But André also tells her that her book failed because she wrote it following the rule of the clinamen. "You set off with a sterile ambition–an ambition of doing something quite new and of excelling yourself."[96] In other words, it is an absolute negation of her previous literary work. For his sake as much as her own, the woman admits that she will write again and that she will find a new way to exist with her son and his wife, to recognize their subjectivity, their independence from her objectification, which is her negation of them. In short, she will learn to love her son and his wife, to accept that the same stars shining down on her and André also shine down on Philippe and Irène, and that her attempted nihilation of them hurts them deeply. She comes to understand that each of them is a crowd and not an atom.

Still, Beauvoir cautions, this is not enough. The dilemmas of time and age expose the failure of our entire civilization. André suggests to the woman philosopher, his companion and partner, that from a self-regarding point of view she may not be able to fulfill her ambition for something quite new (echoes of the clinamen), but that she can still interest readers, she can influence them, make them think, and enrich them. But even when our projects aim at goals that lie beyond the limits of a self-regarding atomistic point of view, what hope do we have that our efforts will not be lost? For men and women who are the least exploited, who can make a place for the Other within, it is a matter of breaking the silence between them, of finding one another again, and of not looking too far ahead. When the the couple sits under the stars, their hands touching, time stops and the fears of old age are allayed by the good fortune of their being together. This is their love; this is how they love one another. Apart from this, they decide to live for the short term. There is no question for them of achieving eternal fame, so that the increased pace of civilization, whereby the present is outdated and lost even before it becomes the past, does not overwhelm them.[97]

But beyond this fortunate pair, fortunate in having interesting work and loving one another, living is a often matter of the exploitation of some groups of human beings by others. Among those who have been most exploited, aging harshly reveals that "the meaning of . . . [their] existence has been stolen from . . . [them] from the very beginning," and that although women and men are allowed to reproduce life, they are not given the opportunity to commit themselves to projects that "people the world with goals, values and reasons for existence."[98] Life without culture, interests, and responsibilities denies transcendence; it denies ambiguity. In order to embrace ambiguity, each and every human being should not look to the future alone and empty-handed. Ambiguity demands that society look upon women and men as useful and mutually influencing at every age, not as atoms able to be negated by other atoms, but as part of a collective in which even the old can be fulfilled as they renew their lives, opening themselves to the other within, and relieve themselves of the weight of the past.[99]

What we are proposing, then, is that although the classical model of nature and the formalist, postmodern framework have suggested an ontology of the new, this is not an ontology that makes it possible to live and act in an ethical manner. We are suggesting that for some situations, for those human encounters where cause and effect matter, where reference makes possible truth and falsity, where choices are made and consequences acknowledged, in these situations, a logic of ambiguity, an acceptance of intuitionism, the admission of the past into the present, the open future, the mutual influence of nonatomistic persons and events, all of this becomes urgently thinkable as we reconceive what it means to be a person and how each of us might be a crowd.

NOTES

PREFACE

Jean-François Lyotard, *The Postmodern Condition, A Report on Knowledge,* trans. Geoff Bennington and Brian Massumi (Minneapolis: University of Minnesota Press, 1984), p. xxiii.

1. Vladimir Tasić, *Mathematics and the Roots of Postmodern Thought* (Oxford: Oxford University Press, 2001), p. 7. Tasić is a mathematician and also writes fiction.

2. Tasić, *Mathematics and the Roots,* p. 8.

3. Tasić, *Mathematics and the Roots,* p. 11.

4. Lyotard, *The Postmodern Condition,* pp. xxiii–xxiv.

5. Lyotard, *The Postmodern Condition,* p. xxiv.

6. Tasić, *Mathematics and the Roots,* p. 129–30.

7. Manfred Frank, *What Is Neostructuralism?,* trans. Sabine Wilke and Richard Gray (Minneapolis: University of Minnesota Press, 1989), p. 217.

8. Tasić, *Mathematics and the Roots,* pp. 131, 136.

9. Frank, *What Is Neostructuralism?,* p. 212.

10. Frank, *What Is Neostructuralism?,* pp. 212–3.

11. Frank, *What Is Neostructuralism?,* p. 213.

12. Tasić, *Mathematics and the Roots,* p. 27.

13. Frank, *What Is Neostructuralism?,* pp. 215–28 for a full account of this.

14. Tasić, *Mathematics and the Roots,* p. 26.

15. Sundar Sarukkai, "Revisiting the 'Unreasonable Effectiveness' of Mathematics," *Current Science* 88, no. 3 (February 10, 2005): pp. 425–23, 417.

16. Tasić *Mathematics and the Roots,* p. 12.

17. Tasić, *Mathematics and the Roots,* p. 13.

18. Edmund Husserl, *Cartesian Meditations, An Introduction to Phenomenology,* trans. Dorian Cairnes (The Hague: Martinus Nijhoff, 1973), pp. 78–79.

19. Husserl, *Cartesian Meditations,* p. 79.

20. Husserl, *Cartesian Meditations,* pp. 79–80.

21. Husserl, *Cartesian Meditations,* p. 80.

22. Husserl, *Cartesian Meditations,* pp. 80–81.

23. Husserl, *Cartesian Meditations,* p. 81.

24. Sarukkai, "Revisiting," p. 417.

25. Sarukkai, "Revisiting," p. 417. Quoted in C. Parsons, "Mathematical Intuition," in *Philosophy of Mathematics: An Anthology,* ed. D. Jacquette, p. 277 (Oxford: Blackwell, 2002).

26. Sarukkai, "Revisiting," p. 417.

27. Tasić, *Mathematics and the Roots,* pp. 31, 27.

28. Bruno Latour, *We Have Never Been Modern,* trans. Catherine Porter (Cambridge, Mass.: Harvard University Press, 1993), pp. 27–28.

29. Latour, *We Have Never Been Modern,* p. 144.

30. Latour, *We Have Never Been Modern,* p. 135. Given Tasić's evaluation of Foucault, Latour seems to be reworking the ground Foucault opened up in his early work.

31. Tasić, *Mathematics and the Roots,* p. 67.

32. Paul Bernays, "Hilbert's Significance for the Philosophy of Mathematics," in *From Brouwer to Hilbert, The Debate on the Foundations of Mathematics in the 1920's,* ed. Paolo Mancosu, pp. 189–197, 189 (Oxford: Oxford University Press, 1998). Bernays (1988–1977) was a Swiss mathematician who worked as an assistant to Hilbert, who made significant contributions to axiomatic set theory.

33. Bernays, "Hilbert's Significance," p. 189.

34. Bernays, "Hilbert's Significance," p. 190.

35. Bernays, "Hilbert's Significance," p. 191.

36. Bernays, "Hilbert's Significance," pp. 191–92.

37. Bernays, "Hilbert's Significance," p. 192.

38. Bernays, "Hilbert's Significance," p. 192.

39. Bernays, "Hilbert's Significance," pp. 192–93.

40. Bernays, "Hilbert's Significance," p. 193.

41. Bernays, "Hilbert's Significance," p. 193.

42. Bernays, "Hilbert's Significance," p. 193.

43. Bernays, "Hilbert's Significance," p. 195. Bernays states this in a slightly different form. He says that it must be impossible to derive the relation that 1 is different from 1.

44. Tasić, *Mathematics and the Roots*, p. 70.

45. Bernays, "Hilbert's Significance," pp. 195–96.

46. Tasić, *Mathematics and the Roots*, p. 67.

47. See http://finitary.ask define.com/ (accessed February 28, 2011).

48. Tasić, *Mathematics and the Roots*, p. 72.

49. Tasić, *Mathematics and the Roots*, p. 75.

50. Tasić, *Mathematics and the Roots*, pp. 75–76.

51. Tasić, *Mathematics and the Roots*, p. 79.

52. Tasić, *Mathematics and the Roots*, p. 83.

53. Tasić, *Mathematics and the Roots*, p. 87.

54. Tasić, *Mathematics and the Roots*, pp. 87–88.

55. Tasić, *Mathematics and the Roots*, p. 89.

56. Tasić, *Mathematics and the Roots*, p. 89.

57. Tasić, *Mathematics and the Roots*, pp. 95–96.

58. Tasić, *Mathematics and the Roots*, p. 97.

59. Tasić, *Mathematics and the Roots*, p. 114.

1. NATURE CALLS

1. Alan D. Sokal, "Transgressing the Boundaries, Towards a Transformative Hermeneutics of Quantum Gravity," *Social Text* no. 46/47 (Spring/Summer 1996): pp. 217–252. The complete text can be viewed online at: http://www.physics.nyu.edu/faculty/sokal/transgress_v2/transgress_v2_singlefile.html. Sokal is professor of physics at New York University. My own interest in Sokal's criticism increased when I realized that an essay in a book I co-edited with my esteemed colleague Constantin Boundas was one of Sokal's targets.

2. Sokal, "Transgressing the Boundaries," p. 217.

3. Steven Weinberg, "Sokal's Hoax," *The New York Review of Books* XLIII, no. 13 (August 8, 1996): pp. 11–15. Emphasis added. Available online at: http://www.physics.nyu.edu/sokal/weinberg.html.

4. Sokal, "Transgressing the Boundaries," p. 217.

5. Richard DeWitt, *Worldviews, An Introduction to the History and Philosophy of Science* (London: Blackwell, 2004), p. 3. The author, Richard DeWitt, is a specialist in the history and philosophy of science, mathematical and philosophical logic, and philosophy of mind.

6. DeWitt, *Worldviews,* table of contents.

7. See for example, David J. Depew and Bruce H. Weber, *Darwinism Evolving: Systems Dynamics and the Genealogy of Natural Selection* (Cambridge, Mass.: MIT Press, 1995), and Eric D. Schneider and Dorian Sagan, *Into the Cool, Energy Flow, Thermodynamics and Life* (Chicago: University of Chicago Press, 2005).

8. J. Bricmont, "Science of Chaos or Chaos in Science?," *Physicalia Magazine* 17 (1995): p. 17. Bricmont is a theoretical physicist in Belgium.

9. Edwin Arthur Burtt, *The Metaphysical Foundations of Modern Physical Science* (Atlantic Highlands, N.J.: Humanities Press, 1952), p. 75. Burtt taught philosophy at the University of Chicago and Cornell University. He cites Galileo, *Dialogues Concerning the Two Great Systems of the World,* p. 40, and "Letter to the Grand Duchess Christina" (1615) in Thomas Salusbury, *Mathematical Collections and Translations,* vol. 1 (London, 1661).

10. Bruce Robbins, "Just Doing Your Job: Some Lessons of the Sokal Affair," *Yale Journal of Criticism* 10, no. 2 (Fall 1997): pp. 467–74. Reprinted by Editors of Lingua Franca, *The Sokal Hoax, The Sham That Shook the Academy* (Lincoln: University of Nebraska Press, 2000), pp. 234–42.

11. Barbara Epstein, "Postmodernism and the Left," originally published in *New Politics: A Journal of Socialist Thought* (Winter 1997): pp. 130–44. Reprinted by the Editors of Lingua Franca, *The Sokal Hoax,* pp 214–29. Epstein is a professor in the History of Consciousness program at UC Santa Cruz.

12. Epstein, "Postmodernism and the Left," pp. 218–19.

13. Tasić, *Mathematics and the Roots,* pp. 87–89.

14. Epstein, "Postmodernism and the Left," p. 219. Epstein cites Joan W. Scott's article "Experience," in Judith Butler and Joan W. Scott, eds., *Feminists Theorize the Political* (New York: Routledge Press, 1992), pp. 22–40, which suggests that the word "experience" is dangerous and opens the way to essentialism and foundationalism (p. 220).

15. Werner Heisenberg, *The Physicist's Conception of Nature,* trans. Arnold J. Pomerans (New York: Harcourt Brace, 1958), pp. 28, 29. Cited in Sokal, "Transgressing the Boundaries," p. 219.

16. Steven Strogatz, "Guest Column: Loves Me, Loves Me Not (Do the Math)," *New York Times*, May 26, 2009, http://judson.blogs.nytimes.com/2009/05/26/guest-column-loves-me-loves-me-not-do-the-math/.

17. Michel Foucault, *Power/Knowledge, Selected Interviews and Other Writings, 1972–1977* (New York: Pantheon Books, 1980), in *The Sokal Hoax*, p. 218. Of equal importance to Epstein is that postmodernism lost its political and social functions and became a largely academic practice.

18. Foucault, *Power/Knowledge*, pp. 82, 80.

19. Foucault, *Power/Knowledge*, pp. 82, 83. Emphases added.

20. Foucault, *Power/Knowledge*, pp. 84, 85, 86. Genealogy doesn't battle institutions directly; rather, it battles the effects of the power of scientific discourse.

21. Foucault, *Power/Knowledge*, p. 90. Political power suspends war but reinscribes warfare in social institutions, economic inequalities, language, and in bodies.

22. Cited in Epstein, "Postmodernism and the Left," p. 222–23.

23. Epstein, "Postmodernism and the Left," p. 223. Emphasis mine. Epstein goes on to regret the "ingroupyness" and concern with who is in and who is out of the intellectual elite that she thinks characterize postmodernists.

24. Meera Nanda, "The Science Wars in India," in *The Sokal Hoax*, pp. 205–13, 206. Originally published in *Dissent* (Winter 1997). See also Meera Nanda, *Prophets Facing Backward: Postmodern Critiques of Science and the Hindu Nationalism in India* (New Brunswick, N.J.: Rutgers University Press, 2004).

25. Nanda, *Prophets Facing Backward*, p. 146.

26. Nanda, *Prophets Facing Backward*, p. 149. These arguments put Nanda in the daunting position of facing down nearly the entire feminist epistemological enterprise.

27. Nanda, *Prophets Facing Backward*, p. 150.

28. Nanda, "The Science Wars in India," in *The Sokal Hoax*, p. 207.

29. Nanda, "The Science Wars in India," in *The Sokal Hoax*, p. 209.

30. Nanda, "The Science Wars in India," in *The Sokal Hoax*, p. 210.

31. Nanda, "The Science Wars in India," in *The Sokal Hoax*, p. 212. Nanda states that Western social constructionist peers have argued that her desire to prove that traditional knowledge is incorrect is a product of her training in biology and that Western science has no democracy-enhancing potential.

32. Paul Boghossian, *Fear of Knowledge, Against Relativism and Constructivism* (Oxford: Clarendon Press, 2006), p. 2.

33. Paul Boghossian, "What the Sokal Hoax Ought to Teach Us," in *The Sokal Hoax,* pp. 174–75. One might find interesting correlations, but as the philosopher David Hume made clear, so far we have not discovered how to prove that physical relations or facts cause mental ones.

34. Boghossian, "What the Sokal Hoax Ought to Teach Us," p. 176.

35. Boghossian, *Fear of Knowledge,* p. 60.

36. See DeWitt, *Worldviews,* pp. 115–24, for a clear account of the Ptolemaic system.

37. Richard Rorty, *Philosophy and the Mirror of Nature* (Princeton, N.J.: Princeton University Press, 1981), pp. 330–31. Cited in Boghossian, *Fear of Knowledge,* pp. 60–62.

38. Boghossian, *Fear of Knowledge,* p. 103. Boghossian overlooks the mathematical substantiation that the Ptolemaic system offers and thereby weakens his own argument, relying only on scripture and observation.

39. Bricmont, "Science of Chaos or Chaos in Science?," p. 11, note 29. Bricmont objects to Stengers' view that ideological claims are operative when thermodynamic entropy is reintegrated with the classical time reversibility of dynamical systems.

40. Isabelle Stengers, *The Invention of Modern Science,* trans. Daniel Smith (Minneapolis: University of Minnesota Press, 2000), p. 64.

41. Stengers, *The Invention of Modern Science,* pp. 6–8.

42. Edmund Husserl, *The Crisis of European Sciences and Transcendental Phenomenology,* trans. David Carr (Evanston, Ill.: Northwestern University Press, 1970), pp. 23–25. Emphasis added.

43. Husserl, *The Crisis,* p. 24. Perhaps too little attention has been paid to Husserl's analysis of what he calls physicalist objectivism.

44. Burtt, *The Metaphysical Foundations,* p. 77. Burtt cites Galileo, "Letter to Kepler, 1610," in Oliver Lodge, *Pioneers of Science* (London: 1913), ch. 4.

45. Tasić, *Mathematics and the Roots,* p. 13.

46. Stengers, *The Invention of Modern Science,* pp. 73, 83. This is particularly interesting in that Galileo presents his arguments in the form of a fictionalized debate between two scientists but then also in the form of a description of his demonstrations.

47. Galileo Galilei, *Dialogues Concerning Two New Sciences*, trans. Henry Crew and Alfonso de Salvio (New York: Dover Books, 1954), pp. 178–79. Galileo's own description of this process is far easier to follow than many explanations of it.

48. Stengers, *The Invention of Modern Science*, pp. 83, 84.

49. Margaret Benz Hull, *The Hidden Philosophy of Hannah Arendt* (New York: Routledge Press, 2002), p. 1. Hull cites Hannah Arendt, *The Human Condition* (Chicago: University of Chicago Press, 1998), p. 17.

50. Hull, *The Hidden Philosophy*, pp. 2–3.

51. Hull, *The Hidden Philosophy* p. 51, citing Arendt, *The Human Condition*, p. 8.

52. Hull, *The Hidden Philosophy*, p. 55.

53. Hull, *The Hidden Philosophy*, p. 28. See Hannah Arendt, *Lectures on Kant's Political Philosophy*, ed. Ronald Beiner (Chicago: University of Chicago Press, 1982), p. 67.

54. Hull, *The Hidden Philosophy*, p. 53.

55. Hull, *The Hidden Philosophy*, pp. 41–42. See Hannah Arendt and Karl Jaspers, *Correspondence: 1926–1969*, ed. Lotte Kohler, trans. Peter Constantine (New York: Harcourt, Inc. 1992), p. 166.

56. Hull, *The Hidden Philosophy*, p. 42. See Hannah Arendt, "Philosophy and Politics," *Social Research* 57, no. 1 (Spring 1990): pp. 73–103, 80.

57. Hull, *The Hidden Philosophy*, p. 43.

58. Hannah Arendt, *The Life of the Mind, One/Thinking* (New York: Harcourt Brace Jovanovich, 1977), pp. 41–42.

59. Arendt, *The Life of the Mind*, pp. 39, 42.

60. Arendt, *The Life of the Mind*, p. 49. This notion is equivalent to Deleuze's conception of percepts and affects as blocks of becoming.

61. Arendt, *The Life of the Mind*, p. 62.

62. Arendt, *The Life of the Mind*, p. 48.

63. Arendt, *The Life of the Mind*, p. 52.

64. Arendt, *The Life of the Mind*, p. 59, 60.

65. Arendt, *The Life of the Mind*, pp. 64–65. Immanuel Kant, *Critique of Pure Reason*, trans. Norman Kemp Smith, (New York: St. Martin's Press, 1965), A70–71; B95–96.

66. Arendt, *The Human Condition*, p. 278.

67. Arendt, *The Human Condition*, p. 324.

68. Contrasting views of Arendt's *The Human Condition*, especially criticisms coming from feminist theorists, are presented by Mary G. Dietz in "Feminist Receptions of Hannah Arendt," in *Feminist Interpretations of Hannah Arendt*, ed. Bonnie Honig, pp. 17–50 (University Park: Penn State University Press, 1995).

69. Arendt, *The Human Condition*, p. 12.

70. Arendt, *The Human Condition*, pp. 13, 22. Aristotle, *Nichomachean Ethics*, i.5, 1096a5.

71. Arendt, *The Human Condition*, p. 14.

72. Arendt, *The Human Condition*, p. 15. Arendt cites F. M. Cornford, *Unwritten Philosophy* (1950), p. 54, for the idea that the death of Pericles and the Peloponnesian War mark the divergence of men of thought from men of action.

73. Arendt, *The Human Condition*, p. 19.

74. Arendt, *The Human Condition*, pp. 20–21.

75. Arendt, *The Human Condition*, pp. 22–23.

76. Arendt has been condemned for her general view of the Greeks by Mary O'Brien, Adrienne Rich, and Wendy Brown. See Mary G. Dietz's account in "Feminist Receptions of Hannah Arendt," in *Feminist Interpretations of Hannah Arendt*, ed. Bonnie Honig, pp. 23–26 (University Park: Penn State University Press, 1995).

77. Arendt, *The Human Condition*, pp. 24, 25.

78. Arendt, *The Human Condition*, p. 26.

79. Arendt, *The Human Condition*, p. 30.

80. Arendt, *The Human Condition*, p. 31.

81. Arendt, *The Human Condition*, pp. 30, 33.

82. Arendt, *The Human Condition*, p. 32.

83. Jean-Pierre Vernant, *The Origins of Greek Thought* (Ithaca, N.Y.: Cornell University Press, 1982), p. 70. Curiously, this process was the result of a reversal of a society governed by speech, unanimity, and a balance of forces, such that "those who made up the city, however different in origin, rank, and function, appeared somehow to be 'like' one another" (p. 60).

84. Vernant, *The Origins of Greek Thought*, p. 53.

85. Vernant, *The Origins of Greek Thought*, p. 64.

86. Vernant, *The Origins of Greek Thought*, p. 75.

87. Arendt, *The Human Condition*, p. 37.

88. Vernant, *The Origins of Greek Thought*, p. 77. Aristotle, *Politics*, 1252b15.

89. Vernant, *The Origins of Greek Thought*, p. 78.

90. Plato, *Republic*, trans. G. M. A. Grube, rev. C. D. C. Reeve in *Plato, Complete Works* (Indianapolis, Ind.: Hackett Publishing, 1997).

91. Arendt, *The Human Condition*, p. 83.

92. Karl Marx, "What Are Wages, How Are They Determined?," in *Wage, Labour and Capital* (Marx/Engels Internet Archive [marxists.org] 1993, 1999): http://www.marxists.org/archive/marx/works/1847/wage-labour/ch02.htm.

93. Arendt, *The Human Condition*, p. 88.

94. Karl Marx, *Economic & Philosophical Manuscripts of 1844*, trans. Martin Mulligan, http://www.marxists.org/archive/marx/works/1844/manuscripts/wages.htm.

95. Karl Marx and Friedrich Engels, *Marx/Engels Selected Works, Volume One* (Moscow: Progress Publishers, 1969), pp. 98–137. Marx/Engels Internet Archive (marxists.org) (1987, 2000): http://www.marxists.org/archive/marx/works/1848/communist-manifesto/ch01.htm.

96. Arendt, *The Human Condition*, pp. 88–89.

97. Arendt, *The Human Condition*, p. 93.

98. Arendt, *The Human Condition*, p. 267.

99. Arendt, *The Human Condition*, pp. 265–66, 268.

100. Arendt points out that in the *Symposium*, the beautiful, what shines forth, is the highest form, but later Plato substitutes the notion of the ideas as standards, measurements, even rules of behavior, thereby eliminating frailty from human affairs and giving the philosopher's deeds and words the same objective certainty given to craftsmen who recall the form of a table in order to make a table (Arendt, *The Human Condition*, pp. 225–26).

101. Burtt, *The Metaphysical Foundations*, p. 76. See Galileo Galilei, *Dialogues and Mathematical Demonstrations*, p. 276.

102. Arendt, *The Human Condition*, p. 267. That the distanced point of view has often been confused with single-point perspective has caused some misunderstandings, so it is important to make the point that the Archimedean point of view is not the same as single-point perspective.

103. Husserl, *The Crisis*, p. 32.

104. Husserl, *The Crisis*, p. 41. Husserl stresses that idealizing and mathematizing proceeds as the methodical objectification of the intuitively given

world. The question of intuition will be addressed but here the emphasis is on mathematical idealization.

105. Arendt, *The Human Condition*, p. 266.

106. Morris Klein, *Mathematics in Western Culture* (New York: Galaxy Books, 1964), p. 184. Rather than explaining why something occurs, as the Greeks and medievals did, Galileo sought a functional relationship, a relation between variables that hold in practically every sphere (p. 185).

107. Klein, *Mathematics*, p. 165.

108. Klein, *Mathematics*, p. 170. "The equation of any curve is an algebraic equality which is satisfied by the co-ordinates of all points on the curve but not by the co-ordinates of any other point."

109. Arendt, *The Human Condition*, p. 266. Arendt cites Burtt, *The Metaphysical Foundations*, p. 106. Emphasis added.

110. Husserl, *The Crisis*, pp. 43–44. Husserl points out that this is Leibniz's idea of a *mathesis universalis*, the science of calculable order whose method is algebra.

111. Arendt, *The Human Condition*, p. 269. Arendt calls this universal science not natural science.

112. Arendt, *The Human Condition*, p. 266. Arendt calls this the Archimedean viewpoint. The argument that the mathematical treatment of the universe lends itself to no philosophical significance was made by Bertrand Russell and anticipates the view of contemporary physicists cited above. Arendt cites J. W. N. Sullivan, *Limitations of Science* (New York: Mentor Books), p. 144.

113. Husserl, *The Crisis*, pp. 42–50. "To it, the world of actually experiencing intuition, belongs the form of space-time together with all the bodily [*körperlick*] shapes incorporated in it; it is in this world that we ourselves live in accord with our bodily [*leiblich*], personal way of being. But here we find nothing of geometrical idealities, no geometrical space or mathematical time with all their shapes" (p. 50).

114. Husserl, *The Crisis*, p. 50.

115. Burtt, *The Metaphysical Foundations*, p. 83. In other words, the distinction between primary and secondary qualities arises.

116. Burtt, The *Metaphysical Foundations*, pp. 83–84. Burtt cites Galileo Galilei, *Opere Complete di Galilei Galilei*, 15 vols. (Firenze 1842), vol. IV, 333, ff. See also Husserl, *The Crisis*, p. 54,

117. Husserl, *The Crisis*, p. 54.

118. Arendt, *The Human Condition*, p. 268.

2. THE NATURAL CONTRACT AND THE ARCHIMEDEAN WORLDVIEW

1. Michel Serres, *The Natural Contract,* trans. Elizabeth MacArthur and William Paulson (Ann Arbor: University of Michigan Press, 1995), p. 22. Originally published in French as *Le Contrat Natural* (Paris: Editions François Bourin, 1992).

2. Serres, *The Natural Contract,* p. 22. As we will see, for Serres this perpetuates a certain originary violence, directed this time against Nature, rather than a Hobbesian war of all against all.

3. Serres, *The Natural Contract,* pp. 8–9. Whether this noise comes from God or society is not clear.

4. Serres, *The Natural Contract,* p. 10. In other words, for Serres, so-called subjective wars between master and slave have been transformed into objective violence against the objective world.

5. Serres, *The Natural Contract,* pp. 12, 14, 21. The conflation of the repetitive dynamics of violence with Nature is questionable. See Thomas Hobbes, *Leviathan* (New York: MacMillan Publishing, 1962).

6. Serres, *The Natural Contract,* p. 20. Perhaps this overestimation of humankind's importance arises from the dialectics. One finds it also, for example, in the neoconservative dialectics of Francis Fukuyama (see below).

7. Arendt, *The Human Condition,* p. 285. Arendt calls this scenario a nightmare, a dreamed world where every dream is real only as long as the dream lasts (p. 286).

8. Serres, *The Natural Contract,* p. 35. Serres' lack of any distinction between science and technology throughout is a limitation of his argument.

9. Serres, *The Natural Contract,* pp. 40–41. The identification of Nature's elements and women is of particular interest, especially as it is one of the few references to women anywhere in this text. The original image of men at sea who must cooperate is Plato's, in *Republic.*

10. Serres, *The Natural Contract,* p. 58.

11. Klein, *Mathematics,* p. 216.

12. Burtt, *The Metaphysical Foundations,* p. 231.

13. Burtt, *The Metaphysical Foundations,* p. 132. Hobbes, *Leviathan,* Bk. 1, Ch. 1.

14. David Ruelle, *Chance and Chaos* (Princeton, N.J.: Princeton University Press, 1991), p. 26. Ruelle is professor of theoretical physics at the *Institut des Hautes Etudes Scientifique,* Bures-sur-Yevettes, France.

15. Ruelle, *Chance and Chaos*, p. 28. The concept of forces is difficult to comprehend, even for physicists.

16. Ruelle, *Chance and Chaos*, p. 28.

17. Burtt, *The Metaphysical Foundations*, p. 244. Isaac Newton, *The Mathematical Principles of Natural Philosophy*, 3 vols., trans. Motte (London: 1803), vol. I, section 9.

18. Depew and Weber, *Darwinism Evolving*, p. 25.

19. Ruelle, *Chance and Chaos*, pp. 28, 29.

20. Ruelle, *Chance and Chaos*, p. 29. Ruelle cites Pierre Simon Laplace, *Essais philosophique sur les probabilitiés* (Paris: Coucier, 1814). Analysis is another term for differential calculus.

21. Depew and Weber, *Darwinism Evolving*, p. 25.

22. Depew and Weber, *Darwinism Evolving*, p. 25.

23. Burtt, *The Metaphysical Foundations*, p. 231. Sir Isaac Newton, *Opticks, or, A Treatise of the Reflections, Refractions, Inflections and Colors of Light*, 3rd ed. (London: 1721), p. 376.

24. Depew and Weber, *Darwinism Evolving*, p. 25.

25. This is the position of William Harper, noted philosopher of science, as expressed in chapter 1 of his forthcoming book on scientific method, *Isaac Newton's Scientific Method: Turning Data into Evidence about Gravity and Cosmology* (Oxford: Oxford University Press, 2011).

26. Isaac Newton, "Rules of Reasoning in Philosophy," in *The World of Physics, Volume 1, The Aristotelean Cosmos and the Newtonian System*, ed. Jefferson Hane Weaver (New York: Simon and Schuster, 1987), p. 508.

27. Harper, *Isaac Newton's Scientific Method*, chapter 1.

28. Klein, *Mathematics*, p. 237.

29. Descartes feared being expelled from Holland and having his books burned when a physician who eventually became the rector of the University of Utrech objected to "Cartesian ideas." See Kurt Smith, "Descartes' Life and Work," revised 02/27/07. http://plato.stanford.edu/entries/descartes-works/. Smith also writes, "Specifically, the Cartesian view denies that physics is grounded in hot, cold, wet, and dry. It argues that contrary to Aristotle's view, such 'qualities' are not properties of bodies at all. Rather, the only properties of bodies with which the physicist can concern him or herself are size, shape, motion, position, and so on–those modifications that conceptually (or logically) entail extension in length, breadth, and depth. In contrast to Aristotle's 'qualities,' the properties (or modes) of

bodies dealt with in Cartesian physics are measurable specifically on ratio scales (as opposed to intensive scales), and hence are subject in all the right ways to mathematics" (Jill Buroker, "Descartes On Sensible Qualities," *Journal of The History of Philosophy* XXIX, no. 4 [October 1991]: pp. 585–611, 596–97).

30. Jefferson Hane Weaver, ed. "Introduction," in *The World of Physics, Volume 1, The Aristotelean Cosmos and the Newtonian System* (New York: Simon and Schuster, 1987), p. 20.

31. The empirical observations were those of Tycho Brahe. Weaver, "Introduction," p. 20.

32. Klein, *Mathematics,* pp. 238, 239.

33. DeWitt, *Worldviews,* p. 3.

34. John Locke, *Second Treatise of Government* (Indianapolis, Ind.: Hackett Books, 1980), p. 8. "In Nature, there is a state of perfect freedom . . . within the bounds of the law of Nature. . . . In a state of equality, no one has more power or jurisdiction than another."

35. Locke, *Second Treatise,* p. 8.

36. Locke, *Second Treatise,* p. 8.

37. Locke, *Second Treatise,* p. 9.

38. Arendt, *The Human Condition,* p. 111.

39. Arendt, *The Human Condition,* p. 111.

40. Arendt, *The Human Condition,* p. 12.

41. Arendt, *The Human Condition,* p. 14.

42. Contrary to the claim made by Hannah Fenichel Pitkin in "Conformism, Housekeeping, and the Attack of the Blob: The Origins of Hannah Arendt's Concept of the Social," in *Feminist Interpretations of Hannah Arendt,* ed. Bonnie Honig, pp. 51–81 (University Park: Penn State University Press, 1995), that Arendt does not define society and the social in *The Human Condition,* Arendt offers a well-developed concept of the origins and meaning of society. The claim that the true meaning of the concept of the social can only be discovered in Arendt's biography commits the intentional fallacy, but also denigrates Arendt as a philosopher.

43. Arendt, *The Human Condition,* p. 40. Thus the public sphere took on, more and more, the characteristics of the private household.

44. Arendt, *The Human Condition,* p. 41. In other words, great words and deeds were no longer valued or even appreciated.

45. Arendt, *The Human Condition,* p. 40.

46. Arendt, *The Human Condition*, p. 41.

47. Arendt, *The Human Condition*, pp. 42–43.

48. Arendt, *The Human Condition*, p. 45. Adam Smith, *The Wealth of Nations* (New York: Bantam Books, 2003).

49. Arendt, *The Human Condition*, p. 46. It is difficult to believe that Arendt's remarkable thesis, so cogent and so well-documented, has received so little attention to this day. It is not simply of historical interest, it is perhaps of the greatest philosophical importance in today's so-called culture wars between natural science and the social sciences and humanities. How did politics, in other words, philosophy, become embedded in science? Are we willing to do something about this? This might be a more important question than has been obvious for a long time.

50. Arendt, *The Human Condition*, p. 47.

51. Arendt, *The Human Condition*, pp. 68–69.

52. Fukuyama, *The End of History and the Last Man* (New York: Free Press 1992), p. 193. See G. W. F. Hegel. *Phenomenology of Mind*, trans. J. B. Baillie (London: 1931).

53. Fukuyama, *The End of History and the Last Man*, p. 194. See Hegel, *Phenomenology of Mind*.

54. Fukuyama, *The End of History and the Last Man*, p. 194. One wonders what the modern natural scientist would think about this claim made by their contemporary.

55. DeWitt, *Worldviews*, p. 9.

56. Burtt, *The Metaphysical Foundations*, p. 220. Burtt cites a letter from Newton to Oldenburg.

57. Locke, *Second Treatise*, Ch. V; Fukuyama, *The End of History and the Last Man*, p. 72.

58. Fukuyama, *The End of History and the Last Man*, ch. 3. Fukuyama is generally associated with the neoconservative position. He endorses, from a dialectical point of view, the mastery of the Earth, just as Serres opposes it from the same point of view.

59. Serres, *The Natural Contract*, pp. 36–37.

60. See especially, John Locke, *Second Treatise*, Ch. III, sect. 16, and all of Ch. V.

61. Fukuyama, *The End of History and the Last Man*, pp. 72–73, 76. Although it is often stated that "[t]he greatest improvements in the productive powers of labour, and the greater part of the skill, dexterity, and judgment,

with which it is anywhere directed, or applied, seem to have been the effects of the division of labour," nevertheless, "when the division of labour has been once thoroughly established, it is but a very small part of a man's wants which the produce of his own labour can supply." Smith, *The Wealth of Nations*, Bk I, ch. 1; Bk I, p. 7.

62. Depew and Weber, *Darwinism Evolving*, p. 74.

63. Arendt, *The Human Condition*, p. 42, note 35. Marx's economic system is more consistent and coherent, more scientific, precisely because it substitutes a generic socialized man for the self-interested man of liberal economics.

64. Depew and Weber, *Darwinism Evolving*, p. 116.

65. Depew and Weber, *Darwinism Evolving*, p. 116.

66. Smith, *The Wealth of Nations*, pp. 2–3.

67. Smith, *The Wealth of Nations*, p. 4.

68. Smith, *The Wealth of Nations*, p. 15.

69. Smith, *The Wealth of Nations*, p. 24.

70. Arendt, *The Human Condition*, p. 88, 90. See Karl Marx, *Wage, Labour and Capital* (Marx/Engels Internet Archive [marxists.org] 1993, 1999): http://www.marxists.org/archive/marx/works/1847/wage-labour/ch02.htm.

71. Arendt, *The Human Condition*, pp. 88–89. See Smith, *The Wealth of Nations*, p. 241.

72. Fukuyama, *The End of History and the Last Man*, p. 77.

73. Fukuyama, *The End of History and the Last Man*, pp. 77–78.

74. Arendt, *The Human Condition*, pp. 255–256. This is the manner in which world alienation has been the "hallmark of the modern age" (p. 254).

75. Frederic L. Bender, *The Culture of Extinction, Toward a Philosophy of Deep Ecology* (New York: Humanity Books, 2003), p. 247. Bender cites Burtt, *The Metaphysical Foundations*, pp. 224–25.

3. SEMI-FREE

1. Arendt, *The Human Condition*, p. 264. Arendt attributes this insight to Ernst Cassirer, *Einstein's Theory of Relativity* (New York: Dover Books, 1953).

2. DeWitt, *Worldviews*, p. 170, 171.

3. Arendt, *The Human Condition,* pp. 261–64. "Under the sign of earth alienation, every science, not only physical and natural science, so radically changed its innermost content that one may doubt whether prior to the modern age anything like science existed at all" (p. 264).

4. Klein, *Mathematics,* pp. 113–15. Kepler was initially Brahe's assistant. Other of Kepler's hypotheses, based on preconceived ideas of harmony in the universe, failed (pp. 113–14; DeWitt, *Worldviews,* p. 141). Brahe gathered, especially, a large amount of empirical data on the observed position of Mars. It is this data that Kepler inherited.

5. Klein, *Mathematics,* p. 237. "Harvey's proof that the blood circulates around the body before returning to the heart reinforced this mechanistic view because it likened the body to a pumping plant with the heart as the pump" (p. 238). Klein refers to La Mettrie (biology), Francois Quesnay (economics), and d'Holback (consciousness).

6. Klein, *Mathematics,* p. 241. Klein points out that Leibniz founded symbolic logic as part of an attempt to represent all ideas symbolically.

7. Klein, *Mathematics,* p. 241.

8. See Kenny Easwaran, "The Role of Axioms in Mathematics," in *Erkentniss* (Netherlands. Kluwer Academic Publishers, 2007), pp. 2–3, http://www.ocf.berkeley.edu/~easwaran/papers/axioms.pdf.

9. Klein, *Mathematics,* p. 243.

10. Klein, *Mathematics,* pp. 24–39. "The Birth of the Mathematical Spirit" is the title of chapter 3 of Klein's book. He cites Lord Kelvin, who called it "the etherealization of common sense" (p. 13).

11. René Descartes, "Rules for the Direction of the Mind," Rule XVI, in *The Philosophical Works of Descartes,* trans. Elizabeth S. Haldane and G. R. T. Ross, vol. I (Cambridge: Cambridge University Press, 1972), pp. 66–67.

12. Descartes, "Rules for the Direction of the Mind," Rule XII, pp. 35, 45.

13. Hobbes, *Leviathan,* pp. 21, 23.

14. Hobbes, *Leviathan,* pp. 28, 33.

15. Hobbes, *Leviathan,* p. 41. This allows politicians to determine men's duties and lawyers to find laws, and to find what is right and wrong in actions.

16. Hobbes, *Leviathan,* p. 41.

17. Hobbes, *Leviathan,* pp. 42, 43, 45.

18. Hobbes, *Leviathan,* p. 43. "I should not say he were in error but that his world were without meaning, that is to say, absurd."

19. Klein, *Mathematics,* p. 245. It seems that Locke was more important in his time than Hume, but in our own Hume is perhaps of greater significance, for reasons I will elaborate.

20. John Locke, *Essay Concerning Human Understanding* (New York: Dover Books, 1959), pp. 121, 122.

21. Locke, *Essay,* p. 123. Only the former is sensation; the latter is reflection.

22. John Locke, *Philosophical Works* (Henry G. Bohn Publisher, 1854), v. 2, Book 4, chapter 4, no. 6.

23. Locke, *Essay,* Book 4, chapter 4, no. 6, p. 172

24. Locke, *Essay,* Book 4, chapter 4, no. 7, p. 172.

25. Locke, *Essay,* Book 4, chapter 4, no. 7, p. 172.

26. Locke, *Essay,* Book 4, chapter 4, no. 8, p. 173. Morality is no less true for not being practiced, Locke claims.

27. Locke, *Essay,* Book 4, chapter 4, no. 8, p. 173. Locke goes on to exclaim that if this were not the case, then everyone would be free to make of the moral or mathematical ideas whatever they please.

28. David Hume, *A Treatise of Human Nature* (Oxford: Oxford University Press, 1968), pp. 87, 75–76. Although in the end, time may be nothing but contiguity.

29. Hume, *A Treatise of Human Nature,* p. 73.

30. Hume, *A Treatise of Human Nature,* p. 400.

31. Ruelle, *Chance and Chaos,* p. 28. Deterministic certainty requires knowledge of forces such as gravity. "For a given system, the forces are at each instant of time determined by the state of the system at this instant. For instance, the force of gravity between two celestial bodies is inversely proportional to the square of the distance between these bodies. Newton now tells us how the variation of the state of a system in the course of time is related to the forces acting on this system."

32. Hume, *A Treatise of Human Nature,* p. 84. Arendt argues that since seventeenth-century scientists had already posited color as a relation to a seeing eye (Galileo) or heaviness a relation of reciprocal acceleration (Newton), the parentage of modern relativism can be traced back to the seventeenth century (Arendt, *The Human Condition,* p. 264).

33. Hume, *A Treatise of Human Nature,* p. 179.

34. Hume, *A Treatise of Human Nature,* p. 91–92.

35. Hume, *A Treatise of Human Nature,* p. 179.

36. Burtt, *The Metaphysical Foundations*, p. 169, 171. The necessity of experimental proofs affirms Hume's skepticism with regard to reason, but ultimately, once added to mathematics, they reinforced its power and authority.

37. Lynn Margulis and Dorian Sagan, "The Universe in Heat," in *What Is Sex?* (New York: Simon & Schuster, 1999), pp. 28–29. Margulis is a well-known evolutionary biologist. Sagan is her son, a science writer. Margulis and Sagan will take this as an argument for a universe that is open and complex.

38. Margulis and Sagan, "The Universe in Heat," p. 31. It was Ludwig Boltzmann (1844–1906) who explained this one-way conversion of energy into heat and friction.

39. Burtt, *The Metaphysical Foundations*, p. 172. Burtt cites Robert Boyle, *The Works of the Honourable Robert Boyle*, 6 vols., ed. Thomas Birch (London, 1672), vol. III, pp. 20, 34, ff.; vol. IV, p. 76, ff.

40. Burtt, *The Metaphysical Foundations*, p. 173. Boyle, *The Works*, vol. III, pp. 429, 13.

41. Burtt, *The Metaphysical Foundations*, p. 177. Boyle, *The Works*, vol. V, p. 177. "I shall express what I call general nature by cosmical mechanism, i.e., a comprisal of all the mechanical affections (figure, size, motion, etc.) that belong to the matter of the great system of the universe."

42. Margulis and Sagan, "The Universe in Heat," p. 29.

43. Eric D. Schneider and Dorian Sagan. *Into the Cool, Energy Flow, Thermodynamics and Life* (Chicago: University of Chicago Press, 2005), p. 26. Schneider is former senior scientist at the National Oceanic and Atmospheric Administration and director of the National Marine Water Quality Laboratory of the EPA. Sagan, as noted above, is a science writer and son of Lynn Margulis, an evolutionary biologist.

44. Schneider and Sagan, *Into the Cool*, pp. 6–7. The meaning of Einstein's equation $E=mc^2$ is precisely the notion that one kind of energy can transform into another, in other words that "matter is a vast potential reservoir of energy" (p. 27).

45. Schneider and Sagan, *Into the Cool*, pp. 28–29. This was documented by Einstein in studies of Brownian motion.

46. Schneider and Sagan, *Into the Cool*, p. 29. They cite astrophysicist Eric Chaisson, *Cosmic Evolution, The Rise of Complexity in Nature* (Cambridge, Mass.: Harvard University Press, 2001).

47. Schneider and Sagan, *Into the Cool*, p. 30. "Edward Lorenz accidentally discovered the field of D chaos while using a computer to model atmospheric trajectories . . . the end points of the trajectories were unpredictable because they were highly dependent on initial conditions and the exact boundary conditions, which could not be determined with enough precision" (p. 30). They cite Garnett Williams, *Chaos Theory Tamed* (Washington, D.C.: Joseph Henry Press, 1977), p. 6.

48. Schneider and Sagan, *Into the Cool*, p. 30. Schneider and Sagan note that demotion of nature's laws into algorithmic rules is a convenience and lure for computational mathematics, but laws are (at least supposed to be) forever, while rules can change. Meioisis, for example, a process of reduction division in which the number of chromosomes per cell is cut in half, did not always exist, but evolved (p. 31).

49. Schneider and Sagan, *Into the Cool*, p. 31.

50. Schneider and Sagan, *Into the Cool*, p. 38. The story of steam engines is perhaps less interesting than the more complex story of organisms.

51. Schneider and Sagan, *Into the Cool*, p. 39.

52. Schneider and Sagan, *Into the Cool*, p. 41.

53. Schneider and Sagan, *Into the Cool*, p. 43. "Burning bright in the forests of night, Blake's tiger uses muscle power drawing sugar energy in the blood, energy stored from the eating of animals feeding on plants, themselves growing off the solar gradient" (p. 43).

54. Isabelle Stengers, *Power and Invention, Situating Science,* trans. Paul Bains (Minneapolis: University of Minnesota Press, 1997), pp. 21–22.

55. Isabelle Stengers and Ilya Prigogine, *Order Out of Chaos, Man's New Dialogue with Nature* (New York: Bantam Books, 1984), p. 61.

56. Stengers, *Power and Invention,* pp. 24, 25. This is the principle of sufficient reason.

57. Stengers, *Power and Invention,* p. 27. The problem with masses of precise data is that usually no theory can handle that much information. This makes idealization, generalization, and approximation a necessity.

58. Stengers, *Power and Invention,* p. 33.

59. Stengers, *Power and Invention,* p. 48.

60. Schneider and Sagan, *Into the Cool*, pp. 47, 48. Ludwig Boltzmann understood that the behavior of heat and gases reflects trends among masses of particles impossible to track individually (p. 45).

61. Ruelle, *Chance and Chaos,* p.113. The ergodic hypothesis still requires a mathematical proof and probably will need to be weakened.

62. Ruell, *Chance and Chaos,* p. 111. The basic or fundamental laws of physics do not include irreversibility, but improbability does factor in (p. 113).

63. Schneider and Sagan, *Into the Cool,* p. 50.

64. Schneider and Sagan, *Into the Cool,* p. 58. The authors point out that it is Jules-Henri Poincaré's recurrence theorem that raises these issues, both for physicists and presumably for Nietzsche. Because of this, Boltzmann came to the conclusion that linear time is the phenomenological experience of beings in certain regions of the universe only (pp. 56–58).

65. See "Love and Hatred," in Dorothea Olkowski, *The Universal (In the Realm of the Sensible)* (Edinburgh and New York: Edinburgh and Columbia University Presses, 2007), chapter 2, for a full explanation of this statement.

66. Margulis and Sagan, "The Universe in Heat," p. 35. Margulis and Sagan point out the amount of mess, garbage, pollution, excrement, etc., the average animal leaves behind, and they argue that local order seems to produce disorder on the edges. They conclude that if this is the case, politicians and governments should be aware of the consequences of order (structure) in an isolated system.

67. Margulis and Sagan, "The Universe in Heat," p. 34.

68. Stengers and Prigogine, *Order Out of Chaos,* p. xxvii.

69. Schneider and Sagan, *Into the Cool,* p. 17.

70. Schneider and Sagan, *Into the Cool,* pp. 15, 16, 18.

71. Schneider and Sagan, *Into the Cool,* p.19.

72. Schneider and Sagan, *Into the Cool,* p. 20. I raise this issue now because I think it will be crucial later in thinking about the limits of a Deleuzian ontology.

73. Schneider and Sagan, *Into the Cool,* p. 21.

74. P. W. Atkins, *The Second Law, Energy, Chaos and Form* (New York: Scientific American Library, 1984), p. viii. Cited in Schneider and Sagan, *Into the Cool,* p. 21. Schneider and Sagan also cite Harold Morowitz, *The Emergence of Everything: How the World Became Complex* (Cambridge: Oxford University Press, 2002), p. 73, for the idea that the molecule "adenine" functions both as a signal for energy transfer and as a major symbolic component of the genetic code. Thus some particles, when they are together, behave as if they have knowledge of one another's presence.

75. Schneider and Sagan, *Into the Cool,* p. 24. In discussions with theoretical physicists, I have found a range of opinions on this subject, includ-

ing the view that this matter was long ago settled. It may be that biologists, chemists, and physicists have rather different views on such matters.

76. Schneider and Sagan, *Into the Cool*, p. 79. The authors attribute this discovery to Alfred Lotka, a physical chemist with an interest in biology. See Alfred Lotka, "The Law of Evolution as a Maximal Principle," *Human Biology* 17 (1945): pp. 167–94.

77. Stengers and Prigogine, *Order Out of Chaos*, p. 12. Equilibrium thermodynamics studies the transformation of energy, and the laws of thermodynamics recognize that although "energy is conserved," when energy is defined as the capacity to do work," nevertheless, nature is fundamentally assymetrical, that is, although the total quantity of energy remains the same, its distribution changes in a manner that is irreversible. See Atkins, *The Second Law*, pp. 8–13; Schneider and Sagan, *Into the Cool*, p. 81; and Ilya Prigogine, *Thermodynamics of Irreversible Processes* (New York: John Wiley and Sons, 1955).

78. Stengers and Prigogine, *Order Out of Chaos*, p. 19. The French title of this book, an earlier and slightly less developed version, reflects the "new alliance" between science and culture

79. Stengers and Prigogine, *Order Out of Chaos*, pp. 19–22.

80. Serres, *The Natural Contract*, pp. 81–83.

81. Stengers and Prigogine, *Order Out of Chaos*, pp. 32–33. Latour picks up this theme from Stengers and Prigogine.

82. Serres, *The Natural Contract*, pp. 82–83. Serres's running together of science and religion, Galileo and Jesus is one of the more disturbing aspects of his analysis. Nature, we will argue, does not make judgments, only humans do. Nature simply appears, leaving humans to understand and interpret these appearances.

83. Stengers and Prigogine, *Order Out of Chaos*, pp. 37–41.

84. Stengers and Prigogine, *Order Out of Chaos*, pp. 42–43.

85. Stengers, *The Invention of Modern Science*, p. 14. Emphasis added. In fencing, to disengage is to perform a maneuver that changes the line of attack.

86. Stengers, *Power and Invention*, pp. 110–11. "I would like to express the deep uneasiness aroused in me by the binary characterization that the modern sciences seem to produce, constructing their identity through opposition with an other" (p. 111).

87. Stengers, *The Invention of Modern Science*, p. 5. Although, as Stengers points out, science does not have the power to make scientists agree with

one another, nevertheless, the concept of a paradigm and of normal science provide both a practical and theoretical model for how to proceed.

88. Stengers, *The Invention of Modern Science*, p. 9. "Do not industry, the state, the army, and commerce all enter into the history of scientific communities on two fronts, both as sources of financing and as beneficiaries of the useful results?" (p. 9).

89. Stengers, *The Invention of Modern Science*, pp. 24, 26. The purification of science led to the idea of a radical break with whatever came before modern science, qualifying the before as nonscience.

90. Stengers, *The Invention of Modern Science*, p. 49. "A great number of actors, all of whom have been, in one way or another, produced by the text, undertake to draw lessons from it. All are situated in the space it has opened; none can claim to have a privileged relation of truth with it" (p. 67).

91. Stengers and Prigogine, *Order Out of Chaos*, pp. 44, 46, 49, 50, 52.

92. Stengers and Prigogine, *Order Out of Chaos*, pp. 57, 59, 60, 61. "If the velocities of all the points of a system are reversed. . . [t]he system would retrace all the states it went through during the previous change" (p. 61).

93. Stengers and Prigogine, *Order Out of Chaos*, p. 77.

94. Stengers and Prigogine, *Order Out of Chaos*, p. 88.

95. Again, this is the subject of chapter 2 of *The Universal*.

96. Stengers and Prigogine, *Order Out of Chaos*, p. 90.

97. Tasić, *Mathematics and the Roots*, p. 17.

4. BURNING MAN

An earlier version of the section of this chapter titled "The Grand Style: The Interesting, the Remarkable, the Unusual" is scheduled for publication as "The Interesting, the Remarkable, the Unusual: Deleuze's Grand Style," in *Deleuze Studies* 5, no. 1 (2011): pp. 118–39.

1. Stengers and Prigogine, *Order Out of Chaos*, pp. 79–290. These theories and others along with their philosophical implications are discussed at length throughout their book.

2. Stengers and Prigogine, *Order Out of Chaos*, pp. 293–94.

3. See, for example, Vesselin Petkov, "On the Reality of Minkowski Space," *Found Phys* 37 (2007): pp. 1499–1502. DOI 10.1007/s10701-007-9178-9. Published online, September 11, 2007. © Springer Science+Business Media, LLC 2007. Science College, Concordia University, 1455 De Maison-

neuve Boulevard West, Montreal, PQ, Canada H3G 1M8. For Bergson's cone of memory see Dorothea Olkowski, *Gilles Deleuze and the Ruin of Representation* (Berkeley: University of California Press, 1999), pp. 104–46.

4. Henri Bergson, *Matter and Memory*, trans. Nancy Margaret Paul and W. Scott Palmer (New York: Zone Books, 1988), p. 168–69. For a clear explanation of special relativity, see DeWitt, *Worldviews*, pp. 207–11.

5. Henri Bergson, *Creative Evolution*, trans. Arthur Mitchell (Boston: University Press of America, 1983), pp. 8–9. "The entire past, present, and future of material objects or of isolated systems might be spread out all at once in space" (p. 8).

6. DeWitt, *Worldviews*, pp. 220–23.

7. Bergson, *Creative Evolution*, p. 10.

8. Bergson, *Creative Evolution*, p. 11.

9. Henri Bergson, *The Creative Mind*, trans. Mabelle L. Andison (New York: Philosophical Library, 1946), pp. 140–41.

10. It is well-known that Bergson suppressed the republication of *Duration and Simultaneity* because of an error in his understanding of Lorentz equations.

11. See for example, Rob Salgado (salgado@physics.syr.edu), "A More Illuminating Look at the Light Cone," (June 15, 1996) (accessed Fall 2009), http://www.phy.syr.edu/courses/modules/LIGHTCONE/lightcone.html.

12. Rob Salgado (salgado@physics.syr.edu), "Einstein-Minkowski, SpaceTime: Introducing the Light Cone," (June 15, 1996) (accessed Fall 2009), http://www.phy.syr.edu/courses/modules/LIGHTCONE/minkowski.html.

13. Stengers and Prigogine, *Order Out of Chaos*, p. 298. By the time scientists began to consider time irreversibility, philosophy had already been relegated to the sidelines. On Bergson, see for example, Bricmont, "Science of Chaos or Chaos in Science?," pp. 23–24.

14. Stengers and Prigogine, *Order Out of Chaos*, p. 300.

15. Schneider and Sagan, *Into the Cool*, pp. xii, 6–7.

16. Schneider and Sagan, *Into the Cool*, p. 81.

17. Schneider and Sagan, *Into the Cool*, p. 82.

18. Stengers and Prigogine, *Order Out of Chaos*, p. 301. "The world of classical science was a world in which the only events that could occur were those deducible from the instantaneous state of the system . . . the objects chosen by the first physicists to explore the validity of a quantitative descrip-

tion . . . were found to correspond to a unique mathematical description that actually reproduced the divine ideality of Aristotle's heavenly bodies" (pp. 305–306).

19. Thomas Kuhn, *The Structure of Scientific Revolutions* (Chicago: University Of Chicago Press, 1996).

20. Stengers and Prigogine, *Order Out of Chaos*, p. 309.

21. Deleuze's reading of Bergson seeks to bring Bergson's philosophy into accord with Deleuze's own views. I have opposed this interpretation of Bergson in the essay "Deleuze and the Limits of Mathematical Time," *Deleuze Studies* 2, no. 1 (2008): pp. 1–24.

22. Gilles Deleuze and Félix Guattari, *What Is Philosophy?*, trans. Hugh Tomlinson and Graham Burchell (New York: Columbia University Press, 1994), pp. 37, 51. Originally published in French as *Qu'est-ce que la philosophie?* (Paris: Les Editions de Minuit, 1991).

23. Deleuze and Guattari, *What Is Philosophy?*, p. 47.

24. Deleuze and Guattari, *What Is Philosophy?*, p. 51. Not surprisingly, no women philosophers seem to inhabit this exalted position.

25. Alain Badiou, *Theoretical Writings*, trans. Ray Brassier and Alberto Toscano (London: Continuum, 2006), p. 3.

26. Badiou, *Theoretical Writings*, pp. 3, 4.

27. Badiou, *Theoretical Writings*, pp. 8–13.

28. Badiou, *Theoretical Writings*, p. 14. See also, Alain Badiou, *Deleuze: The Clamor of Being*, trans. Louise Burchill (Minneapolis: University of Minnesota Press, 1999).

29. Badiou, *Theoretical Writings*, pp. 8, 9.

30. Badiou, *Theoretical Writings*, pp. 10–13.

31. See Badiou, *Theoretical Writings*, pp. 68–82.

32. Badiou, *Theoretical Writings*, p. 4.

33. Deleuze and Guattari, *What Is Philosophy?*, p. 35.

34. Margulis and Sagan, "The Universe in Heat," p. 34.

35. Keith Devlin, *Mathematics: The Science of Patterns. The Search for Order in Life, Mind, and the Universe* (New York: Scientific American Library, 1994), p. 74; Edmund Husserl, *Ideas, General Introduction to Pure Phenomenology*, trans. W. R. Boyce Gibson (New York: Humanities Press, 1969), p. 53. I would propose that Husserl is utilizing this model of differential calculus to solve exactly this sort of problem.

36. Devlin, *Mathematics*, p. 79.

37. Devlin, *Mathematics*, p. 90.

38. Devlin, *Mathematics*, p. 86.

39. Devlin, *Mathematics*, pp. 87, 88.

40. Gilles Deleuze, *Difference and Repetition*, trans. Paul Patton. (New York: Columbia University Press, 1994), pp. 170–82. Originally published in French as *Différence et Répétition* (Paris: Presses Universitaires de France, 1968). Chapter 4 has been translated as "Ideas and the Synthesis of Difference," but the correct translation is "Ideal Synthesis of Difference."

41. Gilles Deleuze, Francis Bacon: *Logic of Sensation*, trans. Daniel W. Smith (London: Continuum, 2004), p. 100. Originally published as *Francis Bacon: Logique de la Sensation* (Paris: Editions de la Difference, 1981), p. 65. Hereafter, references to the French original will appear in brackets.

42. John Casti, *Complexification, Explaining a Paradoxical World Through the Science of Surprise* (New York: Harper Collins, 1994), p. 53.

43. Casti, *Complexification*, p. 55.

44. Deleuze, *Difference and Repetition*, p. 177 [229–30]. Gilles Deleuze, "The Idea of Genesis in Kant's Aesthetics," trans. Daniel W. Smith, *Angelaki: Journal of the Theoretical Humanities* 5, no. 3 (Dec. 2000): pp. 57–70, p. 63.

45. Deleuze, *Difference and Repetition*, p. 177 [229–30]. I have addressed this at length in *The Universal*, pp. 207, 214.

46. Devlin, *Mathematics*, p. 44; Deleuze, *Difference and Repetition*, p. 177 [229–30].

47. Deleuze, *Difference and Repetition*, p. 177 [229–30].

48. Devlin, *Mathematics*, p. 44. "If you have a collection of entities called vectors, an operation of addition of two vectors to give a third vector and an operation of multiplication of a vector by a number to give another vector, and if these operations have the [appropriate properties, they are associative, commutative, distributive, and closed under vector addition], then the entire system is called a vector space" (p. 44).

49. Irving M. Copi and Carl Cohen, *Introduction to Logic* (New York: Macmillan Publishing, 1990), p. 387. For example $(p \vee q)$ may be replaced by $(q \vee p)$ and $(q \cdot p)$ may be replaced by $(p \cdot q)$.

50. The relation between Kant's transcendental Ideas and Deleuze's rigorous mathematics has been worked out in chapter 2 of my book, *The Universal*.

51. Copi and Cohen, *Introduction to Logic*, p. 387. For example $[(p \vee q) \vee r]$ may be replaced by $[p \vee (q \vee r)]$ and $[(p \cdot q) \cdot r]$ may be replaced by $[p \cdot (q \cdot r)]$.

52. Copi and Cohen, *Introduction to Logic*, pp. 705–706. For example: $(p \supset q) \equiv (\sim p \vee q)$.

53. Kant, *Critique of Pure Reason*, A73–74, B98–99.

54. Devlin, *Mathematics*, pp. 46–48.

55. Devlin, *Mathematics*, pp. 86–87.

56. Deleuze, *Difference and Repetition*, p. 135 [176–77].

57. Tasić, *Mathematics and the Roots*, p. 11–12.

58. Kant, *Critique of Pure Reason*, A137–47; B176–87.

59. Deleuze, *Difference and Repetition*, pp. 133–34 [174–75].

60. Deleuze, *Difference and Repetition*, pp. 136–37 [178].

61. Deleuze, *Difference and Repetition*, pp. 139–40 [182].

62. Deleuze, *Difference and Repetition*, p. 143 [186].

63. Deleuze, *Difference and Repetition*, p. 143 [186].

64. Deleuze, *Difference and Repetition*, p. 146 [190]. Deleuze refers to this power to dissolve harmony as the "dark precursor" (p. 145 [189]).

65. Kant, *Critique of Pure Reason*, A333–36; B390–93 and A176–219; B218–66. Gilles Deleuze refers to these Kantian syntheses in *Logic of Sense*, trans. Mark Lester with Charles Stivale, ed. Constantin V. Boundas (New York: Columbia University Press, 1990), pp. 294–95. Originally published as *Logique du sens* (Paris: Les Editions de Minuit, 1969), pp. 242–43. References are to the English version, with the French original (1969) in square brackets. "What after all do we mean by self, world, god? How is it that certain Ideas correspond to the connective, the hypothetical, the disjunctive? Categorical syllogisms, 'All men are mortal,' represent the relations of a concept or idea to a subject. Hypothetical syllogisms, 'If the earth turns, then the sun will rise and set,' are causal, manifesting the relation of a concept or an idea to the manifold of objects in the world of appearance, the synthesis of a causal series. Finally, there is the disjunctive relation, the disjunctive synthesis of parts in a system in relation to objects of thought, 'Either the universe has a beginning or it does not.' This is the relation of a concept or idea to all things in general."

66. Deleuze, *Logic of Sense*, pp. 266–67 [307–8]. "Nature is not collective, but rather distributive. . . . Nature is not attributive, but rather conjunctive; it expresses itself through 'and' and not through 'is'" (p. 267 [308]).

67. Deleuze, *Logic of Sense*, pp. 269 [311]. "In their fall, atoms collide not because of their differing weights but because of the clinamen . . . it relates one atom to another. . . . In the void, the velocity of the atom is equal to

its movement in a unique direction in a minimum of continuous time" (p. 269 [311]).

68. Deleuze, *Logic of Sense,* p. 269 [311].

69. Devlin, *Mathematics,* p. 93. This required a "rigorous theory of approximation processes" and the key idea of a limit (p. 87).

70. Devlin, *Mathematics,* pp. 92–93. So, for example, the differential equation dP/dt = rP describes uninhibited growth where (P)t is the size of some population and r is a fixed growth rate.

71. Devlin, *Mathematics,* pp. 92–93. "Most applications of differential equations in economics are of this nature: the actual changes brought about in an economy by single individuals and small companies are so small compared to the whole, and there are so many of them, that the whole system behaves as if it were experiencing continuous change" (p. 93). For Deleuze, the use of vector fields requires the complete determination of a problem so that "if the differentials disappear in the result, this is to the extent that the problem-instance differs in kind from the solution-instance; it is the movement by which the solutions necessarily come to conceal the problem" (*Difference and Repetition,* pp. 177–78 [230–31]).

72. Deleuze, *Difference and Repetition,* p. 177 [229–30]. For Deleuze, the use of vector fields requires the complete determination of a problem, so to repeat: "if the differentials disappear in the result, this is to the extent that the problem-instance differs in kind from the solution-instance; it is the movement by which the solutions necessarily come to conceal the problem" (pp.177–8 [230–1]).

73. Deleuze, *Difference and Repetition,* p. 179 [232]. Emphases added. Dialectical here refers to Platonic dialectics, not Hegelian dialectics.

74. Deleuze, *Difference and Repetition,* p. 181 [235]. "Differential calculus is not the unimaginative calculus of the utilitarian, the crude arithmatic calculus which subordinates thought to other ends, but the algebra of pure thought, the superior irony of problems themselves" (pp. 181–82 [236–37]). I have discussed the Idea differentiating itself in *The Universal,* pp. 27–30.

75. J. R. Lucas, *The Conceptual Roots of Mathematics, An Essay on the Philosophy of Mathematics* (New York and London: Routledge Press, 2000), p. 401.

76. Lucas, *The Conceptual Roots,* p. 419.

77. Lucas, *The Conceptual Roots,* p. 425, citing Göttlob Frege, *The Foundations of Arithmetic,* trans. J. L. Austin (Oxford: Oxford University Press, 1950), §87, p. 99e.

78. Deleuze, *Difference and Repetition,* pp. 184–86 [238–41].

79. http://mathworld.wolfram.com/Attractor.html. An asymptote is a line that continually approaches a given curve but does not meet it at any finite distance.

80. Casti, *Complexification,* pp. 26–27.

81. Casti, *Complexification,* p. 28. The first attractor is called a fixed point, the second a limit cycle; it describes both clocks and human heartbeats.

82. Casti, *Complexification,* pp. 29–30.

83. Casti, *Complexification,* p. 33.

84. Deleuze and Guattari, *What Is Philosophy?,* pp. 163–67.

85. Deleuze, *Difference and Repetition,* p. 138 [180].

86. Deleuze, *Difference and Repetition,* p. 145 [189].

87. A concise account of these developments can be found at http://www-groups.dcs.st-and.ac.uk/~history/HistTopics/The_rise_of_calculus.html (accessed July 15, 2010).

88. Aristotle, *Metaphysics,* trans. W. D. Ross, in *The Basic Works of Aristotle,* ed. Richard McKeon (New York: Random House, 1970), X, 5, 1054b25.

89. Deleuze, *Difference and Repetition,* p. 139 [182].

90. Marjorie Hass, "Feminist Readings of Aristotelean Logic," in *Feminist Interpretations of Aristotle,* ed. Cynthia A. Freeland, pp. 19–40, 34 (University Park: Pennsylvania State University Press, 1998).

91. Marjorie Hass, "Negation and Difference," *Philosophy Today, Philosophy in Body, Culture, and Time* 44 (2000): pp. 112–18, 112. Hass cites Ludwig Wittgenstein, *Tractatus,* trans. Daniel Kolak (Mountain View, Calif.: Mayfield, 1998), 5.02.

92. Marjorie Hass, "Fluid Thinking, Irigaray's Critique of Formal Logic," in *Representing Reason, Feminist Theory and Formal Logic,* ed. Rachel Joffe Falmagne and Marjorie Hass, pp. 71–88, 75 (New York: Rowman and Littlefield, 2002).

93. Hass, "Feminist Readings of Aristotelian Logic," pp. 35–36; Hass, "Negation and Difference," p. 114.

94. Plato, *Republic,* 524e. Without contrariety and contradiction, would Platonic thought have developed?

95. Gilles Deleuze and Félix Guattari, *Anti-Oedipus,* trans. Robert Hurley, Mark Seem, and Helen R. Lane (Minneapolis: University of Minnesota Press, 1987), p. 287. Originally published in French as *Anti-Oedipe* (Paris:

Les Editions de Minuit, 1972). Determinate conditions are statistical forms (the larger the groups averaged, the less the variation). See note at the bottom of p. 287.

96. Maurice Merleau-Ponty, *The Structure of Behavior,* trans. Alden Fisher (Boston: Beacon Press, 1963), pp. 138–39.

97. Merleau-Ponty, *The Structure of Behavior,* p. 143. Merleau-Ponty emphasizes the unity of the molar as opposed to the molecular aggregate.

98. Casti, *Complexification,* pp. 26–27.

99. http://scienceworld.wolfram.com/physics/AvogadrosNumber .html. The Avogadro Constant, L, is a constant number used to refer to atoms, molecules, ions, and electrons. Its value is 6.023×10^{23} mol^{-1}.

100. Deleuze and Guattari, *Anti-Oedipus,* p. 286.

101. Deleuze and Guattari, *Anti-Oedipus,* p. 288.

102. Deleuze and Guattari, *Anti-Oedipus,* p. 311.

103. See Tasić, *Mathematics and the Roots,* p. 113, for a discussion of the terms structuralism and functionalism.

104. Lucas, *The Conceptual Roots of Mathematics,* pp. 68, 69.

105. Lucas, *The Conceptual Roots of Mathematics,* p. 70.

106. Lucas, *The Conceptual Roots of Mathematics,* p. 72. "Even *l'homme moyen sensuel* can recognize it."

107. Lucas, *The Conceptual Roots of Mathematics,* p. 378. "But that ideal of absolute cogency . . . has proved unattainable" (p. 378).

108. Lucas, *The Conceptual Roots of Mathematics,* p. 381. For example, dialectical justification of recursion allows us to overcome the finitude of incontrovertibility and to show that it is an admissible form of argument. A recursive process is one in which objects are defined in terms of other objects of the same type. Using some sort of recurrence relation, the entire class of objects can then be built up from a few initial values and a small number of rules. See http://mathworld.wolfram.com/Recursion.html.

109. Deleuze, *Difference and Repetition,* p. 144 [187]. "Transcendental empiricism is the only way to avoid tracing the transcendental from the outlines of the empirical" (p. 144 [187]).

110. Deleuze, *Difference and Repetition,* p. 141 [183–184]. It is the same clash as that decried by Plato, but this time without the resolution in harmony.

111. Deleuze, *Difference and Repetition,* pp. 140–141 [183–184]. Without this forcing, Deleuze believes that we remain ignorant or, minimally, habituated.

112. Gilles Deleuze, *Kant's Critical Philosophy,* trans. Hugh Tomlinson and Barbara Habberjam (Minneapolis: University of Minnesota Press, 1984), pp. xi–xii.

113. Deleuze, *Difference and Repetition,* p. 245 [315–16]. Different/ciation indicates both the state of differential relations in the Idea and the qualitative and extensive series in which they are actualized.

114. Lee Smolin, *Three Roads to Quantum Gravity* (New York: Basic Books, 2001), pp. 42–43.

115. Kant, *Critique of Pure Reason,* A434, B462.

116. Kant, *Critique of Pure Reason,* A25.

117. Kant, *Critique of Pure Reason,* A434, B462.

118. Kant, *Critique of Pure Reason,* A440, B468.

119. Kant, *Critique of Pure Reason,* A439, B467.

120. Gottfried Martin, *Kant's Metaphysics and Theory of Science,* trans. P. G. Lucas (Manchester: Manchester University Press, 1955), p. 62. See for example, Casti, *Complexification,* pp. 120–25.

121. Kant, *Critique of Pure Reason,* A70, B95.

122. Kant, *Critique of Pure Reason,* A285, B340.

123. Kant, *Critique of Pure Reason,* A22, B37.

124. Kant, *Critique of Pure Reason,* A163, B204.

125. Klein, *Mathematics,* p. 417. Klein cites Karl Friedrick Gauss, Nikolas Lobatchevsky, and John Bolyai as the important contributors to this discovery.

126. Klein, *Mathematics,* pp. 425, 426.

127. Klein, *Mathematics,* p. 428.

128. Klein, *Mathematics,* p. 429. This was precisely the point Arendt is cited for in a previous chapter.

129. Klein, *Mathematics,* p. 429, 431. Klein cites George Cantor, "The essence of mathematics is its freedom" (p. 431).

130. Kant, *Critique of Pure Reason,* A145, B185.

131. See Olkowski, *The Universal,* pp. 62–65, for an account of this aspect of Deleuze's reading of Kant.

132. Badiou, *Theoretical Writings,* pp. 172–73.

133. Badiou, *Theoretical Writings,* p. 144. This is essentially the same argument as that put forth by Deleuze.

5. PHILOSOPHY'S EXTRA-SCIENTIFIC MESSAGES

An earlier version of the sections of this chapter beginning with "Life and the Human Condition" were published as "Science and Human Nature, How to Go From Nature to Ethics," in James R. Watson, ed., *Metacide, In the Pursuit of Excellence* (Amsterdam: Rodopi, 2010): pp. 43–72.

1. James Glanz, "When Mortals Work on Cosmic Time," *New York Times, Week in Review,* Sunday August 9, 2009, pp. 1, 4. Glanz identifies himself as a former physicist. He has been a science writer and a bureau chief for the *New York Times.*

2. Glanz, "When Mortals Work," p. 4. A tour guide at the pyramid site states that the Mayans left because they failed to rotate their crops and could no longer produce adequate supplies of food.

3. Glanz, "When Mortals Work," p. 4.

4. Bender, *The Culture of Extinction,* pp. 16–17.

5. Depew and Weber, *Darwinism Evolving,* pp. 88–90.

6. DeWitt, *Worldviews,* pp. 204, 301.

7. DeWitt, *Worldviews,* p. 3.

8. Depew and Weber, *Darwinism Evolving,* pp. 85–86.

9. Arendt, *The Human Condition,* p. 111.

10. Arendt, *The Human Condition,* p. 117. Arendt differentiates labor, work, and action. The first is private, the second is something in between, and the third is the public sphere.

11. Arendt, *The Human Condition,* p. 116. Ours is not an era of freedom in the sense that we are tied to necessity.

12. Arendt, *The Human Condition,* p. 133.

13. Arendt, *The Human Condition,* p. 134. The prevalence of tabloids verifies this claim.

14. Arendt, *The Human Condition,* p. 176. By this means, she argues, the ancient Greeks sought immortality.

15. Arendt, *The Human Condition,* pp. 177–79. Arendt contrasts this notion of the unpredictability of action and the effects of noble word and deeds with the predictability necessitated by the mathematical calculations of classical science.

16. Arendt, *The Human Condition,* pp. 190–1, 232.

17. Peg Birmingham, *Hannah Arendt and Human Rights* (Blooming-ton: Indiana University Press, 2006), p. 16. Birmingham's text is crucial for clarifying many of Arendt's concepts that have been misinterpreted due to a lack of understanding of the overall structure of Arendt's thought.

18. Hannah Arendt, *Between Past and Future, Eight Exercises in Political Thought* (New York: Viking Press, 1961, 1968), p. 12. See also: http://www .phys.unsw.edu.au/COURSES/FIRST_YEAR/pdf%20files/Forces%20&%20 Vectors.pdf (accessed March 12, 2011).

19. Arendt, *Between Past and Future*, p. 12.

20. Birmingham, *Hannah Arendt*, p. 24.

21. Arendt, *The Human Condition*, p. 231.

22. Hume, *A Treatise of Human Nature*, p. 79, 71.

23. Arendt, *The Human Condition*, p. 284. Symbols are man-made, meaning they are constructions of the human mind, reflecting human ca-pacities.

24. Arendt, *The Human Condition*, p. 287. When mathematical calcu-lations are unable to be projected onto physical reality, they cease to be of interest to physicists.

25. Arendt, *The Human Condition*, p. 290.

26. Arendt, *The Human Condition*, p. 297. In turn, Arendt argues, this has given way to philosophies of life that describe all phenomena, including human actions, as effects of natural processes.

27. Arendt, *The Human Condition*, pp. 231–32. Thus humanity is the model for the process view of natural science and not the other way around.

28. Casti, *Complexification*, p. 266.

29. Arendt, *The Human Condition*, p. 300.

30. Strogatz, "Guest Column."

31. Sam Vaknin, *Malignant Self-Love, Narcissism Revisited* (Prague and Skopje: Narcissus Publications, 2007), pp. 152–53.

32. Hannah Arendt, *Eichmann in Jerusalem, A Report on the Banality of Evil* (New York: Viking Press, 1963), pp. 23–24.

33. Arendt, *Eichmann*, pp. 22–31.

34. Arendt, *Eichmann*, pp. 22–23; Vaknin, *Malignant Self-Love*, pp. 62–69.

35. Strogatz, "Guest Column."

36. Casti, *Complexification*, p. 41.

37. Devlin, *Mathematics*, p. 96.

38. Devlin, *Mathematics*, pp. 114–18.

39. Devlin, *Mathematics,* pp. 127–28.

40. Devlin, *Mathematics,* pp. 128–29.

41. Devlin, *Mathematics,* p. 129.

42. Devlin, *Mathematics,* p. 130.

43. Devlin, *Mathematics,* pp. 185, 193.

44. Devlin, *Mathematics,* pp. 185, 193.

45. Devlin, *Mathematics,* p. 204.

46. See especially "First Series of Paradoxes of Becoming," in Deleuze, *Logic of Sense.*

47. An earlier version of this material was published as "After Alice: Alice and the Dry Tail," in *Deleuze Studies* 2 (2008): pp. 107–22.

48. I am using Lewis Carroll, *The Philosopher's Alice in Wonderland and Through the Looking-Glass,* introduction and notes by Peter Heath (New York: St. Martin's Press, 1982.), p. 15. This edition is subtitled "The Thinking Man's Guide to a Misunderstood Nursery Classic," but I have found little in the notes to enlighten a thinking woman.

49. Carroll, *Alice in Wonderland,* p. 16.

50. Deleuze, *Logic of Sense,* p. 9 [19].

51. Copi and Cohen, *Introduction to Logic,* pp. 387–88. "In any truth functional compound statement, if a component statement in it is replaced by another statement having the same truth value, the truth value of the compound statement will remain unchanged" (Copi and Cohen, *Introduction to Logic,* pp. 387–88).

52. If p then q = (not p) or q. Devlin, *Mathematics,* p. 48.

53. Deleuze, *Logic of Sense,* p. 75 [93].

54. Carroll, *Alice in Wonderland,* pp. 18–19.

55. Carroll, *Alice in Wonderland,* p. 18.

56. Carroll, *Alice in Wonderland,* p. 20.

57. Mary Tiles, *Mathematics and the Image of Reason* (London and New York: Routledge Press, 1991), p. 72. Bertrand Russell's solution to the paradox was to create a hierarchy of types of objects and a corresponding hierarchy of concepts so that no individual is a member of its own class.

58. Tiles, *Mathematics and the Image,* pp. 79–81. The position is atomist in that it accords reality only to empirical objects and their relations, not to structure (p. 85).

59. Deleuze, *Logic of Sense,* p. 69 [86].

60. Carroll, *Alice in Wonderland,* p. 24.

61. Deleuze, *Logic of Sense,* p. 78 [96].

62. Carroll, *Alice in Wonderland*, p. 24.

63. As we have seen, no causal explanation for the sudden appearance of the creatures is given, thus causality is not restored.

64. Carroll, *Alice in Wonderland*, pp. 30–36.

65. Göttlob Frege, "On Sense and Reference," in *Translations from the Philosophical Writings of Göttlob Frege,* ed. Peter Geach and Max Black (Oxford: Basil Blackwell, 1952), pp. 57–59.

66. Frege, "On Sense and Reference," p. 59.

67. Frege, "On Sense and Reference," p. 60.

68. Frege, "On Sense and Reference," p. 61.

69. Carroll, *Alice in Wonderland*, p. 61.

70. Frege, "On Sense and Reference," pp. 64–65.

71. Carroll, *Alice in Wonderland*, p. 38.

72. Carroll, *Alice in Wonderland*, p. 43.

73. Carroll, *Alice in Wonderland*, p. 47.

74. Carroll, *Alice in Wonderland*, p. 54.

75. Deleuze, *Logic of Sense,* p. 78 [96].

76. Deleuze, *Logic of Sense,* pp. 10–11 [20].

77. Carroll, *Alice in Wonderland*, p. 58.

78. Carroll, *Alice in Wonderland*, pp. 59–60.

79. Carroll, *Alice in Wonderland*, p. 60.

80. Carroll, *Alice in Wonderland*, p. 61.

81. Carroll, *Alice in Wonderland*, p. 61.

82. Carroll, *Alice in Wonderland*, p. 70.

83. Bertrand Russell, *An Inquiry Into Meaning and Truth* (London: Allen and Unwin, 1940).

84. Russell, *An Inquiry,* p. 175.

85. Carroll, *Alice in Wonderland*, p. 74.

86. Russell, *An Inquiry,* p. 175.

87. Carroll, *Alice in Wonderland*, p. 75.

88. Russell, *An Inquiry,* p. 171. Russell argues that assertions have a subjective side and an objective side. The subjective side is found in the expression of the speaker's beliefs or desires. The objective side is the assertion's intention to indicate an object. Russell identifies the significance of a sentence with what it expresses. True and false sentences may be equally significant, but in order for a string of words not to be just nonsense, it must express the beliefs or desires of the speaker. Additionally, if the string of words is nonsense, it cannot have an effect on a hearer.

89. Deleuze, *Logic of Sense,* p. 13 [23].

90. Deleuze, *Logic of Sense,* p. 13 [23].

91. Deleuze, *Logic of Sense,* p. 14 [24].

92. Frege, "On Sense and Reference," p. 59.

93. Frege, "On Sense and Reference," p. 60.

94. Frege, "On Sense and Reference," p. 62.

95. Frege, "On Sense and Reference," p. 63.

96. Deleuze, *Logic of Sense,* p. 21 [33].

97. Deleuze, *Logic of Sense,* p. 22 [34].

98. Deleuze, *Logic of Sense,* p. 22 [34].

99. Carroll, *Alice in Wonderland,* p. 76.

100. Carroll, *Alice in Wonderland,* p. 78.

101. Carroll, *Alice in Wonderland,* p. 78.

102. Carroll, *Alice in Wonderland,* p. 86.

103. Carroll, *Alice in Wonderland,* p. 87.

104. Carroll, *Alice in Wonderland,* p. 92.

105. Carroll, *Alice in Wonderland,* pp. 94, 95.

106. Carroll, *Alice in Wonderland,* p. 102.

107. Carroll, *Alice in Wonderland,* p. 114.

108. Carroll, *Alice in Wonderland,* p. 119.

109. Carroll, *Alice in Wonderland,* p. 119.

110. Catherine Driscoll, "The Little Girl, Deleuze and Guattari," in *Critical Assessments of Leading Philosophers,* vol. 3, ed. Gary Genosko (London and New York: Routledge Press, 2000). Reprinted from *Antithesis* 8, no. 2 (1997); Deleuze, *Logic of Sense,* p. 1[8]. Text provided by the author.

111. Catherine Driscoll, "The Little Girl."

112. Rosi Braidotti, *Nomadic Subjects: Embodiment and Sexual Difference in Contemporary Feminist Theory* (New York: Columbia University Press, 1994), p. 116.

113. Deleuze and Guattari, *Anti-Oedipus,* pp. 283–96.

114. Deleuze and Guattari, *Anti-Oedipus,* p. 276.

115. Deleuze and Guattari, *Anti-Oedipus,* p. 276.

116. Carroll, *Alice in Wonderland,* p. 120.

117. Bergson, *Matter and Memory,* p. 133. For a full account of Bergson's theory of the role of memory in perception, see Olkowski, *Gilles Deleuze and the Ruin of Representation,* ch. 4, especially pages 104–14.

118. Roberto Bolano, *2666*, trans. Natasha Wimmer (New York: Farrar, Straus and Giroux, 2008), p. 831. This is the speech of "Ingeborg," a young German woman who, having survived World War II and various atrocities committed after the war, falls ill with tuberculosis and, we are told, eventually drowns.

119. Devlin, *Mathematics*, pp. 92–93.

120. Devlin, *Mathematics*, p. 98.

121. Devlin, *Mathematics*, p. 98.

122. Simone de Beauvoir, *The Ethics of Ambiguity*, trans. Bernard Frechtman (New York: Citadel Press, 1979), p. 7. Emphases added.

123. Beauvoir, *The Ethics of Ambiguity*, pp. 7, 8.

124. Beauvoir, *The Ethics of Ambiguity*, p. 10. I have extensively discussed Sartre's position in *The Universal*. See especially pages 101–30.

125. Devlin, *Mathematics*, p. 93.

126. Devlin, *Mathematics*, pp. 92–93.

127. Casti, *Complexification*, pp. 27–28.

128. Casti, *Complexification*, pp. 28–29. Most of Deleuze's theoretical formulations are posited in terms of strange attractors where percepts and affects are the contingent boundary conditions. Sartre already used the model of a trajectory. The attractors of his system are probably fixed points, since objectification is implicit in each move from point to point.

129. Casti, *Complexification*, p. 33.

130. Casti, *Complexification*, pp. 92–94.

131. Beauvoir, *The Ethics of Ambiguity*, p. 11.

132. Beauvoir, *The Ethics of Ambiguity*, p. 13.

133. Beauvoir, *The Ethics of Ambiguity*, p. 25.

134. Beauvoir, *The Ethics of Ambiguity*, p. 25.

135. Susan Mapstone, "Non-Linear Dynamics: The Swerve of the Atom in Lucretius *de rerum natura*." http://www.londonconsortium.com/wp-content/uploads/2007/02/mapstonestoicsessay.pdf (accessed July 18, 2009).

136. Beauvoir, *The Ethics of Ambiguity*, p. 25.

6. LOVE'S ONTOLOGY

The epigraph is from Fotini Markopoulou, "Space Does Not Exist, So Time Can." Perimeter Institute for Theoretical Physics (December 1, 2008), http://www.fqxi.org/data/essay-contest-files/Markopoulou_SpaceDNE.pdf.

An earlier version of the sections in this chapter titled "The Joy of Existence" on Beauvoir and ethics is scheduled to appear in a volume edited by Silvia Stoller on Simone de Beauvoir and *The Coming of Age*.

1. Walter P. Van Stigt, "Brouwer's Intuitionist Programme," in *From Brouwer to Hilbert, The Debate on the Foundations of Mathematics in the 1920s*, ed. Paolo Mancosu, pp. 1–22, 5 (Oxford: Oxford University Press, 1998).

2. Henri Bergson, *Time and Free Will, An Essay on the Immediate Data of Consciousness*, trans. F. L. Pogson (New York: Macmillan, 1959), pp. 98–112. Tasić's claim that Bergson lacks a conceptual framework is simply not the case. See my extensive account of Bergson's ontology, "Creative Evolution: An Ontology of Change," in *Gilles Deleuze and the Ruin of Representation*, pp. 118–46.

3. M. A. E. Dummett, "The Philosophical Basis of Intuitionistic Logic," in *Truth and Other Enigmas* (London: Duckworth Press, 1978).

4. Van Stigt, "Brouwer's Intuitionist Programme," p. 7.

5. Van Stigt, "Brouwer's Intuitionist Programme," pp. 6, 7, 8.

6. Van Stigt, "Brouwer's Intuitionist Programme," p. 8

7. Van Stigt, "Brouwer's Intuitionist Programme," pp. 8–9.

8. Tasić, *Mathematics and the Roots*, pp. 40–41.

9. Tasić, *Mathematics and the Roots*, p. 40.

10. Van Stigt, "Brouwer's Intuitionist Programme," p. 9.

11. Van Stigt, "Brouwer's Intuitionist Programme," p. 40.

12. Tasić, *Mathematics and the Roots*, p. 129–30.

13. Van Stigt, "Brouwer's Intuitionist Programme," p. 10.

14. Tasić, *Mathematics and the Roots*, pp. 48–49.

15. Beauvoir, *The Ethics of Ambiguity*, p. 26.

16. Beauvoir, *The Ethics of Ambiguity*, pp. 27–28.

17. Arendt, *Eichmann*, pp. 117–18.

18. Arendt, *The Human Condition*, pp. 254–55.

19. Arendt, *The Human Condition*, pp. 236–37.

20. Seyla Benhabib, "The Pariah and Her Shadow," in *Feminist Interpretations of Hannah Arendt*, ed. Bonnie Honig, pp. 83–104, 99 (University Park: Penn State University Press, 1995).

21. Arendt, *The Human Condition*, p. 177.

22. Arendt, *The Human Condition*, p. 178.

23. Schneider and Sagan, *Into the Cool,* p. 26.

24. Schneider and Sagan, *Into the Cool,* p. 28.

25. Schneider and Sagan, *Into the Cool,* pp. 79–80, 87.

26. Schneider and Sagan, *Into the Cool,* pp. 87, 85.

27. Schneider and Sagan, *Into the Cool,* p. 85.

28. Tasić, *Mathematics and the Roots,* p. 156.

29. Lucas, *The Conceptual Roots of Mathematics,* p. 70.

30. Lucas, *The Conceptual Roots of Mathematics,* p. 72. "Even *l'homme moyen sensuel* can recognize it."

31. http://mathworld.wolfram.com/Algorithm.html. An algorithm is a specific set of instructions for carrying out a procedure or solving a problem, usually with the requirement that the procedure terminate at some point. Specific algorithms sometimes also go by the name *method, procedure,* or *technique.* The word "algorithm" is a distortion of al-Khwārizmī, a Persian mathematician who wrote an influential treatise about algebraic methods. The process of applying an algorithm to an input to obtain an output is called a *computation.*

32. Kant, *Critique of Practical Reason,* pp. 27–29.

33. Kant, *Critique of Pure Reason,* A73–74, B98–99.

34. Kant, *Critique of Practical Reason,* pp. 42–44.

35. Kant, *Critique of Practical Reason,* pp.125, 135.

36. Copi and Cohen, *Introduction to Logic,* p. 387. For example: $[p \circ (q \circ r)] \equiv [(p \circ q) \circ r]$.

37. Copi and Cohen, *Introduction to Logic,* p. 387. For example: $-(p \vee q) \equiv (-p \cdot -q)$.

38. Markopoulou, "Space Does Not Exist," p. 7.

39. Markopoulou, "Space Does Not Exist," pp. 5, 8.

40. Markopoulou, "Space Does Not Exist," pp. 7–8.

41. Bergson, *Matter and Memory,* pp. 168–69 [307–308].

42. Smolin, *Three Roads to Quantum Gravity,* p. 58.

43. Smolin, *Three Roads to Quantum Gravity,* p. 59. Emphasis added.

44. Smolin, *Three Roads to Quantum Gravity,* p. 60.

45. Discontinuous spacetime belongs to the classical system of continuous spacetime. Discrete spacetime is part of the conceptualization of quantum.

46. Smolin, *Three Roads to Quantum Gravity,* pp. 61–62.

47. The concept of intra-activity is that of Karen Barad, *Meeting the Universe Halfway,* (Durham, N.C.: Duke University Press, 2007). I use Barad's

word to describe my own concept of a causal network of interconnected states for which every perspective and every state consists of a multiplicity of cones linked to one another, influencing one another, which is represented by the cover image on *The Universal (In the Realm of the Sensible)*. Barad, however, utilizes Bohr's quantum concepts in her formalist-materialist account of intra-action.

48. Fotini Markopoulou, "The Internal Description of a Causal Set: What the Universe Looks Like from Inside" (November 18, 1999) arXiv: gr-qc/9811053 v2: 1–35, p. 1.

49. Markopoulou, "The Internal Description," pp. 34–35.

50. Fotini Markopoulou, "An Insider's Guide to Quantum Causal Histories" (December 20, 1999) arXiv:hep-th/9912137 v2: 1–4, p. 1.

51. Markopoulou, "An Insider's Guide," p. 2.

52. Markopoulou, "An Insider's Guide," p. 3.

53. Fotini Markopoulou, "Planck-Scale Models of the Universe" (November 7, 2002), arXiv:gr-qc/0210086 v2: 1–19, p. 3.

> Causality still persists even when there is no manifold spacetime. How to describe a discrete causal universe has been known for quite some time, it is a *causal set* (Bombelli et al., 1987; Sorkin, 1990). This is a set of event p, q, r, … ordered by the causal relation $p \leq q$, meaning "p precedes q," which is transitive ($p \leq q$ and $q \leq r$ implies that $p \leq r$), locally finite (for any p and q such that $p \leq q$, the intersection of the past of q and the future of p contains a finite number of events), and has no closed timelike loops (if $p \leq q$ and $q \leq p$, then $p = q$). Two events p and q are unrelated (or spacelike) if neither $p \leq q$ nor $q \leq p$ holds.

> Note that the microscopic events do not need to be the same (or a discretization of) the events in the effective continuum theory. Also, the speed of propagation of information in the microscopic theory does not have to be the effective one, the speed of light, c.

54. This is the primary and possibly most important point of Olkowski, *The Universal (In the Realm of the Sensible)*.

55. Jaak Panksepp, "Affective Consciousness: Core Emotional Feelings in Animals and Humans," in *Cognition and Consciousness* 14, no. 1 (March 2005): pp. 30–80, 11, citing R. D. Lane & L. Nadel, eds., *Cognitive Neuroscience of Emotion* (Oxford: Oxford University Press, 2000).

56. Panksepp, "Affective Consciousness," p. 32.

57. Simone de Beauvoir, "The Age of Discretion," in *The Woman Destroyed*, trans. Patrick O'Brian (New York: Pantheon Books, 1969), p. 12.

58. Beauvoir, "The Age of Discretion," p. 12.

59. Beauvoir, *The Ethics of Ambiguity*, p. 27.

60. Simone de Beauvoir, *The Coming of Age*, trans. Patrick O'Brian (New York: G. P. Putnam, 1972), p. 378.

61. Beauvoir, *The Coming of Age*, pp. 382, 383. Beauvoir notes that some very old people delight in innovation even though they feel themselves unable to participate in it.

62. Beauvoir, *The Coming of Age*, pp. 381, 382. Beauvoir cites many old persons amazed and delighted by the modern world as well as those who refuse it by shutting themselves up in the past.

63. Beauvoir, *The Ethics of Ambiguity*, p. 25.

64. Margulis and Sagan, "The Universe in Heat," p. 32. These are the structures described by nonlinear thermodynamics.

65. Cited in Mapstone, "Non-Linear Dynamics." Mapstone cites Lucretius, *On the Nature of the Universe*, trans. R. E. Latham, rev. John Godwin (London: Penguin Classics, 1994), p. 44.

66. Michel Serres, *The Birth of Physics*, trans. Jack Hawkes (Manchester: Clinamen Press, 2000), p. 21.

67. Deleuze, *Logic of Sense*, p. 269.

68. Serres, *The Birth of Physics*, p. 22.

69. "Morality is physics. An exact knowledge of natural things. . . . Its reduction to the objective is a part of the system. . . . The theory of knowledge is isomorphic with that of being." So says Michel Serres of Lucretius's atomism in *The Birth of Physics*, p. 38.

70. Simone de Beauvoir, *She Came to Stay* (New York: W. W. Norton, 1990), p. 103.

71. Serres, *The Birth of Physics*, p. 22.

72. Beauvoir, *She Came to Stay*, p. 136.

73. Beauvoir, *She Came to Stay*, p. 108.

74. Beauvoir, *She Came to Stay*, p. 127. This negation of the past is the effect of the clinamen. It is a limit or a change of direction in the smallest possible time.

75. Sartre, *Being and Nothingness: An Essay in Phenomenological Ontology*, trans. Hazel Barnes (New York: Washington Square Press, 1971), pp. 489–90. Sartre's explanation seems to be a perfect reflection of the conflicts characterized by objectification in Beauvoir's novel.

76. Beauvoir, *She Came to Stay*, p. 179.

77. Beauvoir, *The Coming of Age,* p. 373.

78. Serres, *The Birth of Physics,* p. 34. "Physics is concerned with weight, heat and fluids. Hence with falling, with the irreversible and with flow. All this needs a slope. The clinamen produces just this inclined path. It quantifies a minimal sense, by which all things have existence and meaning [*sens*]" (p. 35).

79. Beauvoir, *The Coming of Age,* p. 441.

80. See Simone de Beauvoir, *All Men are Mortal,* trans. Leonard M. Friedman (New York: W. W. Norton, 1992) and Beauvoir, *The Coming of Age,* pp. 377–78.

81. Beauvoir, *The Coming of Age,* p. 410.

82. Beauvoir, *The Ethics of Ambiguity,* pp. 7–12.

83. Beauvoir, *The Ethics of Ambiguity,* p. 13. Emphasis added. The "I" must remain at a distance for there to be an ethical stance.

84. Sartre, *Being and Nothingness,* pp. 33–36.

85. Sartre, *Being and Nothingness,* pp. 36–44.

86. Lucas, *The Conceptual Roots,* p. 177.

87. Lucas, *The Conceptual Roots,* pp. 178–79.

88. Beauvoir, *The Coming of Age,* pp. 388–91.

89. Beauvoir, *The Coming of Age,* p. 387.

90. Hass, "Feminist Readings of Aristotelian Logic," pp. 35–36; Hass, "Negation and Difference," p. 114.

91. Beauvoir, *The Coming of Age,* p. 395.

92. Beauvoir, *The Coming of Age,* p. 396.

93. Beauvoir, "The Age of Discretion," pp. 40–41.

94. Beauvoir, "The Age of Discretion," pp. 42, 5.

95. Beauvoir, "The Age of Discretion," p. 82.

96. Beauvoir, "The Age of Discretion," p. 84.

97. Beauvoir, *The Coming of Age,* pp. 379–80.

98. Beauvoir, *The Coming of Age,* p. 542.

99. Beauvoir, *The Coming of Age,* pp. 542–43.

BIBLIOGRAPHY

Arendt, Hannah. *Between Past and Future, Eight Exercises in Political Thought.* New York: Viking Press, 1961, 1968.

———. *Eichmann in Jerusalem, A Report on the Banality of Evil.* New York: Viking Press, 1963.

———. *The Human Condition.* Chicago: The University of Chicago Press, 1998.

———. *Lectures on Kant's Political Philosophy.* Edited by Ronald Beiner. Chicago: University of Chicago Press, 1982.

———. *The Life of the Mind, One/Thinking.* New York: Harcourt Brace Jovanovich, 1977.

———. "Philosophy and Politics." *Social Research* 57, no. 1 (Spring 1990): pp. 73–103.

Arendt, Hannah, and Karl Jaspers. *Correspondence: 1926–1969.* Edited by Lotte Kohler. Translated by Peter Constantine. New York: Harcourt, Inc. 1992.

Aristotle. *Metaphysics.* Translated by W. D. Ross. In *The Basic Works of Aristotle,* edited by Richard McKeon. New York: Random House, 1970.

———. *Nicomachean Ethics.* Translated by A. I. Peck. London and Cambridge, Mass.: Loeb Classical Library, 1937.

———. *Politics.* Translated by Benjamin Jowett. New York: Modern Library, 1943.

Atkins, P. W. *The Second Law, Energy, Chaos and Form.* New York: Scientific American Library, 1984.

Badiou, Alain. *Deleuze, The Clamor of Being.* Translated by Louise Burchill. Minneapolis: University of Minnesota Press, 1999.

———. *Theoretical Writings.* Translated by Ray Brassier and Alberto Toscano. London: Continuum, 2006.

Barad, Karen. *Meeting the Universe Halfway.* Durham, N.C.: Duke University Press, 2007.

Beauvoir, Simone de. "The Age of Discretion." In *The Woman Destroyed*, translated by Patrick O'Brian. New York: Pantheon Books, 1969.

———. *All Men are Mortal*. Translated by Leonard M. Friedman. New York: W. W. Norton, 1992.

———. *The Coming of Age*. Translated by Patrick O'Brian. New York: G. P. Putnam, 1972.

———. *The Ethics of Ambiguity*. Translated by Bernard Frechtman. New York: Citadel Press, 1976.

———. *She Came to Stay*. New York: W. W. Norton, 1990.

Bender, Frederic L. *The Culture of Extinction, Toward a Philosophy of Deep Ecology*. New York: Humanity Books, 2003.

Bergson, Henri. *Creative Evolution*. Translated by Arthur Mitchell. Boston: University Press of America, 1983.

———. *The Creative Mind*. Translated by Mabelle L. Andison. New York: Philosophical Library, 1946.

———. *Matter and Memory*. Translated by Nancy Margaret Paul and W. Scott Palmer. New York: Zone Books, 1988.

———. *Time and Free Will, An Essay on the Immediate Data of Consciousness*. Translated by F. L. Pogson. New York: Macmillan, 1959.

Bernays, Paul. "Hilbert's Significance for the Philosophy of Mathematics." In *From Brouwer to Hilbert, The Debate on the Foundations of Mathematics in the 1920's*, edited by Paolo Mancosu, pp. 189–97. Oxford: Oxford University Press, 1998.

Birmingham, Peg. *Hannah Arendt and Human Rights*. Bloomington: Indiana University Press, 2006.

Boghossian, Paul. *Fear of Knowledge, Against Relativism and Constructivism*. Oxford: Clarendon Press, 2006.

Bolano, Roberto. *2666*. Translated by Natasha Wimmer. New York: Farrar, Straus and Giroux, 2008.

Boyle, Robert. *The Works of the Honourable Robert Boyle*, 6 vols. Edited by Thomas Birch. London, 1672.

Braidotti, Rosi. *Nomadic Subjects: Embodiment and Sexual Difference in Contemporary Feminist Theory*. New York: Columbia University Press, 1994.

Bricmont, J. "Science of Chaos or Chaos in Science?" *Physicalia Magazine* 17 (1995): pp. 3–4, 159–208.

Buroker, Jill. "Descartes On Sensible Qualities." *Journal of The History of Philosophy* XXIV, no. 4 (October 1991): pp. 585–611.

Burtt, Edwin Arthur. *The Metaphysical Foundations of Modern Physical Science*. Atlantic Highlands, N.J.: Humanities Press, 1952.

Butler, Judith, and Joan W. Scott, eds. *Feminists Theorize the Political*. New York: Routledge Press, 1992.

Cabanac, Michel. "What Is Sensation?" In *Biological Perspectives on Motivated Activities*, edited by R. Wong. Northwood, N.J.: Ablex Press, 1992.

Carroll, Lewis. *The Philosopher's Alice in Wonderland and Through the Looking-Glass*. Introduction and notes by Peter Heath. New York: St. Martin's Press, 1982.

Cassirer, Ernst. *Einstein's Theory of Relativity*. New York: Dover Books, 1953.

Casti, John. *Complexification, Explaining a Paradoxical World Through the Science of Surprise*. New York: Harper Collins, 1994.

Chaisson, Eric. *Cosmic Evolution, The Rise of Complexity in Nature*. Cambridge, Mass.: Harvard University Press, 2001.

Copi, Irving M., and Cohen, Carl. *Introduction to Logic*. New York: Macmillan Publishing, 1990.

Deleuze, Gilles. *Difference and Repetition*. Translated by Paul Patton. New York: Columbia University Press, 1994. Originally published in French as *Différence et Répétition*. Paris: Presses Universitaires de France, 1968.

———. *Francis Bacon: The Logic of Sensation*. Translated by Daniel W. Smith. London: Continuum, 2004. Originally published as *Francis Bacon: Logique de la Sensation*. Paris: Editions de la Difference, 1981.

———. *Kant's Critical Philosophy*. Translated by Hugh Tomlinson and Barbara Habberjam. Minneapolis: University of Minnesota Press, 1984.

———. *Logic of Sense*. Translated by Mark Lester with Charles Stivale. Edited by Constantin Boundas. New York: Columbia University Press, 1990. Originally published as *Logique du sens*. Paris: Les Editions de Minuit, 1969.

Deleuze, Gilles, and Félix Guattari. *Anti-Oedipus*. Translated by Robert Hurley, Mark Seem, and Helen R. Lane. Minneapolis: University of Minnesota Press, 1987. Originally published in French as *Anti-Oedipe*. Paris: Les Editions de Minuit, 1972.

Depew, David J., and Bruce H. Weber. *Darwinism Evolving: Systems Dynamics and the Genealogy of Natural Selection*. Cambridge, Mass.: MIT Press, 1995.

Descartes, René. "Rules for the Direction of the Mind," Rule XVI. In *The Philosophical Works of Descartes*, vol. I. Translated by Elizabeth S. Haldane and G. R. T. Ross. Cambridge: Cambridge University Press, 1972.

Devlin, Keith. *Mathematics: The Science of Patterns, The Search for Order in Life, Mind, and the Universe*. New York: Scientific American Library, 1994.

DeWitt, Richard, *Worldviews, An Introduction to the History and Philosophy of Science.* Oxford: Blackwell Publishing, 2004.

Driscoll, Catherine. "The Little Girl, Deleuze and Guattari." In *Critical Assessments of Leading Philosophers,* vol. 3, edited by Gary Genosko. London and New York: Routledge Press, 2000. Reprinted from *Antithesis* 8, no. 2 (1997).

Durie, Robin. "Introduction." In Henri Bergson, *Duration and Simultaneity,* translated by Mark Lewis and Robin Durie. Manchester: Clinamen Press, 1999.

Dummett, M. A. E. "The Philosophical Basis of Intuitionistic Logic." In *Truth and Other Enigmas.* London: Duckworth Press, 1978.

Editors of Lingua Franca. *The Sokal Hoax, The Sham That Shook the Academy.* Lincoln: University of Nebraska Press, 2000.

Epstein, Barbara. "Postmodernism and the Left." *New Politics: A Journal of Socialist Thought* (Winter 1997): pp. 130–44.

Easwaran, Kenny. "The Role of Axioms in Mathematics." In *Erkentniss.* Netherlands. Kluwer Academic Publishers, 2007. http://www.ocf.berkeley.edu/~easwaran/papers/axioms.pdf.

Foucault, Michel. *Power/Knowledge, Selected Interviews and Other Writings, 1972–1977.* New York: Pantheon Books, 1980.

Frege, Göttlob. *The Foundations of Arithmetic.* Translated by J. L. Austin. Oxford: Oxford University Press, 1950.

——. "On Sense and Reference." In *Translations from the Philosophical Writings of Göttlob Frege,* edited by Peter Geach and Max Black, pp. 57–59. Oxford: Basil Blackwell, 1952.

Frank, Manfred. *What Is Neostructuralism?* Translated by Sabine Wilke and Richard Gray. Minneapolis: University of Minnesota Press, 1989.

Fukuyama, Francis. *The End of History and the Last Man.* New York: Free Press, 1992.

Galilei, Galileo. *Dialogues Concerning Two New Sciences.* Translated by Henry Crew and Alfonso de Salvio. New York: Dover Books, 1954.

Glanz, James. "When Mortals Work on Cosmic Time." *New York Times, Week in Review,* Sunday, August 9, 2009, WKI.

Harper, William. *Isaac Newton's Scientific Method: Turning Data into Evidence about Gravity and Cosmology.* Oxford: Oxford University Press, 2011.

——. "Negation and Difference." *Philosophy Today, Philosophy in Body, Culture, and Time* 44 (2000): pp. 112–18, 112.

Hass, Marjorie. "Feminist Readings of Aristotelean Logic." In *Feminist Interpretations of Aristotle,* edited by Cynthia A. Freeland, pp. 19–40, 34. University Park: Pennsylvania State University Press, 1998.

——. "Fluid Thinking, Irigaray's Critique of Formal Logic." In *Representing Reason, Feminist Theory and Formal Logic,* edited by Rachael-Joffe Falmagne and Marjorie Hass. New York: Rowman and Littlefield, 2002.

Hegel, G. W. F. *Phenomenology of Mind.* Translated by J. B. Baillie. London, 1931.

Heinrich, Bernd, and Thomas Bugnyar. "Just How Smart Are Ravens?" *Scientific American,* April 2007, pp. 64–71.

Heisenberg, Werner. *The Physicist's Conception of Nature.* Translated by Arnold J. Pomerans. New York: Harcourt Brace, 1958.

Hobbes, Thomas. *Leviathan.* New York: MacMillan Publishing, 1962.

Honig, Bonnie, ed. *Feminist Interpretations of Hannah Arendt.* University Park: Pennsylvania State University Press, 1995.

Hull, Margaret Benz. *The Hidden Philosophy of Hannah Arendt.* New York: Routledge Press, 2002.

Hume, David. *A Treatise of Human Nature.* Oxford: Clarendon Press, 1968.

Husserl, Edmund, *Cartesian Meditations, An Introduction to Phenomenology.* Translated by Dorian Cairnes. The Hague: Martinus Nijhoff, 1973.

——. *The Crisis of European Sciences and Transcendental Phenomenology.* Translated by David Carr. Evanston, Ill.: Northwestern University Press, 1970.

——. *Ideas, General Introduction to Pure Phenomenology.* Translated by W. R. Boyce Gibson. New York: Humanities Press, 1969.

http://hyperphysics.phy-asTrans.gsu.edu/hbase/pbuoy.html.

http://mathworld.wolfram.com/Algorithm.html.

http://physics.syr.edu/courses/modules/LIGHTCONE/minkowski.html.

Kant, Immanuel. *Critique of Practical Reason.* Translated by Lewis White Beck. Indianapolis, Ind.: Bobbs-Merrill, 1956.

——. *Critique of Pure Reason.* Translated by Norman Kemp Smith. New York: St. Martin's Press, 1965.

Klein, Morris. *Mathematics in Western Culture.* New York: Galaxy Books, 1964.

Kuhn, Thomas. *The Structure of Scientific Revolutions.* Chicago: University of Chicago Press, 1996.

Lane, R. D., and L. Nadel, eds. *Cognitive Neuroscience of Emotion.* Oxford: Oxford University Press, 2000.

Laplace, Pierre Simon. *Essais philosophique sur les probabilities.* Paris: Coucier, 1814.

Latour, Bruno. *We Have Never Been Modern.* Translated by Catherine Porter. Cambridge, Mass.: Harvard University Press, 1993.

Locke, John. *Essay Concerning Human Understanding.* New York: Dover Books, 1959.

——. *Philosophical Works.* Henry G. Bohn Publisher, 1854.

——. *Second Treatise of Government.* Indianapolis, Ind.: Hackett Books, 1980.

Lotka, Alfred. "The Law of Evolution as a Maximal Principle." *Human Biology* 17 (1945): pp. 167–94.

Lucas, J. R. *The Conceptual Roots of Mathematics, An Essay on the Philosophy of Mathematics.* New York and London: Routledge Press, 2000.

Lucretius. *On the Nature of the Universe.* Translated by R. E. Latham. Revised by John Godwin. London: Penguin Classics, 1994.

Lyotard, Jean-François. *The Postmodern Condition, A Report on Knowledge.* Translated by Geoff Bennington and Brian Massumi. Minneapolis: University of Minnesota Press, 1984.

Mapstone, Susan. "Non-Linear Dynamics: The Swerve of the Atom in Lucretius' *de rerum natura*" (2007). http://www.londonconsortium.com/wp-content/uploads/2007/02/mapstonestoicsessay.pdf.

Margulis, Lynn, and Dorian Sagan. "The Universe in Heat." In *What Is Sex?* New York: Simon & Schuster, 1999.

Markopoulou, Fotini. "An Insider's Guide to Quantum Causal Histories" (December 20, 1999). arXiv:hep-th/9912137 v2: 1–4.

——. "The Internal Description of a Causal Set: What the Universe Looks Like from Inside" (November 18, 1999). arXiv:gr-qc/9811053 v2: 1–35.

——. "Planck-Scale Models of the Universe" (November 7, 2002). arXiv: gr-qc/0210086 v2: 1–19.

——. "Space Does Not Exist, So Time Can." Perimeter Institute for Theoretical Physics (December 1, 2008). http://www.fqxi.org/data/essay-contest-files/Markopoulou_SpaceDNE.pdf.

Martin, Gottfried. *Kant's Metaphysics and Theory of Science.* Translated by P. G. Lucas. Manchester: Manchester University Press, 1955.

Marx, Karl. *Economic & Philosophical Manuscripts of 1844.* Translated by Martin Mulligan. http://www.marxists.org/archive/marx/works/1844/manuscripts/wages.htm.

——. "What Are Wages, How Are They Determined?" In *Wage, Labour and Capital,* Marx/Engels Internet Archive (marxists.org) 1993, 1999: http://www.marxists.org/archive/marx/works/1847/wage-labour/ch02.htm.

Marx, Karl, and Friedrich Engels. *Marx/Engels Selected Works,* vol. 1. Moscow: Progress Publishers, Moscow, 1969. Marx/Engels Internet Archive (marxists.org) (1987, 2000): http://www.marxists.org/archive
/marx/works/1848/communist-manifesto/ch01.htm.

Merleau-Ponty, Maurice. *Nature. Course Notes from the College de France.*
Translated by Robert Vallier. Evanston, Ill.: Northwestern University
Press, 2003. Originally published as *La Nature. Notes. Cours de Collège
de France.* Paris: Seuil, 1994.

———. *The Structure of Behavior.* Translated by Alden L. Fisher. Boston: Beacon Press, 1963. Originally published as *La structure du comportement.*
Paris: Presses Universitaires de France, 1942.

Metz, Andre. *Revue de Philosophie,* 1924. Reprinted as "The Time of Ein-
stein and Philosophy, Concerning the New Edition of M. Bergson's
Work, *Duration and Simultaneity.*" In Appendix VI of Henri Bergson,
Duration and Simultaneity. Translated by Mark Lewis and Robin Durie.
Manchester: Clinamen Press, 1999.

Morowitz, Harold. *The Emergence of Everything: How the World Became
Complex.* Cambridge: Oxford University Press, 2002.

Nanda, Meera. *Prophets Facing Backward: Postmodern Critiques of Science
and the Hindu Nationalism in India.* New Brunswick, N.J.: Rutgers University Press, 2004.

———. "The Science Wars in India." *Dissent* (Winter 1997).

Newton, Isaac. *The Mathematical Principles of Natural Philosophy,* 3 vols.
Translated by Motte. London, 1803.

———. *Opticks, or, A Treatise of the Reflections, Refractions, Inflections and Colors of Light,* 3rd ed. London, 1721.

Olkowski, Dorothea. "After Alice: Alice and the Dry Tail." *Deleuze Studies* 2,
No. 3 (2008): pp. 107–22.

———. "Deleuze and the Limits of Mathematical Time." *Deleuze Studies* 2, no.
1 (2008): pp. 1–24.

———. *Gilles Deleuze and the Ruin of Representation.* Berkeley: University of
California Press, 1999.

———. "The Interesting, the Remarkable, the Unusual: Deleuze's Grand
Style." *Deleuze Studies* 5, no. 1 (2011): 118–39.

———. "Science and Human Nature, How to Go From Nature to Ethics." In
Metacide, In the Pursuit of Excellence, edited by James R. Watson, pp.
43–72. Amsterdam: Rodopi, 2010.

———. *The Universal (In the Realm of the Sensible).* Edinburgh and New York:
Edinburgh and Columbia University Press, 2007.

Panksepp, Jaak. "Affective Consciousness: Core Emotional Feelings in Animals and Humans." In *Cognition and Consciousness* 14, no. 1 (March 2005): pp. 30–80.

Parsons, C. "Mathematical Intuition." In *Philosophy of Mathematics: An Anthology*, edited by D. Jacquette. Oxford: Blackwell, 2002.

Petkov, Vesselin. "On the Reality of Minkowski Space." *Found Phys* 37 (2007): 1499–1502. DOI 10.1007/s10701-007-9178-9. Published online: September 11, 2007 © Springer Science+Business Media, LLC 2007.

Plato. *Republic*, Translated by G. M. A. Grube. Revised by C. D. C. Reeve. In *Plato, Complete Works*. Indianapolis, Ind.: Hackett Publishing, 1997.

Prigogine, Ilya. *Thermodynamics of Irreversible Processes*. New York: John Wiley and Sons, 1955.

Robbins, Bruce. "Just Doing Your Job: Some Lessons of the Sokal Affair." *Yale Journal of Criticism* 10, no. 2 (Fall 1997): pp. 467–74.

Rorty, Richard. *Philosophy and the Mirror of Nature*. Princeton. N.J.: Princeton University Press, 1981.

Ruelle, David. *Chance and Chaos*. Princeton, N.J.: Princeton University Press, 1991.

Russell, Bertrand. *An Inquiry Into Meaning and Truth*. London: Allen and Unwin, 1940.

Sartre, Jean-Paul. *Being and Nothingness: An Essay in Phenomenological Ontology*. Translated by Hazel Barnes. New York: Washington Square Press, 1971. Originally published as *L'Etre et Néant, Essai d'ontologie phénoménologique*. Paris: Gallimard, 1943.

Sarukkai, Sundar. "Revisiting the 'Unreasonable Effectiveness' of Mathematics." *Current Science* 88, no. 3 (February 10, 2005): pp. 415–23.

Schneider, Eric D., and Dorian Sagan. *Into the Cool, Energy Flow, Thermodynamics and Life*. Chicago: University of Chicago Press, 2005.

Serres, Michel. *The Birth of Physics*. Translated by Jack Hawkes. Manchester: Clinamen Press, 2000.

———. *The Natural Contract*. Translated by Elizabeth MacArthur and William Paulson. Ann Arbor: University of Michigan Press, 1995.

Sokal, Alan D. "Transgressing the Boundaries, Towards a Transformative Hermeneutics of Quantum Gravity." *Social Text* no. 46/47 (Spring/Summer 1996): pp. 217–52.

Smith, Adam. *The Wealth of Nations*. New York: Bantam Books, 2003.

Smith, Kurt. "Descartes' Life and Work." Revised 02/27/07. http://plato.stanford.edu/entries/descartes-works/.

Smolin, Lee. *Three Roads to Quantum Gravity*. New York: Basic Books, 2001.

Stengers, Isabelle. *The Invention of Modern Science*. Translated by Daniel W. Smith. Minneapolis: University of Minnesota Press, 2000.

——. *Power and Invention, Situating Science*. Translated by Paul Bains. Minneapolis: University of Minnesota Press, 1997.

Stengers, Isabelle, and Ilya Prigogine. *Order Out of Chaos, Man's New Dialogue with Nature*. New York: Bantam Books, 1984.

Strogatz, Steven. "Guest Column: Loves Me, Loves Me Not (Do the Math)." *New York Times*, May 26, 2009, http://judson.blogs.nytimes.com/2009/05/26/guest-column-loves-me-loves-me-not-do-the-math/.

Sullivan, J. W. N. *Limitations of Science*. New York: Mentor Books, 1963.

Tasić, Vladimir. *Mathematics and the Roots of Postmodern Thought*. Oxford: Oxford University Press, 2001.

Tiles, Mary. *Mathematics and the Image of Reason*. London and New York: Routledge Press, 1991.

Vaknin, Sam. *Malignant Self-Love, Narcissism Revisited*. Prague and Skopje: Narcissus Publications, 2007.

Van Stigt, Walter P. "Brouwer's Intuitionist Programme." In *From Brouwer to Hilbert, The Debate on the Foundations of Mathematics in the 1920s*, edited by Paolo Mancosu, pp. 1–22. Oxford: Oxford University Press, 1998.

Vernant, Jean-Pierre. *The Origins of Greek Thought*. Ithaca, N.Y.: Cornell University Press, 1982.

Weaver, Jefferson Hane, ed. *The World of Physics, Volume 1, The Aristotelean Cosmos and the Newtonian System*, New York: Simon & Schuster, 1987.

Weinberg, Steven. "Sokal's Hoax." *The New York Review of Books* XLIII, no. 13 (August 8, 1996): pp. 11–15.

Wheeler, John Archibald. *A Journey into Gravity and Spacetime*. New York: Scientific American Library, 1990.

Williams, Garnett. *Chaos Theory Tamed*. Washington, D.C.: Joseph Henry Press, 1977.

Wittgenstein, Ludwig. *Tractatus*. Translated by Daniel Kolak. Mountain View, Calif.: Mayfield, 1998.

INDEX

affective sensations, 143

algebra, 19

algorithm: definition, 194; demotion of nature's laws, 175n48; mathematical, 134, 135; state of universe, 47

Alice in Wonderland, 103–18

analytic philosophy, xiii, xv; of language, xxii

appearance(s), 12–13

Archimedean point of view, xxi, xxii, 17, 25, 31, 32, 93, 131, 134, 137, 141, 165n102; and Deleuze, 63; logic, 88; ontology, 89

Archimedes, 76

Arendt, Hannah, xxi, xxii, xxiii, 7, 20, 25, 55, 93, 128, 134; on Adolf Eichmann, 101, 129; on Ancient Greeks, 11–17, 30; banality of evil, 135, 138; on determinism and freedom, 47; on earthly alienation, 39–40, 62; on economics, 30–31, 35–37; feminist views of, 164n68; finitude of individuals, 95; forgivenness, 129; human action, 96, 130; *The Human Condition,* 95–99, 170n42; on labor, 95, 188n10; on Locke, 29; misinterpretations, 188n17; natality, 96, 97, 103, 129, 130, 134; noble words and deeds, xxii, 30, 58, 96, 99, 130, 134; ontology of becoming, 134; parallelogram of forces, 96; on Plato, 165n100; *vita activa,* 13–14, 30, 32, 33, 90, 96, 99

Aristotle, 13, 61; common sense, 133–34; identity, 134; qualities, 169n29; representationalism, 133; substance, 81, 133; unity in a genus, 78

assemblage: of affects and percepts, 74; contingency of, 75

association, xiv, xxii; of ideas, 32, 43, 45, 72; logical, 78, 79, 138; rules of, 68, 69; transcendental, 71

atom(s), 72–73; Ancient atomism, 74; as objects of thought, 72

atomistic individuals, xxii, 32, 34, 79, 95, 133, 135, 139, 140, 142, 152

attractor, 75, 137; Idea as, 79; limit cycle, 121; strange, 121–22

axiom(s), xvi; consistency in, xvii; contradiction in, xvii; definition, 40; geometric, xvi; law of excluded middle, 127; logical compatibility in, xvii; logical dependency in, xvii

axiomatic method, xvii

Badiou, Alain, 64–65, 89–90; the grand style, 64, 89–90; rigorous mathematics, 64

Beauvoir, Simone de, xxii, xxiii, 93, 128, 144–52; "The Age of Discretion," 153; *All Men are Mortal,* 150; being and nothingness, xii, 93, 121, 122, 146; clinamen, xxii, 93, 128, 145–47, 148, 149, 151, 152, 155; *The Coming of Age,* 148, 149; dualism, 119; ethics, 126, 128, 146, 148, 150, 152, 154; *The Ethics*

165n104; immanent temporality, xv; passive genesis, xiv, passive synthesis, xiv; the pre-given world, 20–21; on reason and habit, 45
hybrids, xvi; thinking machine, xvi
hypothetical proposition(s), 105; and causal relations, 105, 107

Idea, 116–17, 79; as attractor, 67, 79, 84; dialectical, 82; indeterminate, 84; as signification, 79
identity, 109, 110; and common sense, 107
imaginary number(s), xix
immanence: field of, xx; plane of, xxii
incompleteness, xviii
intersubjectivity, xiii
intuition, xiv; in Descartes, 41
intuitionism, xiv, xxiii, 126–28, 156; and building, 126, 142; and human nature, 130; and mathematical truth, 127; and time, 127, 131
intuitionistic logic, 135, 151–52; as logic of ambiguity, 135; and time evolution, 141
intuitionists: mathematical, xv, 151–52
invisible hand, 35

Jaspers, Karl, 11

Kant, Immanuel, xiv, xvi, 11, 64, 150; antinomies, 85–86; antinomy, xiv; a priori intuition, xiv, xvi; axioms of intuition, 88–89; common sense, 70, 87; disinterested aesthetic pleasure, 137; faculties, 70–71, 87; free play of faculties, 84; good sense, 70, 87; I think, 70; Ideas of Reason, 67, 182n65; Imagination, 61, 71, 74, 76, 83, 88, 89; logical categories of relation, 137; object = x, xiv; practical reason, 138; schematism, 70; second antinomy, 85–88; sensible intuition, 86; sublime, 71; thing-in-itself, 12, 86; transcendental idealism, 87, 89; transcendental Ideas, 70–71; transcendental philosophy, 57, 69;

understanding, 13, 45, 70, 74, 75, 85, 86, 87, 89; and universal moral law, 135, 137
Kepler, Johannes, 25, 28, 172; laws of planetary motion, 40
Kuhn, Thomas, 63

labor, 13, 16–17, 31, 36; division of, 37; labor-power, 16–17, 36–37; and property, 29
language game, xii
language system, xiii
Large Hadron Collider, 91–92, 97
Latour, Bruno, xv–xvi
law of nature, xx, 3, 18; reason as, 29
Leibniz, Gottfried, 25, 67–68, 76, 84, 93; calculus of infinitesimals, 83, 93; symbolic logic, 172n6
Leventhal, Richard M., 92
life: philosophy of, 15–16, 95, 97
life-world, 20–21
light-cone, 60–61, 139–40, 141–42; mutually influencing, 152; past, 142
linguistic turn, xi, xii, xv
Locke, John, 21, 28, 95, 133; *Essay Concerning Human Understanding,* 43; as Newtonian science, 42; on mathematics, 42, 173n27; on moral knowledge as mathematical, 43; and property, 29, 31
logic, xv, 10, 69, 103–104, 118; and algebraic geometry, 138; of ambiguity, 126, 135, 152, 156; Boolean, 141; contradiction, 78; contrariety, 78; of identity, 127; intuitionistic, 135, 151–52; mathematical, xvii; negation, 77–78; predicate, 102
logical rules of replacement, 104–105
Lucretius, 72–73; clinamen, 72, 122, 145, 149
Lyotard, Jean-François, xii

Markopolou, Fotini, 125, 138; on causal sets, 141; geometry as emergent matter, 138; Heyting algebra, 141; on light cones, 140; on space and time